THE WORKS COUNCIL

THE
WORKS COUNCIL

A GERMAN EXPERIMENT IN
INDUSTRIAL DEMOCRACY

By

C. W. GUILLEBAUD

FELLOW OF ST JOHN'S COLLEGE
CAMBRIDGE

CAMBRIDGE
AT THE UNIVERSITY PRESS
1928

CAMBRIDGE
UNIVERSITY PRESS

University Printing House, Cambridge CB2 8BS, United Kingdom

Cambridge University Press is part of the University of Cambridge.

It furthers the University's mission by disseminating knowledge in the pursuit of education, learning and research at the highest international levels of excellence.

www.cambridge.org
Information on this title: www.cambridge.org/9781316509517

© Cambridge University Press 1928

First published 1928
First paperback edition 2015

A catalogue record for this publication is available from the British Library

ISBN 978-1-316-50951-7 Paperback

PREFACE

The present volume is the result of a number of years' close study of the German Works Councils. I have spent a portion of each year since 1919 in Germany investigating at first hand the operation of the Works Councils Act. I am glad to have this opportunity of thanking the many Government officials, employers, members of Works Councils, Trade Union officials and others with whom I have discussed this problem, for the unfailing courtesy with which I have been received and for the time that they have sacrificed in assisting me in my researches.

There is a certain danger that the writer of a monograph on a particular institution may, without realising it, come to identify himself too closely with the fortunes of the institution which he is studying, and may thereby be led to adopt an uncritical attitude towards it. I have endeavoured throughout to guard against this danger and to treat the efforts and achievements of the Works Councils impartially, though with that measure of sympathy which is necessary if the workings of an essentially human institution are to be understood and appreciated.

The writing of this book was completed in December 1926, at a time when the Reports of the German Factory Inspectors were not available for 1926. The detailed study of the Works Councils has therefore not been carried beyond the middle of that year. But the Reports of the Factory Inspectors, which were published in 1927, and other information that I have been able to procure, show that the Works Councils were functioning throughout 1926 in very much the same way as in the preceding year, while the general economic environment remained substantially unaltered.

v

PREFACE

It was originally my intention to make a comprehensive survey of the Shop Steward movement, Whitley Committees, and voluntary Works Councils in England, in order to make a detailed comparison of conditions and tendencies in the two countries. I collected a good deal of material for this purpose, but found subsequently that the time at my disposal was insufficient to enable me to carry out this plan, and I have been compelled to confine myself to Germany. I hope, however, that it will be found that the history of the German experience with statutory Works Councils will provide material of value for those who are concerned with this side of the labour movement in England.

I wish to express my gratitude to Mr I. L. Evans for helping me with the proofs, and to my aunt, Mrs Alfred Marshall, for reading the whole of the manuscript and for providing the index.

C. W. GUILLEBAUD

ST JOHN'S COLLEGE
CAMBRIDGE
July 1927

CONTENTS

CONTENTS

CONTENTS

CHAPTER I

The Origins of the German Works Councils Act of February 4, 1920

The German Works Councils Act of February 4, 1920, is the child of two parent ideas—the one constitutional, the other essentially revolutionary.

The influence of this dual parentage is very closely to be seen in the early struggles over the Council system, in the crystallisation of this system in the Constitution and the Works Councils Act, and in the subsequent history of the operation of this Act.

The first indications of the new problems which arose with the growth of the factory system in Germany are to be found in a resolution put forward by the Industrial Commission of the revolutionary National Assembly, which met in Frankfurt in 1848, calling for the compulsory issue of works rules (disciplinary regulations, etc.) by a "Factory Committee" consisting of the factory owner and elected representatives of the employees. The rules were to be approved by a district "Factory Council" elected by the Factory Committees in the district. The proposal was frustrated by the collapse of the Revolution, but remained one of the most keenly desired reforms in the programme of German labour. Finally in 1891, shortly after the fall of Bismarck, an amending Act was passed to the Industrial Code (*Gewerbeordnung*) which satisfied to a small extent the aspirations of labour. The issue of works rules (*Arbeitsordnung*) was made obligatory in all factories and businesses subject to the Industrial Code, employing more than 20 workers, and provision was made for the permissive constitution of workers' committees. These committees, where they existed, were entitled to be consulted before the promulgation of works rules, though the employer was not required to give effect to any of the modifications put forward by the workers' committee of his factory.

In 1905 the election of workers' committees was made obligatory in Prussia in all mining undertakings employing 100 or more workers, and in 1909 "safety men" elected by the workers were introduced in the mining industry and the functions of the workers' committees were slightly extended. Apart from this single industry there was no further legal recognition of works representation of the employees between 1891 and 1914. The efforts of labour during this period were concentrated on the struggle for recognition of the Trade Unions and for the consolidation of their organisation. By 1914 there existed only a few thousand of the permissive workers' committees constituted under the Act of 1891, and in any case their powers were so small that they possessed no practical importance. On the other hand, the system by which shop delegates were appointed by the Trade Unions to act as their local representatives in the individual factories was prevalent in the large-scale industries, though their activities were not recognised or approved by the employers, except in a few cases where they were constituted by Collective Agreement between Trade Unions and employers.

With the outbreak of the War the position of the Trade Unions underwent a vital change. Hitherto they had been struggling, often unsuccessfully, to defend the right of association against the opposition of practically the whole of the employers; now they found themselves courted by the Government and treated with deference by the employers. The shop delegates were recognised and used as a means of control over the enforcement of agreements between the Trade Unions and the employers. Far-reaching concessions were made in order to range the Trade Unions beside the Government and to maintain a united "home front". Finally in 1916 the adoption of the Hindenburg munition programme necessitated the passing of the Auxiliary Service Act, which was designed to mobilise the whole of industry and of the male civilian population for the prosecution of the War. As was the case with the Munitions Acts in Great Britain, the sentiment of organised labour in Germany was very strongly opposed to many of the provisions of the Auxiliary Service Act. One of the chief concessions, with which the Government sought to placate the Trade Unions and to diminish their opposition to this measure, was the constitution of workers' committees (composed both of wage-earning and

2

salaried employees) in all undertakings coming within the scope of the Act, which employed more than 50 workers in all. The direct functions given to these committees were not large: they were to be the organ of the employees in the factory, and were to bring to the notice of the employer any complaints or wishes expressed by the employees in regard to the organisation of the factory or to wages or other labour conditions. Over and above this, special tribunals were set up to which the workers' committees had an independent right of appeal in case of disputes with the management. The tribunals, which were called *Schlichtungsausschüsse* (Conciliation Boards), were composed of three representatives of the employers and three representatives of the employees with a Chairman appointed by the War Board.[1] The Conciliation Boards were empowered, if they could not bring about an amicable agreement, to make decisions which were binding on both parties. The legal powers of these workers' committees set up under the Auxiliary Service Act were small, but their practical authority varied widely from one undertaking to another. In some cases, under the pressure of war production, the committees were able to extract very considerable rights and privileges from the employers, in much the same way as the Shop Stewards in Great Britain were able to take advantage of the strength of their bargaining position. In Germany, also, these workers' committees were looked at somewhat askance by the leaders of the Trade Unions.

The end of the War in November 1918 was followed by two important measures—the one being a voluntary agreement between the employers and the Trade Unions, and the other an administrative Order of the new Government. On November 15, 1923, an agreement was concluded between the Trade Unions and the Employers' Federation which provided for the setting up of Joint Industrial Alliances (*Arbeitsgemeinschaften*), consisting of representatives of employers and employees in equal numbers, to which was delegated the task of drawing up a programme for the period of economic demobilisation. A central Joint

[1] The composition of these tribunals, which became later one of the corner stones on which the Works Councils Act of February 4, 1920, was founded, was modified by the Order of December 23, 1918, and again by the Order of October 30, 1923.

Industrial Alliance was set up for the whole of Germany, and German industries were divided into 14 groups each of which had its own Joint Industrial Alliance. This organisation had a good deal in common with the Whitley Councils in England. In joining with the employers in these Joint Alliances the socialist Trade Unions sacrificed one of their dearest principles—that of the refusal to co-operate with the employers in securing the peaceful regulation of industrial conditions under the system of private enterprise. On the other hand, they gained the unconditional recognition of the method of Collective Agreements regulating wages and other labour conditions; it was agreed that disputes should be referred to joint arbitration boards, and the employers accepted the continuance of the workers' committees set up by the Auxiliary Service Act of 1916. Soon after the conclusion of this agreement the Government issued their famous Order of December 23, 1918,[1] which Karl Legien, the most influential leader of the socialist Trade Unions, described as "The Great Charter of Labour".

This Order regulated in detail the operation of Collective Agreements; it reorganised the system of Conciliation Boards;[2] and, finally, it made provision for the constitution of workers' committees, in all establishments employing 20 or more workers, which were to be responsible, in conjunction with the employer, for supervising the execution of Collective Agreements and for furthering peaceful industrial relations.

With the Order of December 23, 1918 was reached the apparent climax of the whole of the preceding evolutionary process, based as it was on the extension of the powers of the Trade Unions and on the legal and practical recognition of their right to bargain on equal terms with associations of employers. The outbreak of the German Revolution in November 1918, however, had introduced into the situation a new and very potent factor—the influence of Russian revolutionary ideas. Many of the most active leaders of the German Revolution drew their inspiration from the events which had led to the setting-up of the Russian Republic of the Soviets and were ardent partisans of the device of using Councils of Soldiers, Workers and Peasants

[1] See below, pp. 36–8.   [2] See below, pp. 22–4.

4

as a method of transferring all power in the State into the hands of the proletariat.

The use of such Councils as revolutionary organs has an interesting history. As early as 1647–9 the Levellers' Movement in England was associated with the formation of Soldiers' Councils to which it was endeavoured to join Councils of Citizens. For a brief period the movement threatened to become dangerous, but the success of Cromwell and Fairfax in re-establishing discipline in the Army led to the collapse of the agitation.[1] During the period of the Commune in the French Revolution of 1789 Councils of Citizens were formed as political organs elected by and directly responsible to local groups. Similar Councils, but more distinctively representative of the workers as such, reappeared in the short-lived Commune in Paris in 1871, and again in a much clearer and more definite form in the abortive Russian Revolution of 1905. In Russia the weakness of the Trade Union movement and the reactionary policy of the Government afforded a strong incentive to the spread of revolutionary ideas through agitators working in the factories, and the revolutionary leaders, taught by the failure of 1905, set themselves to organise revolt based on the factory as a nucleus or "cell". The War of 1914 collected millions of men under arms and thus facilitated the work of propaganda. When the Czar's Government collapsed in 1917 the more extreme elements in the factories formed themselves into Councils, which became grouped together in district organisations and finally, in cooperation with Councils of Soldiers and Peasants, constituted a national Congress of Councils. For a time the Congress existed side by side with the Duma and then, with the victory of the Communists, swept the Duma aside and took over political and economic control throughout the country.

Thus the success of the Russian Revolution of 1917 appeared to be based on and bound up with the Council system. This fact gave to Workers' Councils an enormous prestige in all countries in which revolutionary socialism had taken a strong hold, for it appeared that at last the long-sought-for weapon had been forged

[1] Cf. Gooch, *English Democratic Ideas in the Seventeenth Century*, chs. IV and V; Firth, *Cromwell's Army*, ch. XIV.

5

which would enable the proletariat to attain to supreme power. Outside Russia, however, it was only realised by very few that, once the Revolution had been carried through, the whole of the political and executive power was assumed by a few men working through political Councils of Communists; while the factory Committees or Councils were relegated to the subordinate work of, at best, representing the immediate interests of the employees in each of the nationalised undertakings, the management of which was at least as autocratic as in the days of private enterprise. In most cases, moreover, the Russian factory Councils soon fell into the hands of the Communists and represented not so much the point of view of the workers, as the policy of the management.

In Germany the Revolution broke out in November 1918 with a suddenness and a completeness which surprised no one more than the Trade Union leaders who were the official heads of the German labour movement. In Germany, as in England, the war-time restrictions on the right to strike and the continual increases of wages due to the competition of the war industries to secure labour, had temporarily weakened the influence of the Trade Union leaders and diminished their control over their members. Officially, German labour had been throughout the War on the side of the Government and in favour of the prosecution of the War, and only a small minority had stood out and opposed it. This minority, belonging to the left wing of the labour movement, had gradually become convinced that the only way to bring the War to an end was to bring about a revolution, as in Russia. They therefore deliberately sowed the seeds of revolution wherever the ground seemed favourable, but above all in the large factories in the industrial districts. At the same time, the soldiers who had been fighting on the Eastern Front and who were transferred to the West after the collapse of Russia, brought with them the story of the Bolshevik success and of the means by which it had been achieved. It was in the Baltic ports, where the fleet had so long been cooped up, and in the industrial districts that the Revolution originated, and from thence it spread rapidly all over Germany. In most cases Soldiers' Councils were first formed, but these were soon joined by Workers' Councils. In Berlin an Executive Council was set up and six People's Commissars were appointed—Ebert, Scheidemann and Landsberg as representatives of the Majority Socialists, and Dittmann, Haase and Emil Barth, representing the Independent Socialists.

It very soon became apparent that there was a fundamental cleavage of opinion between the different sections of German labour in regard to the future form of government. The greater number of the Independent Socialists, led by Däumig and Müller, were in favour of an out-and-out Soviet or Councils State. The catch-words, "All power to the Councils" and "The Dictatorship of the Proletariat", which had already done duty in Russia, began to be heard throughout Germany. On the other side were the Majority Socialists of the Social Democratic Party. Their leaders, experienced Trade Unionists of the stamp of Ebert, Scheidemann and Noske, were men who put their faith and their hopes in democratic parliamentary institutions after the English pattern. For them the events in Russia since 1917 afforded a warning rather than an example to be followed, and they were determined if possible to avoid the fate of the Kerensky Government. The strength of the two sections was measured at the first general Congress of Councils held in Berlin, December 16–20, 1918. At this Congress the standpoint of the Majority Socialists carried the day and a decisive resolution in favour of parliamentary government and the election of a Constituent Assembly on January 19, 1919, was adopted. A Central Council was also elected to "safeguard the results of the Revolution" and to supervise the actions of the provisional Government. At the end of December the three Independent Socialist members of the Government resigned and went into active opposition. The elections to the National Assembly in January resulted in the formation of a Government based on a majority composed of Social Democrats, Democrats, and the Centre Party. The Independent Socialists and Communists found themselves in a small minority in the Assembly. In this election the political aims of the adherents of a Soviet State were definitely rejected by the great majority of the electorate. But the issue still hung for a time in the balance, for the Spartacists broke out in armed revolt, hoping to imitate the success of the Bolsheviks in the Russian Revolution. In the end the victory lay, though by a narrow margin, with the parliamentarians, backed up as they were by the powerful and disciplined Trade Union organisation.

The Central Council referred to above resigned its mandate and its legal powers on the convocation of the National Assembly. At the second Congress of Councils held from April 8 to 14, 1919, a second Central Council was elected, which was not recognised by the Government and which, moreover, ended by falling into the hands of the anti-Councils party.

With the disbandment of the Army the Soldiers' Councils soon disappeared, but the political Workers' Councils (those set up in connection with local government) survived for a longer period. They had, however, to contend with the opposition of the officials, who had all been reinstated in their former positions by the new Government, with financial difficulties, and with the absence of any effective central leadership.[1] By degrees they lost all semblance of power and finally vanished without leaving any impress on local government.

It was otherwise with the revolutionary industrial Workers' Councils, which were very strong in some parts of Germany, particularly in and around Berlin and the chief industrial districts, and which in some cases were well organised regionally. These Councils were not formed under the Order of December 23, 1918; they arose spontaneously out of the revolutionary enthusiasm of a section of German labour. The aim of these bodies was to supersede what they regarded as the bureaucratic and official-ridden organisation of the Trade Unions, by a new type of organisation based solely on the Councils system and imbued with the revolutionary spirit in contrast to the timid reformist socialism of which the Government and the Trade Union leaders

---

[1] Some of the leaders of the left wing were in favour of an exclusively Soviet State—i.e. a Councils system without a parliament (Däumig, Müller), others of a Councils organisation working on an equal footing with a parliament (Haase, Kautsky), and others of Chambers of Labour (to include employers) exercising political functions alongside parliamentary government (Kaliski, Cohen). The multitude of counsels confused the workers and weakened the force of the revolutionary movement.

were adherents. The struggle which developed for the leadership of German labour is described in Chapter III. Here we are concerned with the effects of the Councils agitation in causing a new and vitally important Article to be added to the German Constitution by the Constituent Assembly at Weimar.

The draft of the Constitution presented by the Government contained no mention of the Councils. As late as February 25, 1919, Scheidemann, the head of the Government, declared officially: "No member of the Cabinet contemplates, or has ever contemplated, the incorporation of the Councils system in any form, whether in the Constitution or in the administrative machinery". The immediate result of this declaration was to produce a very dangerous internal situation. The pronouncement was too reactionary for the majority of the workers. A general strike broke out among the metal workers in Berlin and those employed in many of the chief industries of Westphalia and Central Germany. The Cabinet realised that they had gone too far in their attitude of negation towards a movement which had in a large measure caught the imagination of the masses and, under the influence of Erzberger, they sought for a formula that would quiet the storm they had aroused. On March 5, 1919, Scheidemann gave a written undertaking that the Workers' Councils should be "recognised in principle as a representation of the workers' interests, and be anchored in the Constitution". A month later the Government issued its proposals for organising and making use of the Councils in the form of an amendment to one of the draft Articles of the Constitution. This amendment, with slight modification, was adopted by the Assembly and included in the Constitution as Article 165, being placed in the group of Articles entitled "Fundamental Rights and Duties of Germans".

Article 165, the precise wording of which is of great importance, runs as follows:

Wage-earning and salaried employees are called upon to co-operate, with equal rights in common with employers, in the regulation of wages and of working conditions as well as in the whole economic development of production. The organisations on both sides and the agreements entered into by them are recognised.

For the purpose of safeguarding their social and economic interests

9

the wage-earning and salaried employees are entitled to be represented in Workers' Councils for each establishment, as well as in Regional Workers' Councils organised for each industrial area, and in a Federal Workers' Council.

The Regional Workers' Councils and the Federal Workers' Council join with the representatives of the employers and of other interested sections of the community to form Regional Economic Councils and a Federal Economic Council for the accomplishment of all economic tasks and for co-operation in the execution of the socialisation laws. The Regional Economic Councils and the Federal Economic Council shall be so constituted as to represent all important occupational groups in accordance with their respective economic and social importance.

Drafts of Bills of fundamental importance relating to social and economic policy, before being introduced into the Reichstag, shall be submitted by the Federal Government to the Federal Economic Council for an expression of its views. The Federal Economic Council has the right itself to initiate such Bills. Should the Federal Government not approve of such Bills it is nevertheless bound to introduce them into the Reichstag, together with a statement of its own views. The Federal Economic Council may delegate one of its own members to appear before the Reichstag in support of its Bill.

Supervisory and administrative functions in questions assigned to them may be delegated to the Workers' Councils and to the Economic Councils.

The Reich alone has power to determine the organisation and duties of the Workers' and Economic Councils respectively, as well as their relation to other self-governing bodies.

The very skilful wording of this Article for the time being stilled the popular clamour, and the work of drafting the rest of the Constitution was able to proceed.

A great deal turns on the precise interpretation of that co-operation "with equal rights" (*gleichberechtigt*) accorded to labour by the first paragraph of the Article. There can be no doubt that the Government intended, and the whole course of subsequent history has shown this to be the case, to maintain the integral features of the industrial system (subject to any measures of socialisation), and to recognise the existence of divergent interests between employers and workers, while setting up an additional representative machinery by which these special interests of labour and the common interests of labour, the employers and the community in the furtherance of production could be facilitated. The attitude of the Government is

10

well shown in the following extract from the official memorandum accompanying the draft of Article 165:

> The worker as such strives for the direct intensive realisation of his interests in his employment and in public affairs: at the same time he endeavours to reach out beyond the status of employee and to attain to co-operation in the productive process itself, which hitherto has been controlled by the employer alone. He desires no longer to live and die merely *quâ* worker performing certain defined tasks, without any comprehension of the economic system as a whole; he feels the need of looking out beyond his work bench to the economic process in its entirety, of contributing thereto his practical knowledge and experience and of co-operating in the development of production. All these aspirations, mingling with new vital forces, are producing an intellectual movement which is permeating the whole body of labour, and whose value must be recognised by legislation.

Many of the workers, however, took the above-mentioned phrase more at its face value, and believed that the system of direct occupational representation foreshadowed would at least give to labour an equal voice with the employers in industrial matters, and would effectively abolish the autocratic one-sided control of the employers in industry.

The German Constitution was adopted on July 31, 1919, and the Government at once proceeded, in consultation with employing and labour interests, to prepare a Bill for the establishment of Works Councils, this being the first stage in the edifice of labour representation contemplated by Article 165 of the Constitution. The Government's Bill was laid before the National Assembly on August 16, 1919, and gave rise immediately to an enormous amount of controversy. The employers had recovered somewhat from their first fright after the Revolution, when they had been only too ready to agree to what then seemed the relatively mild proposals contained in Article 165, lest much worse things should befall them. They now marshalled their forces to defend their interests against the attempts of the Independent Socialists and Communists to widen the scope of the Bill and to give to the Works Councils a substantial measure of power independent of the employers. At the same time the Bill caused a very serious discord and discussion within the ranks of the Trade Unionists, especially those

11

belonging to the socialist Trade Unions, for the question immediately arose whether the Works Councils should be subordinated to the Trade Unions or whether, as the more radical members desired, the Councils should constitute a separate organisation distinct from the Trade Unions and destined, if successful, subsequently to supersede the latter. Even amongst the left wing Socialists there were widely divergent views as to the precise form in which the Council system should become crystallised in the economic machinery of the country. The Majority Socialists were backed up to the utmost by the employers, who were at least as much concerned to fetter the Works Councils and to confine them within the organisation of the Unions. Of the latter the employers were not afraid, but they were thoroughly alarmed at the pretensions of those who supported the Council system.

Throughout the latter part of 1919 the influence of the radical element was perceptibly diminishing and the fear of a successful Spartacist revolt was gradually passing away. The old-established Trade Union leaders gradually regained control over the bulk of their members, and thus found themselves able to steer the course of the new Works Councils measure into "safe" channels—safe, that is, so far as the maintenance of the pre-existing Trade Union predominance in labour organisation was concerned.

The discussion of the Works Councils Bill lasted from August 16, 1919, to February 4, 1920; every clause was fiercely debated and numberless amendments proposed. The representatives of the employing interests were able to take advantage of the reaction from the excesses of the period immediately following the Revolution to secure the adoption of many alterations in their favour, but the feeling was still much too strong for them to be able to draw all the teeth from the measure. The Act in its final state is much longer and more complicated than the original draft of the Government, and bears all over it the stamp of compromise. The result is a law which, to those who were the protagonists of the Council or Soviet system, is a bitter disappointment, a mere shadow of that for which they had hoped, even though to most employers it represents an unwelcome encroachment on their rights and responsibilities as managers of industry and commerce. The swing round of opinion and of the balance of power between the early months of 1919 and the beginning of 1920 was such that the Works Councils Act, as it at length emerged from its long period of gestation, appeared to most of its supporters as but an anaemic and sickly child, quite unworthy of the parent ideas expressed in Article 165 of the Constitution, and of the revolutionary spirit which helped to inspire that Article.

CHAPTER II

The Machinery of the Works Councils Act

THE COMPOSITION, ELECTION AND PROCEDURE
OF WORKS COUNCILS[1]

The German Works Councils, unlike the Works Committees under the Whitley scheme in England and most of the voluntary Works Councils in England and America, are not joint bodies holding their meetings in association with the employer. The German Councils are composed of employees alone, and the employer has no right to attend their meetings unless he is invited or has called a meeting in order to discuss a particular matter with the Council.

The Works Councils are constituted under a legislative Act which empowers their election in all establishments[2] above a certain size (five employees being the minimum for the election of a Works Steward and 20 for the election of a Works Council).[3] The membership of the Council ranges from three, in establishments where fewer than 50 persons are employed, up to a maximum of 30 where there are 15,000 or more employees.[4]

---

[1] For reasons of space I am compelled to give here only the barest outline of some of the most important provisions of the Works Councils Act, the full text of which will be found in translation in Appendix i.

[2] The term "establishment" is extremely comprehensive; it includes all public and private undertakings, together with administrative offices, and thus covers agricultural, industrial, commercial and financial enterprises of every kind with the exception of shipping. The unit of organisation is the establishment and not the undertaking, though a Central Works Council may under certain conditions be appointed for an undertaking composed of a number of separate establishments.

[3] In the case of agriculture and forestry a minimum of 20 *permanent* workers is necessary for the election of a Works Council and of 10 permanent workers for that of a Works Steward.

[4]

No. of employees	No. of members of Works Council	No. of employees	No. of members of Works Council
20–49	3	800–999	10
50–99	5	1,000–1,499	11
100–199	6	1,500–1,999	12
200–399	7	2,000–2,499	13
400–599	8	2,500–2,999	14
600–799	9	3,000–3,499	15

A peculiarity of German labour legislation and labour organisation is the distinction made between wage-earners and salaried employees. This distinction is carried into the Works Councils, which are composed of two Sectional Councils (a Wage-earners' Council and a Salaried Employees' Council), each solely competent to deal with matters affecting its own group, but joining together to form the Works Council in all questions concerning the employees as a whole.

All employees in an establishment, without distinction of sex, nationality or period of employment, who have attained the age of 18 years, are entitled to vote at the election of a Works Council. But a candidate for election is required to be a German national, who is not less than 24 years of age, and who has worked six months in the establishment and three years in the trade. He must also have completed his period of training; hence, though apprentices may vote, they may not be elected to serve on the Council.

The election of the Works Council is managed by an Election Committee of three appointed by the retiring Council.[1] The members of the Works Council are elected by the direct votes of the employees, by secret ballot, and in accordance with the system of proportional representation. It may be noted that the election procedure is exceedingly complicated.[2] Elections are held annually and the term of office is for one year.

The office of Works Councillor is honorary, all necessary expenses incurred being paid by the employer. For any working

No. of employees	No. of members of Works Council	No. of employees	No. of members of Works Council
3,500–3,999	16	9,000– 9,999	24
4,000–4,499	17	10,000–10,999	25
4,500–4,999	18	11,000–11,999	26
5,000–5,499	19	12,000–12,999	27
5,500–5,999	20	13,000–13,999	28
6,000–6,999	21	14,000–14,999	29
7,000–7,999	22	15,000 and over	30
8,000–8,999	23		

[1] If the Council fails to do this, or if the undertaking is newly established, or one in which the Council has lapsed, the duty of nominating an Election Committee falls on the employer, who must select the three senior employees for this purpose.

[2] The text of the election regulations is translated in Appendix II.

time lost during the exercise of his official duties, a Councillor must be paid the full remuneration (including an allowance for overtime, if any is being worked) appropriate to an employee of his class. It is unlawful for the Works Council to collect contributions from the employees to be used for any of the purposes of the Council. Thus the Council must always be financially dependent on the employer.

The procedure of the Council is not regulated in detail by the Act but is in the hands of the Chairman, who is elected by a majority vote of the members of the Council and who is empowered to convene a meeting whenever he considers desirable. He must call a meeting on the demand of not less than one-fourth of the members of the Council or if the employer wishes to discuss any matter with the Council. Minutes must be kept of all meetings, which must contain at least the text of resolutions and the majority by which they are passed. They must be signed by the Chairman and one other Works Councillor.

The principle is laid down that, as a general rule and wherever possible, the Works Council must meet outside working hours. The sole responsibility for deciding that a case of urgent necessity has arisen rests with the Chairman,[1] who must give proper notice to the employer of his intention to call a meeting during working hours.

Meetings of the Works Council are private, but may be attended by one representative of each of the Trade Unions to which its members belong. These representatives attend on invitation and are allowed to take part in the proceedings but not to vote. The employer has corresponding rights in the case of those meetings of the Council at which he is entitled to be present.

The Chairman is entitled to convene a meeting of the Works Assembly[2] when he considers it necessary, and is required to do so on the demand of the employer or of not less than one-fourth of the

[1] The employer is powerless to withhold his consent even if he considers that there is no justification for the decision of the Chairman. He can, however, subsequently appeal to the competent Labour Court, and, in a bad case, secure a ruling that the Chairman, having abused his powers, is no longer fit to act as a Works Councillor.

[2] The Works Assembly consists of the whole body of employees in an establishment, including those who are not entitled to vote in the election of the Works Council.

16

employees with voting rights. The Works Assembly must normally be held outside working-hours, and it is only permissible to depart from this rule if the consent of the employer has first been obtained. The Works Assembly may discuss all matters which come within the competence of the Works Council (it is not empowered to discuss other matters, e.g. political questions); it may pass resolutions approving or disapproving of the conduct of the Council, or directing it to take certain steps. But it has no power to compel the Council to follow its instructions, nor can it force the Council to resign. A right of appeal to a Labour Court is, however, provided, both for the employees and the employer, against the Works Council on the ground of "gross misfeasance of duty". If the Court considers that the accusations brought forward have been proved it may revoke the mandate, either of an individual Works Councillor or of the whole Council.

THE DUTIES AND POWERS OF WORKS COUNCILS[1]

The Works Council as a whole is required (i) to co-operate (in an advisory capacity) with the employer in promoting efficiency of production;[2] (ii) to co-operate in the introduction of new labour methods;[2] (iii) to promote peace within the establishment,[3] and, in case of a dispute with the employer, to appeal to the Conciliation Board if a settlement cannot be reached by negotiation; (iv) to supervise the execution of awards affecting the employees as a whole; (v) to come to an agreement with the employer in regard to works rules applicable to all employees,

---

[1] The functions summarised here are discussed in detail in Chapter v below. Their precise wording, which is very important, is contained in Sections 66–90 of the Act (Appendix I, pp. 261–8).

The duties and powers of the Works Steward are in general the same as those of the Works Council and of its Sectional Councils. The one exception of importance consists in the fact that the Works Steward is not empowered to appeal to the Labour Court against the dismissal of any of his fellow-employees.

[2] Works Councils in establishments "which serve political, trade union, military, religious, scientific, artistic or other similar purposes" are exempted from both these duties in so far as their fulfilment "would conflict with the essential aims of these establishments".

[3] A Works Council, as such, must never foment or lead a strike within the establishment for which it is elected.

and, if no agreement can be reached, to appeal to the Conciliation Board whose decision is final in respect of all rules other than those relating to working-hours; (vi) to defend the workers' right of association; (vii) to reconcile grievances received from the Sectional Councils of wage-earning and salaried employees; (viii) to take steps to prevent accidents and injury to health and to co-operate with the Factory Inspectors; (ix) to participate in the administration of works welfare schemes.

Finally, it is laid down that the management of an undertaking, and the management only, is responsible for carrying out all decisions arrived at in co-operation with the Works Council. The Works Council has no right to issue orders on its own initiative or to interfere with the executive functions of the management, nor can it require the employer to follow its advice in regard to the conduct and organisation of the business.

The duties of the Sectional Councils are similar to those of the Works Council as a whole, except that they refer to all cases in which the interests of either the wage-earners or the salaried employees are concerned, e.g. the fixing of wages and other working conditions, the regulation of working-hours, holidays, etc., subject in all cases to the priority of ruling Collective Agreements. In one chief respect very important powers are given to the Sectional Councils and not to the Works Council as a unit. An employee who has been dismissed may protest, on certain specified grounds, to his Sectional Council against his dismissal. If the Council after investigating the case comes to the conclusion that his protest was justified, but is unable to persuade the employer to rescind his decision, it may appeal to the Labour Court, which can take evidence on oath. If the Court rules that the dismissal was unjustifiable it can compel the employer to choose between the alternatives of re-employing the man or compensating him on a scale fixed by the Court.

In order to facilitate the execution by the Works Council of its official duties (especially those relating to its joint responsibility with the management for promoting the efficiency of the establishment) the Works Council as a unit is given new and far-reaching powers. The Council is entitled (a) to elect one or, in some cases, two of its members to sit on the Control Boards of

18

all joint stock companies or private undertakings which have a Control Board, such members being unpaid but having full voting rights; (b) to demand access to information on all proceedings of the business which affect the contract of service or the activities of the employees, including the wages books and any other information required for checking the execution of existing Collective Agreements; (c) to require the employer to make a quarterly report dealing with the position and progress of the enterprise and the industry generally and, in particular, with the output of the undertaking and the anticipated demand for labour; (d) to be informed by the employer, as long as possible in advance, of his intention to engage or dismiss a large number of employees; in the event of projected dismissals on a large scale the employer must discuss with the Council any means that can be taken to avoid hardship; (e) to require, in all large industrial or trading establishments,[1] the presentation of an establishment balance sheet and profit and loss account for the preceding business year, together with any necessary explanations.

Finally, special protection is given to Works Councillors against victimisation. With certain specified exceptions a Works Councillor may not be dismissed without the concurrence of the Council of which he is a member, but where the Council refuses its consent the employer is entitled to appeal to the Labour Court, whose decision is final and binding on both parties. If the Court decides in favour of the employee (which it must do if it holds that the employer's action has been due to discrimination against the Councillor on the ground of his office, or if the reason given is otherwise inadequate) the employer is required unconditionally to cancel the notice of dismissal. The employer must continue to keep the worker concerned in his employment until the Labour Court has given its decision.

[1] Establishments in which there are not less than 300 employees in all (both wage-earning and salaried employees) or 50 salaried employees.

THE SETTLEMENT OF DISPUTES ARISING OUT OF
THE WORKS COUNCILS ACT

The rights of the Works Councils and Works Stewards to "co-operate" with the employers in the regulation of dismissals and other important matters entrusted to them by the Act are subject to the power of either side to appeal to a tribunal for decision. In some cases this decision is binding on both parties, but in some it has the nature of a recommendation without mandatory force. It is clear therefore that the nature and composition of these tribunals are of the utmost importance in the operation of the Act, for a great part of the effectiveness of its provisions depends on the decisions given in cases of dispute. This is the more apparent when account is taken both of the complexity and frequent obscurity of the Act and of the rigidity with which legal provisions are commonly interpreted in Germany. The position is complicated by the fact that different tribunals are competent for different parts of the Act and that certain of its original provisions have been altered by the Conciliation Order of October 30, 1923. In the following pages the present state of the law (1926) in regard to appeals will first be set out, and then a description given of the composition of the various tribunals to which disputes can be referred.

The following types of disputes are to be distinguished:

1. Disputes of an administrative character (within the Works Council or between the Council and the employer or the Council and the body of employees) over
   (a) the necessity for constituting a workers' representative body, and the composition of such a body;
   (b) eligibility to vote or to be a candidate for election;
   (c) organisation, competence and procedure of a workers' representative body;
   (d) liability of the employer for expenditure incurred under the Act;
   (e) elections of Works Councils and Works Stewards.

The competent body under the Works Councils Act to give decisions in all the above cases was the Regional Economic Council. Owing to the fact, however, that these bodies have not yet been set up, other tribunals were appointed in their place. Down to the end of 1923 this duty was given in most parts of Germany to the Factory Inspectors. Since the new Conciliation Order of October 30, 1923, all these appeals come before the Labour Courts. In the case of undertakings which extend over more than one State, the Federal Economic Council is the competent tribunal. The decisions given are in every case final, in the sense that they are not subject to appeal, though they are not directly enforceable at law.

2. Disputes over the formation and dissolution of a Common Works Council for several establishments.

3. Disputes over the compulsory retirement of a workers' representative body or of any of its members.

In both the above cases, the original tribunals appointed under the Act were the Regional Economic Councils, for which were substituted *ad interim* the statutory Conciliation Boards. Since the new Conciliation Order these appeals come before the Labour Courts, whose decisions are final.

4. Disputes over the engagement or dismissal of employees or the dismissal of members of workers' representative bodies.

Under the Act the Conciliation Boards were the competent tribunals, but since the new Conciliation Order the Labour Courts, whose decisions are final and have legal effect.

5. Disputes over the drafting of statutory works rules (*Arbeitsordnung*).

The statutory Conciliation Board remains the competent tribunal. Its decisions are final and may be made binding by the Board on both parties, except in regard to disputes over the duration of working hours.

6. Disputes of a collective character arising out of the exercise by the Works Council or Works Steward of the right to represent the interests of the employees, and to co-operate with the employer in the determination of conditions of employment.

The statutory Conciliation Board is the competent tribunal, or any other board of arbitration or conciliation agreed upon between the two parties. In these disputes the decision takes the form of a recommendation which is not binding, unless the competent authority under the Ministry of Labour makes use of its powers to declare the award to be binding on both parties.

It will be seen that there are three tribunals which at present are competent to deal with disputes under the Works Councils Act: the unofficial Boards of Conciliation and Arbitration, the statutory Conciliation Boards, and the Labour Courts.[1] Before describing the composition and procedure of these bodies it is desirable to make some reference to the part played by the Factory Inspectors during the first three years of operation of the Works Councils Act.

The Factory Inspectors constitute the chief supervisory organ of the State for controlling the great mass of protective labour legislation in Germany. Their authority extends not merely over factories and workshops but over all establishments which come under the scope of the Industrial Code (*Gewerbeordnung*). It is to them that the statutory works rules are submitted for approval, and they are empowered to decide on the necessity for modifications in the duration of the working-day. Their annual reports since 1920 show that they have been in very close touch with the activities of the Works Councils and that their influence has been of great importance in the evolution of these bodies. They have not merely acted as the competent tribunals in disputes over the constitution, procedure, etc., of Works Councils, but they have in many instances mediated between Works Councils and employers, and have played an important part in drawing the attention of both sides to the correct interpretation and practical application of the provisions of the Works Councils Act. By this means they have often prevented serious troubles, and have lessened materially the number of cases taken before the Conciliation Boards. Wherever in the course of their inspections they have found establishments in which representative bodies under the Act have not been set up, they have urged the employees, often with success, to make use of their legal rights and to elect representatives to protect their interests. The rôle of the Factory Inspectors in the operation of the Works Councils Act

---

[1] Where the recovery of sums of money in excess of 300 marks is at issue the ordinary Courts of Justice are also competent and appeals can be carried to the *Reichsgericht* (Supreme Court of Civil Law).

has been of the utmost importance, and no small part of such success as many of the Councils have achieved is due to their efforts.

The unofficial Boards of Conciliation and Arbitration are tribunals to which labour disputes may be submitted under Collective Agreements, as a rule with a joint undertaking on the part of both sides to accept the awards given. Their composition varies in different cases. They have priority over the statutory Conciliation Boards, in the sense that the latter are only competent to deal with a dispute when there is no provision in the Collective Agreement for reference to an unofficial Conciliation Board, or when the latter Board has been unable to settle a dispute which has come before it. These unofficial Boards of Conciliation and Arbitration have only played a relatively small rôle in connection with disputes between employers and Works Councils, partly because the latter are statutory bodies, and are not constituted by collective agreement, and partly because the competence of the unofficial Boards of Conciliation and Arbitration to deal with disputes arising out of the Works Councils Act is very limited.

The statutory Conciliation Boards are those before which most of the important disputes under the Works Councils Act were brought prior to the issue of the new Conciliation Order in October 1923. Down to the end of 1923 the composition of the Conciliation Boards was determined in accordance with the Order of December 23, 1918, which in turn was based partly on the Auxiliary Service Act of 1916. During the War Germany was divided into District Commands, in each of which there were several administrative areas known as *Ersatzkommissionen.* A Conciliation Board was set up for each *Ersatzkommission,* and this organisation was retained when the system was revised in 1918. In the case of State undertakings and administrations special Conciliation Boards were set up in order to secure uniformity of conditions in such undertakings. In each area a panel composed of representatives of employees and employers selected by the organisations on both sides, and of independent Chairmen nominated by the State Governments, was constituted. In the event of a dispute the Board consisted of three employers and three employees. Of these, four were members of the panel, while the remaining two—one employer and one employee, with special knowledge of the technical aspects of the dispute—were nominated *ad hoc*. The Board thus constituted was empowered to elect one of its members as Chairman, but if the members could not agree on a Chairman, or if from the outset they desired an impartial Chairman, they proceeded to elect him from the panel. If a Board, composed only of employers and employees, was unable to give a decision in a dispute owing to the voting being equal on both sides, an impartial Chairman had to be elected to hear the case and he then had the casting vote. Before these Conciliation Boards came not merely collective disputes over Collective Agreements but also the great mass of individual disputes arising out of the provisions of the Works Councils Act, in particular those relating to the protection of the workers and their representatives against dismissal.

Under the new Conciliation Order of October 30, 1923, the number of Conciliation Boards has been greatly reduced,[1] their composition has been altered, and many disputes which previously came before them have been handed over to the Labour Courts. As before, the Conciliation Boards are set up by the appropriate Minister in each of the States, but this location is now determined by industrial rather than by territorial considerations. A Conciliation Board for a dispute is composed now of an impartial Chairman and two representatives of the employers' and two representatives of the workers' organisations. The non-permanent members of the Boards have been abolished and the presence of an impartial Chairman is obligatory instead of, as formerly, only optional. The impartial Chairmen are nominated by the Minister concerned after receiving the opinion of the economic organisations of employers and employed. He also appoints the representatives of the employers and employees, but is bound by the lists put forward by their organisations. The office is unpaid and cannot be refused except on specified legal grounds. The members of the Boards hold office for three years, but can at any time be called upon to resign by the Minister.

[1] In 1924 there were 105 Conciliation Boards in the whole of Germany as compared with about 250 in 1923.

In the event of a dispute the Chairman alone hears the case in the first instance and endeavours to bring the parties to an agreement; only in the event of his failing to secure an agreement does he proceed to select two representatives of the employers' and two of the employees' organisations. The Board thus constituted re-hears the case and pronounces an award.

The Chairman, in making his selection of the members, is governed by the nature of the dispute, and, so far as possible, acts in accordance with the wishes of both sides. The competence of the Conciliation Boards is restricted to collective disputes arising either out of the Collective Agreement or out of Works Agreements between the employer and the Works Councils, as all individual disputes are now dealt with by the Labour Courts. The competent Conciliation Board to deal with a dispute is the Board established for the area in which the workers concerned are employed. Representation by lawyers is not allowed, but an employer can be represented by his manager (*Prokurist*), or other permanently authorised representative, while the employees can be represented by the Works Council or by Trade Union representatives. In practice it is not uncommon, in the case of a dispute between a Works Council and an employer, for the former to be represented by a Trade Union official. When either side appeals to the Conciliation Board the Board is empowered to compel the attendance of a representative of the other side— a fact not without importance when account is taken of the burden thus imposed on the smaller firms who cannot afford to delegate whole-time officials for this purpose. The whole of the costs of conciliation proceedings are borne by the State. The essential principle of the operation of Conciliation Boards is that so far as possible the two parties should be brought to an agreement and that an award (*Beschluss*) should never be made until all attempts to achieve an agreement have failed. The decision contains the opinion of the Board as to the best and most appropriate solution of the dispute but it is not binding on the parties concerned, in the absence of official intervention. If it is accepted by both parties, whether before or after the decision is given, it becomes *ipso facto* a Collective Agreement and as such has legal effect. A decision of a Conciliation Board may be declared binding on both parties in the event of a dispute of major importance, but this procedure seldom or never comes into question in the case of disputes between employers and Works Councils. Finally, mention must be made of the Conciliation Officers (*Schlichter*) who, with the Minister of Labour of the Reich, are empowered to declare decisions to be binding on both parties. The Conciliation Officers are a small number of persons (in 1924 there were 20 for the whole of the Reich) who are appointed by the Reich and are empowered to take out of the hands of the Conciliation Boards any disputes which are of special importance. They can declare any decision of a Conciliation Board to be binding on both parties, while the Minister of Labour of the Reich can declare any decision of a Conciliation Officer to be similarly binding.

The Labour Courts are of long standing in Germany, being descended from the *Conseils de Prud'hommes* established by Napoleon I throughout France. After the fall of Napoleon these Councils remained in operation in German territory on the left bank of the Rhine and similar institutions were later set up in other parts of the country. A further step was taken by the Industrial Code of 1869 which provided that industrial labour disputes could be decided by the communal authorities. Finally the system was regulated definitively by the Industrial Courts Act (*Gewerbegerichtsgesetz*) of 1890, which was followed by the Commercial Courts Act (*Kaufmannsgerichtsgesetz*) of 1904.

An Industrial Court[1] must be set up in all communes with over 20,000 inhabitants and may be set up by any commune or group of communes. The Court consists initially of one or more Chairmen, together with their deputies, and a panel of employers and employees. The Chairman is elected by the municipality; he must be neither an employer nor an employee and is, as a rule, either a judge or a high government official. The other members of the Court are elected in accordance with the principles of proportional representation by secret ballot by the employers and employees who are over 20 years of age and are resident in the district for which the Court is established. The members must be

---

[1] With slight modifications, the same composition, procedure, etc., holds for the Commercial Court.

over 25 years of age. They are unpaid but receive compensation for loss of time and for travelling expenses. For each dispute the Court consists normally of three members—the Chairman, one representative of the employers and one of the employees. The Industrial Court is competent to deal with all individual disputes between employers and employees arising out of the contract of employment and, in particular, with those disputes now referred to it under the Works Councils Act. In contrast to proceedings before a Conciliation Board, the Court can require either party to a dispute to take the oath. Lawyers are not allowed to plead but the Court can appoint and hear experts. In disputes arising out of the Works Councils Act the normal procedure of the Industrial Court is modified in the sense, firstly, that the Works Council as such can plead before the Court, while in all other cases only the individual or his permanent representative can plead; and, secondly, that the costs of the case, which in other disputes fall as a rule on the losing party, are borne by the Reich when the Works Council is the losing party. In Works Council disputes two quite distinct methods of procedure are provided.[1] In disputes under Sections 82–90 of the Act, i.e. those relating to the engagement or dismissal of employees, the Court is empowered to give a decision (*Schiedspruch*) which has the immediate force of law. In all other disputes referred to it under the Works Councils Act the Court can only give an award (*Beschluss*) which, though final in the sense that there is no appeal against it, is not legally binding on both parties. It is held that in this latter category the functions of the Court are not those of a Court of Law, but represent the intervention of a public tribunal in disputes of an administrative rather than a legal character. In practice these awards are as effective in almost all cases as the legally binding decisions. In the case of disputes in which only an award is given, an oath cannot be required of the witnesses, there are no costs and the presence of witnesses and experts cannot be compelled. It is not necessary in these cases for there to be

[1] In the new Conciliation Order, the Industrial and Commercial Courts are for the first time referred to officially as "Labour Courts" in connection with their functions in regard to the Works Councils. They are in fact provisional Labour Courts. The final regulation of these Courts is the subject of a new Bill which it is proposed shortly to pass into law.

an actual hearing and evidence can be submitted in writing. In general, the whole of the methods and procedure of the Industrial and Commercial Courts are designed in order to accelerate the settlement of disputes as much as possible.

The recent modifications in the system of dealing with disputes under the Works Councils, which has just been described, are the result of the experience of the functioning of the Conciliation Boards during the first three years of operation of the Act. In many ways this experience was not wholly satisfactory. In so far as the Boards acted as true conciliation bodies in disputes of a general character between the Works Councils and their employers, no objections could be raised against the manner in which they functioned. They were not, however, only concerned with this type of dispute, but also with innumerable disputes of a strictly legal character arising out of the application of particular provisions of the Act to individual cases. For this type of dispute they were very inadequately equipped, especially as it was not compulsory for a Board to sit with an independent Chairman.

The inevitable result was a great mass of conflicting decisions, many of which gave evidence of crass ignorance of legal principles and of the proper interpretation of legal provisions. By degrees a large body of precedents grew up which were often used as the basis for subsequent decisions. But the precedents themselves were often of very doubtful validity and merely perpetuated abuses. In any case each Board was a law unto itself; its decisions were final and subject to no appeal to a higher tribunal.[1] The personnel of the Boards for different disputes was fluctuating, and any particular Board was not even bound by a decision given in a precisely similar case by a different Board belonging to the same panel. Thus there was always a chance that a case which had been decided one way on one day would be decided differently on the next. However, the likelihood of conflicting decisions was much less in one and the same area than it was between different areas. In important cases a great

---

[1] The rulings of the Minister of Labour of the Reich have played a considerable rôle in practice. In specially important questions of interpretation the Minister has given rulings which have been widely adopted as authoritative and as governing the practice of the Boards.

deal naturally depended on the personality and attitude of the impartial Chairman who, when present, had the casting vote. A peculiarity, moreover, of the position of the Conciliation Boards was that in no case did their awards have legal effect, even when they were binding on both parties. In order for an award to be put into force in the case, for instance, of the payment of compensation to an employee who had been improperly dismissed, the employee had to appeal to the Industrial or Commercial Court, or where these did not exist, to an ordinary Court, for a judgement against the employer. Although the award of the Board was final in all questions of fact and of the conclusions to be drawn from the facts, it was liable to review by the Court in respect of the legal competence of the Board to give an award in the particular case and of the observance by the Board of the prescribed legal procedure. The result of this was, firstly, considerable delay in securing the legal enforcement of an award, and, secondly, in very many cases, the Court decided that there had been some legal irregularity and refused to enforce the award. Many Courts also interpreted their powers in regard to awards rather widely and quashed them on general legal grounds when they disagreed with the reasons given by the Board for arriving at its decision. The whole system was also very costly in its operation. Disputes involving a few marks often involved several hours' discussion before a Board of seven members. If witnesses or important documents were not available the case had to be adjourned to another day, with a further loss of everybody's time. Then the case often had to come up again before a Court of Law for enforcement. The financial costs fell on the Reich and were quite an appreciable burden, but the greater real cost was the loss of time to the officials, employers and employees composing the Courts.

The chief manner in which the Conciliation Order of 1923 took account of these objections was by removing from the competence of the Conciliation Boards all the individual disputes which had taken up so large a part of their time during the past three years and which involved, in a large measure, legal questions with which the Boards were scarcely fitted to deal. The duplication of work caused by the need for judicial enforcement of awards was thus also obviated. There are not lacking, however, those who regret the change and who hold that many of the individual disputes which now come before the Labour Courts involve broad social as well as legal issues. The essence of the work of the Conciliation Boards has been the decision of such issues on broad practical grounds, rather than in accordance with rigid legal formulas and there is a danger, especially when the Labour Courts become incorporated in the general legal system of the country, of the loss of a very valuable elasticity and freedom from doctrinaire formalism in dealing with labour disputes.

The Industrial and Commercial Courts, or, as they are now termed in their capacity as adjudicators under the Works Councils Act, the Labour Courts, have in common with the Conciliation Boards the important characteristic that their decisions and awards are not subject to appeal, except on purely legal grounds in certain cases, where the legality of the procedure is called in question. Hence here also the same repetition of conflicting decisions is to be observed as in the case of the Conciliation Boards. Some remarkable instances of this were cited by a speaker at a Congress of Works Councils.[1] On March 12, 1924, the Industrial Court of Königsberg decided, in the case of two disputes, that the members of the Works Council enjoy the protection of Section 96 of the Act in the event of a lock-out—i.e. that the consent of the Works Council as a whole is necessary for their dismissal.[2] On the same day the same Court, but with a different membership, gave an exactly converse ruling in another dispute over the same issue. Again, in the question whether the consent of the Court to the dismissal of a Works Councillor has retroactive effect, three different opinions have been expressed. The superior Provincial Court of Stettin in a recent decision declared without reservation in favour of the retroactive effect of such consent; the Industrial Court of Würzburg held that the consent should only have retroactive effect if

[1] *Protokoll der Konferenz des Reichsbeirats der Betriebsräte...der Metall-industrie*, December 28–30, 1924.
[2] Failing that consent the employer could, of course, appeal to the Labour Court to substitute its consent for that of the Council.

it was forthcoming within a reasonable time after the notice of dismissal; finally, the Provincial Court of Leipzig denied the possibility of retroactive effect and declared that the notice of dismissal only began to operate as from the date on which the Court proclaimed its consent. These instances could be multiplied indefinitely. A speaker at the Conference expressed the opinion that the cause of such unfortunate differences in judgements by the Courts was to be found, partly in the obscure drafting of the Works Councils Act, but mainly in the lack of understanding on the part of the members of the Courts of the social problems of the present day. The latter part of this comment raises the highly controversial issue as to the true functions of the special Courts called upon to give decisions in labour disputes. The view of organised labour is that broad considerations of social policy should have the dominant influence, while the employers very naturally stand out for an exceedingly rigid legal interpretation of statutory provisions. Most legal authorities who have not made a special study of labour problems also incline to the latter view, which is certainly calculated to appeal strongly to the legal mind. In general, it may be said that, despite the disadvantages resulting from the absence of unity of judgements, the Labour Courts have played an indispensable part in the practical operation of labour legislation in Germany, and that their success has been largely attributable to their familiarity with the special characteristics of labour disputes, to their informal procedure, and to their endeavours (even though not always successful) to promote social justice.

It is the intention of the Government to make drastic changes in the system of Labour Courts in the near future, as can be seen from the text of a Government Bill which was adopted by the Reichsrat in February 1926 preparatory to its submission to the Reichstag.

The Bill provides for the abolition of the Industrial and Commercial Courts, and for the transfer of the functions hitherto allotted to them to the new Labour Courts which are to be competent in all civil legal disputes between employers and employees. There are three stages—the Labour Court, i.e. the Court of first instance; the Provincial Labour Court, to which appeal can be made from the first Court if the sum in dispute exceeds 300 marks or if the Labour Court itself regards a decision of the higher Court on a question of principle as desirable; lastly, the Labour Court of the Reich, the final Court of Appeal in labour disputes. The Labour Courts of first instance are composed of an ordinary judge who is appointed by the Department of Justice, as Chairman, and two members (*Besitzer*), of whom one is representative of the employers and one of the employees.

The composition of the Provincial Labour Courts is similar to that of the lower Labour Courts except that the Chairman must be a Provincial Court Judge. The Supreme Court is composed of the highest judges, together with an equal number of legal experts in labour matters and of representatives of employers and employed.

Lawyers are to be admitted in most actions to plead in the Courts.

By these means it is proposed, at length, to secure unity of judicial decisions interpreting statutory provisions. It remains to be seen whether this unity will not have been attained at too high a cost for, on the one hand, the existing system has had the great merits of celerity and finality, while, on the other, the incorporation of the Labour Courts, even though to only a modified extent, into the normal judicial system of the country, is likely to lead to a more rigid application of legal principles to labour questions. It has been pointed out above that many of the so-called "individual disputes" which now come before the Labour Courts involve important questions of public policy; hence the personal attitude of the judges to such questions becomes a matter of great public importance. On these grounds many Trade Union leaders are opposed to the Bill in its present form and would even prefer the maintenance of the present *status quo* to the proposed new regulation. The admission of lawyers to plead, especially in the Courts of first instance, is a very obnoxious proposal to the Trade Unions. It should be observed, however, that the retention of the representation of the employers and employed on the Courts is an important concession to those who wish to preserve the special character of the existing Courts.

32

CHAPTER III

The Works Councils and the Trade Union Movement

THE TRADE UNION MOVEMENT IN GERMANY

The German Trade Union movement had developed before the War on lines which differed in important respects from the movement in England, though it resembled the latter in that it was almost entirely organised in the form of Craft Unions. In the early years of the 'nineties the movement was still very weak and the Unions were small local organisations, confined sometimes to individual works and sometimes to particular industrial districts. They had to contend against restrictive legislation and against the active and determined opposition of the employers all over the country. Despite these unfavourable conditions, the 20 years which preceded the War of 1914 witnessed a great expansion and consolidation of the forces of the Unions. Powerful Craft Unions arose whose membership was drawn from all parts of the country; a highly organised and centralised system of administration was built up; and the policy of submitting disputes to arbitration and of securing Collective Agreements regulating the wages, hours and other conditions of employment for large masses of workers, was followed with ever-increasing success. By 1914 the total membership of German Trade Unions was 8,450,000 and they already played a leading rôle in the relations between labour and the employers in many of the important large-scale industries.

The chief contrast, however, between the development of Trade Unionism in Germany and in England lay, and still lies, in the great divisions existing within the ranks of organised labour. In 1914 the "Free" Trade Unions had a membership of 2,500,000 confined to those workers who formally acknowledged the validity of the Marxian doctrine of the *Klassenkampf* and accepted the Social Revolution as the ultimate goal of their efforts. The "Free" Trade Unions were thus organised on a definitely socialist basis and though they might be driven by practical necessity to parley and negotiate with the employers, their avowed aim was the ultimate elimination of private capitalists and their replacement by the State under the control of the workers. At the same time the "Free" Trade Unions themselves contained every variety of opinion, from the most diluted type of reformist socialism to extreme advocacy of syndicalism and immediate revolution by violence. The second most powerful body of Trade Unions, the "Christian" Unions, had a membership of 342,000. They were to be distinguished from the "Free" Trade Unions mainly by their explicit rejection of the Class War as a working principle and of the tenets of revolutionary socialism in general, and by their willingness to co-operate with the employers in seeking to secure industrial peace and the greater productivity of industry, in so far as this was compatible with the legitimate interests of the workers. The "Christian" Unions were composed mainly of Catholics and their chief strength was in the industrial districts of the Rhineland and the Ruhr. Just as, politically, the "Free" Trade Unions were associated with and represented by the Social Democratic Party, so also the members of the "Christian" Unions adhered to the Catholic Centre Party. Hence the antagonism between the two Unions in matters of Trade Union policy was also reflected in the political sphere.

The third organisation of Trade Unions—the Hirsch-Duncker Unions—had a membership just before the War of 107,000. Without any special political or religious bias, the Hirsch-Duncker Unions, whose origins went back as far as 1868 to the beginnings of the Trade Union movement in Germany, were in closer sympathy with the aims and methods of the "Christian" than with those of the "Free" Trade Unions. Their outlook was that of the Manchester Liberals. They opposed the Bismarckian reforms as State-socialist paternalism and stood for self-help and for the organisation of the workers on orthodox Trade Union lines, as embodied in the Trade Union movement in England in the 'seventies and 'eighties of the last century. To a greater extent than the "Christian" Trade Unions, they were opposed to strikes, except in the last resort, and frequently refused to follow the lead of the "Free" Trade Unions when the latter called their men out on strike. The membership of the three organisations described above numbered at the outbreak of war in 1914 approximately 3,000,000—i.e. they comprised the overwhelming majority of all the Trade Unionists in Germany, and of these 3,000,000 as many as 2,500,000 belonged to the "Free" or socialist Trade Unions.

The remaining Unionists were either organised as purely religious Unions—Catholic bodies based on the Pope's Encyclical "Rerum Novarum" of 1891—or as "Independent Unions", many of the latter of which had syndicalist tendencies.

Finally, there should be mentioned the "Pacifist" Unions (*Wirtschaftsfriedliche Vereine*), usually stigmatised as "Yellow" Unions. These had 280,000 members in 1913 (they are not included in the total of 3,450,000 given above). The "Yellow" Unions were organised with the express purpose of co-operating with the employers in defence against the fighting organisations, especially of the socialist Unions, and of helping to preserve industrial peace. As a rule their funds were either openly or secretly subsidised by the employers, and they were based mainly on the individual works or establishment, in the form of Works Unions (*Werkvereine*). Their influence was greatest before the War in the very large undertakings, in which they were not infrequently able to frustrate the policy of the other Unions.

The War drew large numbers of Unionists into the Army; as many as 1,400,000 members of the "Free" Trade Unions were under arms in September 1918. At the end of 1916 the membership of these Unions had fallen to 945,000, but from then on the numbers increased, partly owing to the entry of women employed in the munition industries. By September 30, 1918, the "Free" Trade Unions numbered approximately 1,500,000. Despite this enforced reduction of membership, the War brought a great stimulus to the whole movement. The urgent needs of war-time production constrained the rulers of Germany to make concessions of an important character to the Unions, longstanding restrictions on their activities were removed, and their leaders were treated as part of the machinery of administration. The freedom of action of the Trade Union was, however, still far from complete, strikes were dealt with severely and meetings and other Trade Union activities were often prohibited by the Generals in charge of the military commands into which Germany was divided during the War. Although the workers on the State railways were, for the first time, allowed to form themselves into a Union, this permission was only granted on the undertaking being given that the Union would not make use of the strike weapon.

The relations between the employers and the Trade Unions varied greatly in different industries and in different parts of the country and though, in a few cases, Joint Industrial Alliances (*Arbeitsgemeinschaften*) were constituted, the majority of employers remained as before hostile and opposed to any recognition of the Unions. Hence their powers in practice depended on the degree of recognition that they were able to extort from the employers. In the munitions industries, in particular, the strength of their position under war conditions was considerable, and the employers found themselves constrained to treat with them and to allow very appreciable rights to the Shop Stewards who were their representatives in the factories.

The collapse of the War and the outbreak of the Revolution in October 1918 resulted, after a very short period of chaos, in the formation of a Government consisting wholly of Trade Union leaders and, for a long time, even after the representatives of other parties had been included in the Government, organised labour remained the strongest political force in the country. Under its influence the old disabilities were finally removed. The freedom of association was guaranteed by the new Constitution, which also promised the workers an important voice in the determination of their industrial conditions. The eight-hour day was established by law and, in some ways most important of all, the Order of December 23, 1918, was issued. This Order regulated almost the whole system of Collective Agreements between employers and Trade Unions and gave to the Trade Unions a new and far more comprehensive control over the determination of wages, hours of work, etc., than they had ever had before the War. It almost amounted to a new constitution for labour, with the Trade Unions legally recognised as the executive and legislative representatives of the workers. The Order of December 23,

1918, is of such fundamental importance in regard to the functions of the Trade Unions that it is desirable to summarise briefly its main provisions, if only because the scope of the activities of the Works Councils under the Act must be understood as being limited and bounded by the functions which have been allocated exclusively to the Trade Unions.

Under this Order, Collective Agreements are agreements made between groups of workers and a single employer or a number of employers, which lay down the conditions regulating the conclusion of individual labour contracts. On the workers' side some form of organised Union is an indispensable condition, though the Union need only comprise the workers in a single undertaking. Once a Collective Agreement has been arrived at and signed by the authorised representatives of both sides it becomes binding on all employees and employers who, by their membership of the Union or Federation concerned, were parties to the Agreement. It cannot legally be modified except in favour of the employees and only then, provided that the Agreement itself does not contain provisions expressly excluding the possibility of such modifications. It is true that, in practice, a modification of the Agreement might become operative by mutual consent, but it would always be open to any individual employee to appeal to the competent Court on the ground that his contract with his employer was not in accordance with the principles laid down by the Collective Agreement. If he was able to establish his contention, the Court would be bound to rule that the contract must be altered to conform to the Agreement. The majority of Collective Agreements provide for the submission of disputes to agreed arbitrators or Conciliation Boards whose decisions, if accepted by both parties, have the effect of an Agreement. The Order also provides for the setting up of Conciliation Boards[1] (*Schlichtungsausschüsse*) to which either party can appeal in case of a dispute. If both parties accept the award it immediately comes into operation, and is enforceable, but if either party refuses to adhere to it the award is not operative. Finally, by a vital provision, the Federal Minister of Labour is given power to decree that any existing

[1] See above, p. 23.

Collective Agreement, "which has acquired predominant importance in the district covered by it", shall be binding on all persons engaged in the area and trade, or section of a trade, to which the Agreement applies. Hence, where an Agreement is declared universally binding in this way, both employers and employees who were not originally parties to it are legally compelled to adhere to its provisions. If the Collective Agreement in question is a Federal one, then all employers and workers in that trade or occupation throughout Germany become subject to it.

The legal sanction given by the Order of December 23, 1918, to Collective Agreements freely concluded between employers and Unions of workers was carried an important stage further by the Conciliation Order of November 30, 1923, which empowered the Federal Minister of Labour and the newly constituted Conciliation Officers (*Schlichter*) to give a binding decision in any collective dispute. An award may be declared binding, even though it is rejected by one or both parties, if "the settlement made by the award is equitable, due regard being had to the interests of both parties, and if its enforcement is necessary on economic and social grounds". A compulsory award has precisely the same legal effect as a voluntarily concluded Collective Agreement, inasmuch as in both cases the organisations on either side are required, not merely to abstain from any positive action against the settlement, but also to use all their influence with their members to secure its recognition in practice. If, for example, an employer refuses to adhere to the Agreement, his Federation must put pressure on him up to the point even of excluding him from the Federation. Any failure to do this, or actual support by a Federation (or a Trade Union), renders the organisation in question liable in civil law for all damages and losses resulting from such action. In practice, however, these powers of compulsory arbitration, which enable the State to put an end at any time to a collective dispute, have hitherto been used somewhat sparingly. It is also true, both in the case of compulsory awards and of the voluntary Collective Agreement, that it is rare for either party to have recourse to the civil law and to bring an action for damages.

38

The tendency since the War has been in the direction of widening the sphere of operation of Collective Agreements and bringing more and more aspects of the labour contract within their scope. In many industries and trades, wages and the wage system, hours of work, overtime, holidays, apprenticeship and often questions of works discipline (works rules) as well are regulated by Collective Agreement. The expansion of the number of workers covered by Collective Agreements can be seen in the following table:[1]

At end of	No. of Collective Agreements	No. of establishment	No. of employed persons		
			Total	Females	Salaried employees
1912	10,739	159,930	1,574,285	—	—
1913	10,885	143,088	1,398,597	—	—
1914	10,840	143,650	1,395,723	—	—
1918	7,819	107,503	1,127,690	—	—
1919	11,009	272,251	5,987,475	—	—
1920	11,624	434,504	9,561,323	1,665,115	—
1921	11,488	697,476	12,882,874	2,729,788	—
1922	10,768	890,237	14,261,106	3,161,268	1,930,754

The relative stability of the number of Collective Agreements is noteworthy as indicating the decreasing importance of Agreements made in respect of a single firm and the growth of Agreements made between associations of employers and workpeople. In March 1924, 1470 Collective Agreements were in operation which had been declared by the Ministry of Labour to be binding on all those employed in the occupation in question in the area covered by the Agreement. Of these 78 were Federal Collective Agreements covering the whole country.

The growth of the importance of Collective Agreements was favoured by the deliberate policy of the Government, by the withdrawal of the opposition of the employers and by the necessities of the troubled and ever-changing economic conditions which followed the Revolution. But an essential concomitant and condition of this expansion was the growth in the numbers and influence of the Trade Unions. As in most other industrial countries, the end of the War brought with it an immense and very rapid accession of strength to the Trade Union movement

[1] *Reichsarbeitsblatt*, May 16, 1924.

in Germany. To the millions of men who were suddenly demobilised and thrust upon the labour market, the Trade Unions appeared as an effective aid against exploitation and as offering an indispensable assistance in finding work under reasonable conditions.

The changes in the membership of Trade Unions are shown in the following table:[1]

(In Thousands)

End of	"Free"	"Christian"	Hirsch-Duncker	End of	"Free"	"Christian"	Hirsch-Duncker
1913	2,525	342	107	1922	7,822	1,034	231
1918	2,866	539	114	1923	5,809	807	216
1919	7,337	1,001	190	1924	4,024	613	147
1920	8,032	1,106	226	1925	4,183	588	158
1921	7,752	1,029	225				

The year 1920 saw the maximum increase in the numbers of the great Unions. The membership remained a little below this level until the year 1923, when the complete collapse of the currency followed by the hardships of the stabilisation period occasioned a very great falling off in numbers. The "Free" Trade Unions were the worst affected, their membership decreasing to approximately 4,000,000 by June 1924. This great crisis in the movement was in part a direct consequence of the too rapid expansion in the preceding period, which had drawn into the ranks of the Unions millions of workers, most of whom had little or no understanding of the true aims and methods of Trade Unionism. When the reaction came and the Unions were for a time powerless to resist cuts in wages and the extension of hours, these workers grew disheartened and deserted the movement as rapidly as they had joined it. The progress of inflation destroyed the value of the accumulated funds of the Unions and made it difficult if not impossible for them to continue unemployment and other benefits, while the same causes, together with the growth of unemployment on a great scale, made the weekly contributions to the Union funds a heavy burden. An additional unfavourable factor was the dissensions

[1] From *Jahrbuch der Berufsverbände im deutschen Reiche*. The available figures for the other Trade Unions are incomplete and not always comparable from year to year. Their relative importance, however, has greatly diminished since the War.

and disunity within the Unions and the discontent of the rank
and file with the policy of the leaders. Many workers ceased to
belong to any organisation at all, while others joined the ranks of
syndicalist and communist Unions. Since the middle of 1924,
however, there has been a marked change in the situation. The
three great Unions have consolidated their forces and won back
some of the ground they had lost. Their finances are now on a
much sounder basis and they have been successful in many cases
in securing rises in wages and reduction in overtime.

THE STRUGGLE FOR THE CONTROL OF
THE WORKS COUNCILS

When the Works Councils Act came to be drafted, in a period
of considerable revolutionary ferment, the leaders of the Trade
Union movement were exceedingly anxious to ensure that the
Works Councils should not be given such powers as would enable
them to form a rival organisation of German labour, with the
result of weakening the dominant position to which the Trade
Unions had attained and imperilling the whole system of Collective Agreements under which labour conditions were being
regulated on a uniform basis over large industrial areas. The
history of the Russian Revolution had shown that the leadership
of the whole body of industrial workers in a country could be
wrested from the hands of the Trade Unions and transferred to
an entirely different body of men without experience of Trade
Union traditions and imbued rather with feelings of hostility
towards their aims and methods.

To prevent, if possible, a similar development taking place in
Germany, was one of the chief concerns of the Trade Unions and
of the legislature. Thus, while the first section of the Works
Councils Act is drawn in very wide terms and describes the purpose of the constitution of Works Councils as being "to protect
the common interests of the employees as against the employer",
it is made clear in subsequent sections (Sections 8, 20, 31, 37, 47,
66 (3) and 78 (1, 2, 3)) that the intention of the framers of the Act
was that the Works Councils should act as subsidiary and subordinate organs of the Trade Unions, with distinct if comple-
mentary functions.

The provisions of all these sections exemplify the care taken by the framers of the Works Councils Act to prevent the Councils from encroaching on the sphere of operations of the Trade Unions, and the wording of many of them was due to the Trade Union representatives in the Reichstag.

As soon as the Works Councils Act had been passed, the radical elements in German labour gathered together their forces in a determined endeavour to capture the new Works Councils machinery and to use it as a weapon in their struggle against the conservative and moderate policy of the leaders of the Trade Union movement. Defeated though they had been in every attempt to secure political functions for the Works Councils, or even to obtain for them any wide measure of independent powers in the economic sphere, the leaders of the Communists and the Independent Socialists still hoped that the Councils could be welded into a revolutionary agency. Revolution by force of arms had failed, but there remained the hope that an organisation of Works Councils, imbued with the communist or syndicalist spirit, would afford a means of rendering the existing capitalist system unworkable and thus of bringing about the Revolution on Russian lines which they so ardently desired.

The left wing of the German labour movement was opposed to the traditional policy of the Trade Unions, not merely because of its "reformist" character, but also because the administration of the Unions was centralised and bureaucratic. It was contended that the official leaders had betrayed the true interests of the working classes during the War, owing to their whole-hearted support of the Government in the prosecution of the War. Events had proved them to be wrong over that great issue. Was it not more than likely that here also they were pursuing a false policy? Hence, throughout the country, there arose an ably conducted and bitter campaign against the "mandarins" of the Trade Unions and their pretensions to stifle the Works Councils by bringing them under the aegis and control of the central organisation of the Trade Unions. In Berlin, where the radical element was very strong, an independent Works Councils Bureau was set up, to which 26,000 Councils in and around Berlin were affiliated. The general instructions of the Trade Unions were ignored and many "wild strikes", as unofficial strikes are called in Germany, were fomented.

In the meantime, the Trade Unions' headquarters had been active in their own defence. They possessed the immense advantage of being in control of an elaborate and widespread machinery and of being able to get into immediate touch with their members and, in particular, with their local officials throughout the country. As soon, therefore, as the first elections to the Works Councils were due to be held, lists of candidates were drawn up for each works by the Unions and were presented for election. The opposition had no such organisation and had to depend in most cases entirely on local and unco-ordinated action. At the same time, a Works Council Bureau was set up by the "Free" Trade Unions at their headquarters in Berlin, consisting of four members of the *Allgemeiner Deutscher Gewerkschaftsbund* (A.D.G.B.) and three members of the Afa or central organisation of salaried employees' Trade Unions.

Finally, special Works Councils newspapers were brought out and financed by the A.D.G.B., the Afa, and a large number of individual Unions. These journals devoted considerable space to urging upon their readers the need of loyalty to their Trade Unions and of being guided in all important questions by the advice of their Union leaders.

The decisive point in this conflict of policy and principle came in October 1920, when the A.D.G.B. and the Afa summoned the first National Congress of Works Councils belonging to their organisations. The Congress was held in Berlin and lasted for three days. In all 953 delegates were present from all parts of Germany. The debates were animated by a great deal of feeling on both sides. The party in opposition to the official leaders urged that the Trade Unions, by their organisation and historical development, were essentially non-revolutionary. The Works Councils represented a new and vital force in the German labour movement and must not be allowed to be stultified by the centralised bureaucratic organisation of the Unions. The Works Councils must be permitted to develop on their own lines, untrammelled by the cautious advice of the Union leaders, or, indeed, by the many restrictive provisions of the Act itself; it was not too late to save the Revolution if the Councils were true to the genius of their own institution. They must not shrink from the fact that the adoption of this policy would inevitably lead to civil war.

On the other side it was contended that the Works Councils were essentially economic rather than political institutions. The German people was not ripe for an immediate revolution in the sense of the expropriation of the capitalists and the taking over of the whole productive process by the workers. The Works Councils were a new and valuable weapon to be used in working towards the socialist State, but they could only safely achieve this purpose if they carried out their functions in the closest co-operation with the Trade Unions.

The course of the proceedings revealed that by far the greater number of the delegates to the Congress were adherents of the official view and, finally, the following resolution was passed by an overwhelming majority:

It is incumbent on Labour to develop the power, which lies in it as a class, to the maximum extent; to make use of this power in action; and to avail itself of all means which can serve this purpose. Important tasks are imposed on the Works Councils through their position in the productive process, and they have a great responsibility to shoulder. The Works Councils find their support in the Trade Unions, which remain, as before, the chief protagonists in the economic sphere, in the struggle between Capital and Labour. The Works Councils must base themselves on the Trade Unions because they can only accomplish their tasks if they are certain of the support of the Trade Unions. The development of the Trade Unions into powerful industrial unions is exclusively a matter for the Trade Unions themselves.

The Works Councils are to be organised within the Trade Unions. A separate organisation of the Works Councils, whether local or central, is undesirable; apart from its effect in hindering the activity of the Trade Unions it would nullify the effective representation of the interests of the workers by the Works Councils. On the other hand, a local grouping of the Works Councils in conjunction with the local Committees of the A.D.G.B. and of the Afa, as well as the establishment of a Central Bureau jointly with the Central Bureau of the Trade Unions, is necessary. The Congress agrees to the local organisation of the Works Councils and the formation of a Central Bureau for the Reich, but only on the basis of the principles of the A.D.G.B. and of the Afa. The Consultative Committee to be elected by the Congress is instructed, in co-operation with the Executive Committee, to make preparations for the elections to the District Economic Councils as soon as the Districts are defined.

THE INCORPORATION OF THE WORKS COUNCILS IN THE TRADE UNION ORGANISATION

With the passing of the resolution referred to in the preceding section, the way was clear for the Trade Unions to proceed with the work of incorporating the Works Councils within their organisation.

This was effected, firstly, by setting up special machinery designed to preserve to the Unions a general control and supervision over the policy of the Works Councils and also, in part, by the Unions' control over the elections to the Councils.

In the case of the "Free" Trade Unions, the general principle adopted was that the Works Councils in each district should be subject to the direction and guidance of the local District Committees of the Unions. For this purpose 15 industrial groups were recognised, and every Works Council is now classified as belonging to one or other of these groups, the determining factor in each case being the nature of the undertaking and not the occupation or craft of the workers.[1]

Each member of a Works Council who belongs to the "Free" Trade Unions is required to register his name with the local Trade Union Committee, which informs him to which industrial group he belongs. All the Works Councils members in a given industrial group in each district elect a small Committee (*Gruppenrat*) composed of five representatives of the Councils and not less than two Trade Union representatives. The latter are thus able to influence the Works Councils in the direction of uniformity along the general lines of Trade Union policy. The intention of the Unions is that the *Gruppenrat* as such should not concern itself with Trade Union matters, but rather with the economic problems of the industry in question and, in par-

---

[1] Industries are grouped as follows: banking, insurance and commerce; building; textiles and clothing; chemical industries; liberal professions; printing and paper industries; wood industries; agriculture; food stuffs; leather; smelting and metal industries; state and municipal services; transport; mining; social insurance.

ticular, should act as a centre for the collection of economic information from all the Works Councils in its area. The *Gruppenrat* reports at intervals to a plenary meeting of all the local Works Councils members in the industry together with representatives of every Union in the area.

The different industries are linked together by a General Assembly of the Works Councils, consisting of delegates from the Works Councils belonging to all the 15 industrial groups in the locality and also delegates from the Trade Unions. It is significant that a minimum period of one year's membership of a Trade Union is a necessary qualification for election to the General Assembly. The conduct of the business of the General Assembly itself is in the hands of a Central Council, the Executive Committee of which is composed of five members of the Central Council and five Trade Union representatives.

The chief features of this organisation of the Works Councils are: (a) the care taken to prevent the Councils from encroaching on any of the normal functions of the Unions; (b) the large representation of Trade Union officials on the various bodies representing the Works Councils and, in particular, on the Executive Committee of the Central Council; (c) the whole representative machinery, so far as the Works Councils are concerned, is purely local and there is no permanent central organisation of the Works Councils provided for the country as a whole. Since the passing of the Works Councils Act in February 1920, there has been only one Federal Congress of Works Councils officially convened by the A.D.G.B. Unofficial Congresses have been held under the auspices of the Communists, but the official leaders of the Trade Union movement have thrown the whole of their weight and influence against the holding of Congresses, which they feared might lead to the establishment of a rival organisation which would endanger their centralised control over labour policy.

In practice, the Works Councils in some of the great industrial districts of Germany have gone beyond the general principles laid down by the A.D.G.B. and the Afa, and have formed important district organisations of Works Councils. A number of these bodies have been created or controlled by the Syndicalists and Communists as a direct attempt to establish a rival organisation to that of the Trade Unions.

The most important communist Trade Union is the Union of Manual and Brain Workers (*Union der Hand- und Kopfarbeiter*), formed in 1921, which is based definitely on the Councils as a method of organisation. The chief strength of this Union is in the Ruhr mining district, and the following table is instructive as showing that, in this area, the Communists and Syndicalists enjoy a degree of representation on the Councils which is out of all proportion to their relative strength in the Trade Union movement as a whole.[1]

Ruhr Mining District

Trade Unions	Works Councils members				Percentage of total members			
	1921	1922	1924	1925	1921	1922	1924	1925
Socialist Unions	1223	1195	1038	1275	45·67	41·70	33·85	43·30
"Christian" Unions	459	590	627	687	17·14	20·59	20·45	23·33
Hirsch-Duncker	18	38	32	26	0·67	1·33	1·06	0·88
"Yellow" Unions	—	1	11	10	—	0·03	0·36	0·33
Syndicalist and Communist Unions	850	942	1310	893	31·74	32·87	42·72	30·32
Polish and other Unions, and unorganised	128	100	48	53	4·78	3·48	1·56	1·84
Total	2678	2866	3066	2944	100·0	100·0	100·0	100·0

If the conditions represented by these figures held good over the rest of Germany, it would clearly be idle to say that the communist danger in the Councils had been overcome, though the figures for 1925 show a great falling off in the representation of the Communists. But, in fact, in other parts of the country the Communists have only a very insignificant place on the Councils and, taking German mining as a whole, their proportional strength in the years under review was only about one-half what it was in the Ruhr Councils, while in most other industries and districts their strength is very slight. In most parts of the country the district organisations of the Works Councils have

[1] In 1922 the *Union der Hand- und Kopfarbeiter* had 162,000 members, and the chief syndicalist Union, the *Freie Arbeiter Union Deutschlands*, 62,000 out of a total Trade Union membership of more than 10,000,000.

47

been either initiated or captured by the socialist Trade Unions, which have used them as a means of consolidating their power over the Councils. Nevertheless, so long as the Syndicalists and Communists are able to maintain so great a hold over the Councils as they continue to do in the very important Ruhr mining area, it is impossible to regard them as a negligible factor in the situation, or to speak of the menace to the Trade Unions as entirely overcome.

It is worthy of note that the attitude and relations of the "Christian" Trade Unions towards the Works Councils have always been different from those of the socialist Unions. The "Christian" Unions have never been confronted with the possible secession of great numbers of workers, imbued with the revolutionary spirit which was so widespread in 1919 and 1920. Consequently they have not had to fear the Works Councils as a rival type of organisation nor to take special precautions against them; on the contrary they have welcomed them from the first and regarded them as a useful and valuable piece of social machinery. On the whole, the co-operation here between the Unions and the Works Councils has been closer and more cordial than in the case of the socialist Unions.

One consequence of this is the more organic and comprehensive organisation of the Works Councils, as can be seen in the case of the "Christian" Union of Textile Workers, where there is a four-fold grouping.[1]

The functions of these Councils are set out as follows:

(a) The discussion of all economic and social questions which specially concern the interests of the textile industry or the workers employed therein.

---

[1] 1. In each locality there is a Textile Workers' Council with a Committee of eight members, half of whom are representatives of the Works Councils and half of the local Trade Union officials.

2. In each main industrial centre there is a District Textile Workers' Council to which the individual Textile Workers' Councils send one representative for each ten members. This has an Executive Committee of eight constituted in the same manner as in the case of the local Councils.

3. There is a Federal Textile Workers' Council for the whole Reich elected by the District Councils, with an Executive Committee of 16 members, of whom eight are elected by the District Councils and eight are nominated by the Central organisation of the Textile Workers' Union.

4. There are branch Councils for the separate crafts (spinners, weavers, etc.) within the industrial districts.

(*b*) The general and technical education of the members of the Works Councils, in order to enable them to accomplish the tasks entrusted to them under the Works Councils Act in the interests of the whole body of textile workers and in furtherance of the economic prosperity of the individual undertakings and the industry as a whole.

(*c*) The collection of statistics relating to wages and prices, and of information necessary for drawing up wage proposals; the giving of advice to officials of the Union and co-operation with them in the negotiation of Collective Agreements; and finally the supervision of such Agreements in operation.

(*d*) The strengthening of the Union and the furtherance of the closest possible understanding between the Works Councils and the organs of the Trade Union. The whole of the costs of the above organisation are met out of the funds of the Union.

A second instrument in the hands of the Trade Unions consists in their control over the election to the Works Councils. At each new election a list of candidates is put forward by each of the great groups of Unions represented in the works (socialist Unions, "Christian" Unions, etc.). The loyalty of all the other members of the group in the works is then engaged to vote for the candidates on the official list and considerable pressure is exerted to prevent the putting forward of rival lists. In many cases this is successful and the nominees of the Unions are adopted without opposition from the members concerned. Where the Union feels itself sufficiently strong, it may require each candidate to sign an undertaking that he will, if elected, resign his office at any time if he finds himself in conflict with the wishes of his electors or of the Trade Union and is asked either by the Union or a majority of his electors to withdraw.[1] Such an undertaking is, however, alien both to the letter and to the spirit of the Works Councils Act, which gives to the members of the Council an irrevocable mandate for one year (save in cases of gross misconduct).

Except in the Ruhr and in Berlin the control exercised by the Unions over elections to Works Councils was fairly complete

---

[1] Winschuh, *Betriebsrat oder Gewerkschaft* (1922), p. 76.

between 1920 and the end of 1923, but it received a great set-back in 1924, when millions of workers left the Unions and became either completely unorganised or grouped themselves into one of the loosely formed communist or syndicalist organisations. As the latter are concerned even more to oppose the policy of the Unions than to obstruct the employers in the conduct of their businesses, the Unions found themselves confronted by numbers of Works Councils which entirely repudiated their authority and which at times were willing to conclude agreements with the employers that were contrary to the declared policy of the Unions, and at others to foment "wild strikes" unauthorised and unrecognised by the Unions. The practical disadvantages of this position of independence were, however, not long in showing themselves, especially as the industrial situation was such that the bargaining strength of the employers was enormously greater than it had been at any time since the Revolution. During 1925 the Trade Unions consolidated their position and recovered a portion, though a small one, of their lost members. At the same time the employers ruthlessly dismissed Works Councillors whose activities were obnoxious to them, sometimes even temporarily closing down the whole of their works, in order to deprive them of the protection of the Act. All these factors combined to strengthen again the influence of the Unions and to give them a greater voice both in the election and the policies of the Works Councils.

A third and very important sphere of Trade Union influence is to be found in the powers given by the Works Councils Act to the Councils to invite delegates of their Unions to be present at Council meetings and also at meetings of the Works Assembly. Extensive use has been made in practice of this power, and the officials of the Unions have been able to exercise a moderating and enlightening influence on the policy of the Works Councils, many of whose members lack the education and experience necessary to carry out their functions with success and efficiency. The Union officials themselves, however, are not always as conversant as they should be with the technicalities of the Works Councils Act, as witness the following passage in the Report of the Factory Inspectors for the district of Erfurt, 1923-4:

It was often observed that the Trade Unions endeavoured to take certain rights out of the hands of the Works Councils and took the initiative in negotiations which were properly the concern of the Councils. Works Councillors have frequently complained to the Inspector that they were given incorrect advice by the Unions in legal questions, and in one instance the desire was expressed that he should convene a meeting of the Works Councillors in all branches of industry in the area, without the knowledge of the Trade Unions, in order to explain certain questions in a lecture.

Even apart from the numerous cases where Works Councils have been under the influence of syndicalist or communist leaders, friction is apt to arise between members of the Councils and the local officials of the Unions.

The latter are not always very tactful in their dealings with the Councils, while the different angle from which they view questions of policy sometimes leads to conflicts with the Unions, which stand out for the rigid uniformity of the "Common Rule", whereas the Works Councils are more ready to permit deviations in the productive interests of their own concerns. A certain amount of mutual jealousy and rivalry for the effective leadership of the workers is also inevitable.

Nevertheless it remains true that the successful functioning of the Works Councils is dependent primarily on the backing they receive from the Unions, and it is much more common for the members of Councils to complain of insufficient support from the Unions than of excessive zeal on their part. Except in the very large concerns, the employer is rarely inclined to pay much attention to the representation of the Works Council unless he knows that it has a powerful Union at its back. On countless occasions it has been the presence of Trade Union officials at meetings of the Council, or their advice and assistance in the background, which has prevented the employer from taking advantage of the ignorance and lack of experience of the members of the Council. It is not too much to say that, despite all its statutory powers, the Works Council as an institution is impotent unless it is based upon the organised strength and financial resources of the Unions. It is the realisation of this fact which, more than anything else, has accounted for the success of the Unions in incorporating the Works Councils into their organisation. The dependence of the Works Councils on the Unions has been strikingly shown by the course of events in 1924 and 1925, when depression of trade hit the Councils even more hardly than the Unions. The Councils virtually disappeared except where the Unions retained some of their power, while, apart from those who belonged to Trade Union organisations, there were only few employees who had the courage and the self-sacrifice to allow themselves to be elected to serve on the Councils.[1]

There remain to be mentioned two other directions in which the Trade Unions are able to exert influence over the trend and development of the Works Councils. These are in the first place the Works Councils schools and secondly the Works Councils press. Both of these activities are discussed at some length subsequently, and it is sufficient here to draw attention to their evident importance in moulding opinion in directions which are in harmony with the principles adopted and followed by the central organisations of the Trade Unions.

THE WORKS COUNCILS AND THE FREEDOM OF ASSOCIATION

While it is broadly true that the fears cherished at first by the Trade Unions that their position of leadership in the labour world would be undermined by the Works Councils have proved hitherto to be exaggerated, the Works Councils Act has created new conditions which were not foreseen by the legislature and have led to considerable abuses in practice.

It is laid down in Section 66, Clause 6, that it is the duty of the Works Council to safeguard the employees' right of association. But other sections of the Act afford opportunities, which have not hitherto existed, for the infringement of this right of association in ways which it is impossible in practice to guard against.

In the first place, there is the possibility that the Works Council will not concern itself to take up a legitimate complaint where the individual or section of employees concerned is not

[1] Cf. Reports of Factory Inspectors for Baden for 1925, p. 16.

organised at all or belongs to a different organisation. The writer was once informed by the Chairman of the Works Council in a large firm that his first enquiry to any worker who came to him for advice or with a complaint was "Are you a Trade Unionist?" If the answer was in the negative he read him a lecture on the neglect of his duties to his fellow-workers, which caused the man to depart hurriedly, glad to escape from so unfriendly a reception.[1]

Of much greater practical importance than this mere neglect of the interests of the unorganised worker is the scope, given by the sections relating to the engagement and dismissal of workers, for the penalising of the unorganised and, in particular, of employees belonging to rival organisations.

Reference has already been made above to the antagonism between the "Free" Trade Unions and the "Christian" Trade Unions and the other smaller Unions, which are all apt to be characterised by the "Free" Trade Unions by the opprobrious epithet "Yellow"[2]—i.e. friendly to the interests of the employers. In the case of the engagement of workers the only rights given to the Works Council by Section 78, Clause 8, are those of agreeing on certain general principles with the employer and it is explicitly laid down that these principles must not contain any provisions which make employment dependent on the adherence or non-adherence of the worker to any particular political party or Trade Union organisation. The Works Council has no legal claim to control the exercise by the employer of his power of engaging workers within the framework of the agreed principles. But in practice the Council is often able to influence the choice of the particular employees who are taken on. Thus one writer states that the Chairman of the Wage-earners' Council is normally in close touch with the porter at the gate of the works and can secure that applicants who do not belong to his organisation are discouraged. Again the Chairman will often have occasion to communicate with his colleague who is a member of the local Labour Exchange Committee, and who can send to the works applicants who are of the same way of

[1] Cf. also Reports of Prussian Factory Inspectors for 1921, p. 450.
[2] See above, p. 35.

thinking. The Chairman, being notified beforehand by telephone, can take steps to facilitate their engagement.[1]

The opportunities for infringing the freedom of association are however greatest in the case of dismissals, where the legal powers of the Works Council are much more extensive than in the case of engagements. Where a worker has been dismissed he must apply in the first instance to his Sectional Council; if the latter refuses to take up his case the worker has no redress and cannot appeal to the Labour Court on his own behalf. If he could prove that the Council had refused solely on the ground that he did not belong to a particular organisation, he could no doubt secure the dissolution of the Council on the ground of gross abuse of its official duties. But in the nature of things this would be very difficult to establish and, in any event, his dismissal would still stand. A considerable number of cases have occurred in which the employer has been forced by the Works Council, under threat of strike, to dismiss employees on the sole ground that they were not members of the Union to which the Council belonged. Where such instances have been brought officially to the cognisance of the Conciliation Board or Labour Court they have generally resulted in the compulsory dissolution of the Council involved and, in some cases, even in the imprisonment of the offending Works Councillors.[2]

Again, where large numbers of workers have to be dismissed on economic grounds, the Works Council is empowered by the Act to co-operate, and in practice the employer is accustomed, as a rule, to throw upon the Works Council the task of selecting those who are to be dismissed. The opportunity which this offers for discrimination in favour of the friends and colleagues of the Council is patent, though it is perhaps of smaller aggregate importance than the case of the individual employee, where the proof of unfair discrimination is also so much harder to establish. The "Christian" Unions have suffered so much from this sort of treatment that their leaders have pressed hard, but so far unavailingly, for an amending Act which would modify, in par-

[1] Winschuh, *Betriebsrat oder Gewerkschaft* (1922), p. 45.
[2] Reports of Prussian Factory Inspectors for 1921, pp. 495, 512, and for 1922, p. 213.

ticular, Section 86, in the sense that a dismissed employee who is unable to secure the support of his Sectional Council shall be able to bring his own case before the Court. This, however, would have the great objection of eliminating the important function of the Council of sifting out cases of dismissal and preventing the time of the employer and the Court being wasted by appeals in which the employee is obviously entirely in the wrong. It must not be imagined that this short-sighted policy of discrimination against members of minority organisations—a policy which can at any time recoil on its authors' heads with an alteration in the composition of the body of employees—is dictated by the responsible leaders of the Unions concerned. No doubt in some cases the district lodges of the Unions are at fault, but to a large extent the cause is to be found in the practical advantages of a uniform policy within the works, and in the desire of the Council members elected by the majority group to retain office and to strengthen their influence and hold over the employees who are their electors. In the long run, a Works Council, which is actuated by partisan motives and sacrifices the interests of the employees in the works as a unit to the interests of an external organisation, is likely to forfeit the respect and confidence both of the employees and the employer and to seek in vain for that solidarity of support which is so essential to the successful carrying out of its functions.

THE WORKS COUNCILS AND COLLECTIVE BARGAINING

It has already been stated that the negotiation with the employers of Collective Agreements regulating wages, hours and other conditions of employment, has for long been the cardinal policy of the Trade Unions, but it is precisely in this most vital point of their defences that the Works Councils Act has opened up new and dangerous possibilities of a breach. The Collective Agreement represents a norm to which both parties can appeal and one which is not susceptible of modification by individual agreement, except where such modification is to the advantage of the employees.[1]

[1] See above, p. 37.

Now the existence of the Collective Agreement renders it more difficult for the workers of a particular concern to extract specially favourable terms from their employer, even though he is in a position to grant them. The employer in turn is generally a member of an Employers' Federation and is more or less tightly bound to abide by the terms which have been negotiated between the Trade Union and his Federation. The Agreement can thus become a reason or at least an excuse for refusing to increase wages. Even before the War this had often given rise to friction and to complaints of incompetent and timid leadership in the Unions. Since the War, with the enormous accession of numerical strength to the Unions and with the spread of a radical spirit amongst the workers, this friction and discontent has immensely increased, to the great detriment of the labour movement as a whole.

The Works Councils Act has in some ways aggravated and intensified these disruptive tendencies. The employees in each establishment have now a properly elected recognised body of representatives through whom they can approach and bargain with the employer. Moreover, the Councils are required by the Act to supervise the putting into effect of the ruling Collective Agreements in respect of their own establishments; but they complain that they have no say in the determination of those Agreements, which are negotiated solely by the Trade Union officials. As these Agreements tend to cover an ever-wider sphere of industrial relations, the Councils find themselves to some extent reduced to a mere organ of inspection, responsible not so much to their immediate electors as to the Trade Unions. Even where no Collective Agreement exists, the Act requires the Works Council to negotiate, in most cases, in conjunction with the Trade Unions and under these conditions it is not difficult for the employer to play off the one against the other. Although in theory a Collective Agreement merely lays down minimum rates of wages and other conditions of employment, the tendency is naturally for these to become the established rates throughout the whole industry. But the Works Councils, with their representatives on the Control Board of every Company and with the right of inspection of the balance sheet and profit and loss account of all large businesses, are in a particularly strong position for knowing when conditions are favourable for extracting improved conditions. The employer, in such cases, will often take refuge in the Collective Agreement and will appeal to the Union representatives to preserve discipline amongst their members. Thus the Union is continually being put in the invidious position of acting as a brake and a restraining influence upon its members. The Works Council, in turn, finds itself with divided loyalties and may decide that its duty to its electors is more direct and immediate than its duty to the Trade Union to which its members belong. An additional factor of some importance, which weakened the position of the Trade Unions during the later stages of the great period of inflation that came to an end in November 1923, was that wage rates became linked automatically to cost of living index numbers—i.e. coefficients of inflation. The direct influence of Trade Union organisations on wage rates was lessened, and membership of the Unions was rendered less attractive. This is one of the explanations of the tremendous decline in membership which all Unions experienced in the latter part of 1923; while the subsequent hardships of the stabilisation period, when the level of real wages was intolerably low, made the payment of Union contributions impossible in many cases.

Unemployment, as measured by the official figures, rose from 6·3 per cent. in August 1923 to 28·2 per cent. in December 1923, while at the latter date 42·2 per cent. of those in employment were working short time. Thus, very suddenly, the employers regained the "strategic initiative" which had been in the hands of the workers ever since the Revolution of November 1918. The cumulative effects of the above changes have been of the utmost importance in influencing the relations of the Works Councils to the Trade Unions and of both to the employers.

The great change in the relative bargaining strength of the two parties in the labour market has been reflected in the very active, and to some slight extent successful, attempts of the employers to wean the workers from their allegiance to the Unions by concluding specially favourable agreements with them on the basis of a "Works Agreement" (*Betriebsvereinbarung*) in place of a

Collective Agreement between the organisations on both sides. During the inflation period it was not uncommon for an employer, whose order book was full, to compound with his Works Council in order to avoid trouble, and to grant terms which were superior to those under the ruling Collective Agreement. In such circumstances there is a tendency for the Council to appear to the workers to be a more efficient form of labour organisation than the Trade Union and one, moreover, possessing the advantage of not requiring any financial contributions. It was, however, after the end of the inflation, when the Trade Unions, temporarily crippled by the loss of nearly all their reserves and suffering from a great decrease in membership and consequently in prestige, were with difficulty consolidating their resources, that the employers developed to the fullest extent their propaganda in favour of local Works Agreements. The employers have discovered a new magic in the formula *Werksgemeinschaft*, or Works Community, i.e. a community of interest between all those engaged in an undertaking—the interest of the employees in high wages and salaries, of the employer in low real costs and high profits, each alike dependent upon the successful conduct of the undertaking as a whole. For the employers the attractiveness of the *Werksgemeinschaft* lies in the possibility it affords of cutting adrift from the Collective Agreement, with all its rigidity, and of determining wage rates once more by individual bargaining. In this case, however, it is contemplated that the bargaining should be, not between the employer and each separate worker, but between the employer and his own employees as a body—a *Betriebsvereinbarung* or Works Agreement in place of the *Tarifvertrag* or Collective Agreement. It is contended that the mass regulation of wages, hours and other conditions of work has been unsatisfactory in its results, that it has prevented firms working under unfavourable competition from competing with their more fortunate rivals, and so has increased unemployment. The individual employer feels that he should be free to strike a bargain with his own employees; in certain directions he may be able to offer them more favourable terms than those secured under the Collective Agreement, in return for concessions on other points of vital importance to him.

The dread of unemployment has undoubtedly been responsible for some of the Works Agreements which have been concluded. Sometimes the employer has made his agreement with the Works Council, while at other times he has gone over the head of the Works Council and has appealed to the whole body of employees to accept his terms in preference to the alternative of the closing-down of the factory. In such cases, the Works Council, powerless to intervene, has been forced to acquiesce in an arrangement of which it disapproves but which it cannot resist.

The Hours of Work Order of December 21, 1923, which virtually repealed the eight-hour day established by previous legislation, tended, on the one hand, to check the movement towards Works Agreements, inasmuch as extensions of the working-day were permitted as a result of Collective Agreements between organisations of employers and employees, while the intention of the Act was that such extensions would not become legally operative as a result of Works Agreements. On the other hand, the employers, realising that individual agreements with their own operatives would be much easier to attain than agreements with the Unions, were stimulated to seek for ways of evading the intention of the Order. To some extent they have been successful in doing this by means of working arrangements with their employees, who have preferred to acquiesce in the proposals of the employer rather than be unemployed. To some extent also they have been aided by the legal obscurity of the term Tarifvertrag, and by the uncertainty whether an agreement between the Works Council representing the body of workers in a particular undertaking and the employer can ever be a "Collective Agreement" in the legal sense of the word.

It is held by good authorities that under certain conditions this can be the case, i.e. where the Works Council is specifically empowered by the employees to negotiate a Collective Agreement on their behalf with the employer. In this case the body of workers form themselves effectively into a Trade Union. They cannot, however, legally do this and still retain membership of an outside Union which has concluded a general Collective Agreement with the employers—for any agreement concluded under such conditions would be legally null and void, even though in practice, owing to the weakness of the Unions, it might be effective. Although the term Works Agreement (*Betriebsverein-barung*) has made its appearance in the statute book, it is still, in contrast to the Collective Agreement, without legal effect—with the solitary exception of the statutory clauses of the works rules (*Arbeitsordnung*). Not merely does the Collective Agreement always take priority over the Works Agreement, but the latter does not legally bind either the employer or employees, nor does it exclude the possibility of individual contracts between the employer and any of his employees, which deviate from the terms of the Works Agreement. At present there is a strong movement in Germany in favour of giving legal effect also to the Works Agreement, while retaining the priority of the Collective Agreement, but opinion is by no means unanimous on this proposal.[1]

The practical difficulties encountered by the Unions in enforcing Collective Agreements are aggravated by their loss of membership, which often means that the majority of the employees in a works are non-Unionists, and further by the existence of different Unions (the socialist, "Christian", Hirsch-Duncker Unions, etc.) pursuing different policies in many cases. The method of proportional representation applied to the election of employees to the Works Councils ensures the representation of minority groups on the Councils, and therefore renders it the more difficult for the Councils to pursue a uniform policy dictated by any one Union.

The employers, on their side, make no concealment of their desire to use the Works Community, as they conceive it, as a means of restoring direct negotiation with their workpeople:

The Trade Unions must cease to regard the Works Councils merely as their officials in the works.... The Works Council as an organ of the Trade Union inevitably results in the intrusion of the Trade Union

[1] An enormous literature has grown up round the legal issues involved in the Works Agreement. Cf., in particular, Flatow, *Betriebsvereinbarung und Arbeitsordnung* (1923); Schuldt, *Die Betriebsvereinbarung* (1925); Kaskel, *Arbeitsrecht* (1925), pp. 21–27; *Die sozialen Probleme des Betriebes* (1925), edited by Potthoff. Also many recent articles in *Die Arbeit*, *Die Gewerkschaftsarchiv*, *Arbeitsrecht*, and other periodical literature.

organisation in the works and thereby frustrates any hope of a fruitful Works Community.[1]

In January 1925 courses were held by employers' organisations for works managers, etc., at which these were instructed as to the methods of forming a Works Community.[2] Stress was laid on the value of works welfare schemes, such as the provision of sports facilities, housing, canteens, etc., which would tend to link the employee closer to his place of work.[3] It was even declared that, not merely Trade Unions, but also associations of employers, were harmful and superfluous as interposing between the employer and his own workpeople: the ideal of the future must be to cultivate anew the old close personal relationship between employer and worker. It may be noted that this policy of decentralisation, so far as relations between employers and employed are concerned, does not correspond in any way to a decentralisation of industrial organisation in general; for the consolidation movement in German industry has proceeded with added vigour since the War.

While this reaction on the part of the employers against the Collective Agreement and their preference for the Works Agreement is, to some extent, based on a not unreasonable desire for a greater degree of elasticity in the determination of wages and conditions of employment, which would take into account the great existing variations both in the industrial requirements of different undertakings and in the composition and attitude of mind of the employees, it also unquestionably reflects a revival of the former antagonism of the employers against the Trade Unions as a type of labour organisation. Since the end of 1923 the employers, strengthened by the change in the industrial situation, have been able to take advantage of the weakness of the Unions to open a new industrial offensive against them.

Reference has already been made to the Joint Industrial Alliances (*Arbeitsgemeinschaften*) established at the end of the War by the central organisations of the employers and the Trade

[1] Dr Meissinger, "Die Betriebsgemeinschaft", in *Die sozialen Probleme des Betriebes* (1925).
[2] Nörpel in *Die Arbeit*, April 15, 1925.
[3] Cf. also Winschuh, "Die psychologischen Grundlagen der Werksgemeinschaft", in *Die sozialen Probleme des Betriebes*.

Unions. The terms under which the Joint Alliances were established comprised, *inter alia*, the full and complete recognition of the Trade Unions, and the renunciation by the employers of the support given to the "Yellow" Unions, which had been the most favoured devices before the War for fighting the socialist Unions. These Alliances, however, met with lively opposition on the part of the more radical section of the labour movement, as conflicting with the principle of class warfare; at the same time they were by no means popular with the employers. Hence it is not surprising that they should have fallen into abeyance and ceased to have any practical bearing on industrial relations. Thus the employers have found themselves with unfettered hands, free to make use of every weapon available to them in their struggle against the Trade Unions—and in particular, free to take up again the support of the "Yellow" Unions.

The new enthusiasm of the employers for the Works Agreement is in reality a part of the plan of campaign for utilising those who have broken away from the great Unions to drive breaches into the principle of collective bargaining. Thus a Works Council can become the executive head of what is in effect a "Yellow" Union, composed of a majority of workers in the undertaking, who, in return for certain benefits in respect of employment, welfare schemes, holidays on full pay, etc., follow the lead and pursue the policy of the employer. An organisation has been created in the form of the *Vaterländische Arbeitnehmerbewegung*, which is the successor of the "Yellow" Works Unions of pre-war days, and the policy of which is voiced in a weekly publication—*Die Werksgemeinschaft*. Against these disruptive manœuvres of the employers the Trade Unions have thrown the whole of their weight. By means of their schools, their newspapers, and their organisation throughout the country, they have warned their members and the workers as a whole against the conclusion of Works Agreements along the lines sought by the employers. For the Trade Unions it has been a vital struggle for existence and for the maintenance of everything for which they have fought and which they have attained during long years of strife. Works Agreements involve the undermining of the Collective Agreement and its replacement by a series of locally concluded bargains. The Unions are on strong ground when they urge that if the employers succeeded in their aim of eliminating Trade Union influence from the determination of wage rates, etc., the local Works Councils would be powerless to strike good bargains and all the advantages would accrue to the employers. Moreover, the Unions are opposed to Works Agreements for reasons of a more general character. They are afraid of joint agreements between the employers and Works Councils, the result of which might be the exploitation of the community as a whole. They regard the notion that the Councils could ever control the productive resources of the country as a wild revolutionary dream and as most undesirable even if it was feasible. During the maintenance of the existing industrial system, the Unions hold that they, and they alone, hold a mandate to secure the furtherance of the wider interests of the workers and to lay down the broad lines of labour policy, while under a socialist system their organisation and leadership would still be essential for the orderly control of the whole productive process in the collective interests of the community.

The struggle outlined in the preceding pages is still proceeding and it is not yet possible to give a final verdict on the issue; nevertheless all the indications hitherto point to the victory of the Trade Unions and to their ultimate success in warding off the assaults of the employers on the principle of the Collective Agreement. Although their loss of membership since 1923, and the dissensions within their ranks, have enabled the employers at times to use the Works Councils to further their aims, in many cases, where the Unions have been strongly represented in the Councils, they have been able to put up a resistance in detail which has often been more effective than the opposition of the Union as a body. The following statement of a well-known Trade Union leader bears witness to the value of the Councils to the Unions:[1]

The importance of the Works Councils to the Trade Union movement lies in the fact that the Works Councils, precisely at this time, act in most undertakings as well-knit cells of trusty adherents and as the organisers of a leading group of avowed supporters of the movement.

[1] Seidel, "Aufstieg und Krise der Gewerkschaftsbewegung", in *Die Gesellschaft*, April 1924, p. 81.

The value of such nuclei has shown itself for the first time in many Unions in the perilous months of the second half of the year 1923, and it will be still more clearly demonstrated in the coming days in which the mass of new Trade Union members, still untrained, short sighted, and only loosely bound to the movement, must be led in struggles involving many sacrifices.

The recurrent complaints of the employers that the Works Councils too often follow blindly the lead of the Unions testify to the strength of the control of the latter in practice.

THE WORKS COUNCILS AND THE STRUCTURE
OF TRADE UNIONISM

In Germany, even more than in England, the desirability and feasibility of changes in the organisation and structure of Trade Unionism have been under discussion since the War. The German Trade Unions, before the War, were built up on a craft basis and consisted for the most part of sharply demarcated bodies of workers, most of whom had served an apprenticeship to their trade and who belonged predominantly to the skilled occupations. With the growth, however, of Unionism amongst unskilled workers, many of the Craft Unions widened their scope to the extent of also admitting unskilled workers belonging to the same trades. Side by side with the Craft Unions there grew up Industrial Unions embracing workers in a large number of different trades but engaged in a single industry. This took place, sometimes through the amalgamation of Unions, and sometimes through the creation of a general Union to cover all those in a given industry. Except for one outstanding Union— the Metal Workers' Union—the development of Industrial Unionism was still relatively weak before the War. But during and since the War the movement towards industrial consolidation has made very great strides, especially in the direction of vertical combines, comprising workers of very different trades and degrees of skill. With the extension also of the Collective Agreement, regulating the wages and working-conditions of vast masses of workers, the tendency has been to simplify the wage tariffs by grading the workers into a small number of groups for wage purposes, the group classification being made dependent on skill, apprenticeship, length of service, etc., irrespective of craft or occupation. Under modern conditions, although a single Craft Union may be in a position to exploit a quasi-monopolist position and extract high wages for its members, the wages of the whole body of the employees are dependent on the economic position and capacity of the industry as a unit, and individual successes may be won at the expense of the remainder of the workers. Thus supporters of the Industrial Unions contend that only a comprehensive Union covering all the workers can hope to negotiate on equal terms with the employers and to extract the maximum available for all concerned.

Even though there are far fewer separate Unions in Germany than in England (in the A.D.G.B. 44 Unions; in the "Christian" 18 Unions: as compared with about 1135 in England), the disadvantages resulting from the representatives of perhaps five or six Unions negotiating with a single employers' organisation, have been frequently experienced. The radical-communist element in German labour has also exerted its influence strongly in favour of Industrial Unionism, on the ground that an Industrial Union, acting in accordance with a single policy, could bring a whole industry to a standstill, without the employers having the possibility of keeping part of their works running, or of playing off one section of organised labour against another.

In addition to the foregoing factors the widespread existence of Works Councils must be recognised as an important though subsidiary element in the situation. The Works Council, by the very nature of its composition, is an Industrial Union in little; it is a microcosm of all the units available for organisation throughout an industry. Irrespective of sex, craft or skill, the Works Council is elected by and represents the whole of the employees, both wage-earning and salaried, in an establishment. It thus cuts across all the pre-existing lines of Trade Union organisation. The Works Council, like the Industrial Union itself, is a product of the intensive demand, which has been one of the outstanding features of the German labour movement since the War, for a share in the wider aspects of the control of industry and of the productive process as a whole. At the same time the practical co-operation between the diverse interests of different classes of workers within the individual industrial establishments, which has been effected through the institution of Works Councils, has in turn exercised an influence on the attitude of the workers towards the structure and form of organisation in the wider unit of the Trade Union. There can be no doubt also that many of the leaders of the Union movement feel that both their control over the general policy of the Works Councils, and the practical support and backing of the Councils by the Unions, would be much easier and more effective if the ultimate basis of organisation were the same for both. It is a significant fact that, when the "Free" Trade Unions (the A.D.G.B.) came to incorporate the Works Councils within their organisation, they formed them into 15 great industrial groups corresponding to the usual classification of all forms of industry in Germany.[1] Thus from the outset no attempt was made to group them on craft lines, although this was the prevailing form of structure of the Unions comprised within the A.D.G.B.

The outcome of all these forces was seen in a resolution passed by a great majority at the Congress of "Free" Trade Unions held in Leipzig in 1922. The resolution points out that the evolution of industrial organisation in Germany has been away from the old type of specialised undertaking requiring a particular kind of skill, and has brought about the typical large-scale undertaking of the present day with its great variety of products and processes. It goes on to say:

In the struggle of the Trade Unions for better wages and working conditions the closely organised body of employers must be opposed by a solid union of workers grouped in large efficient industrial organisations.... The tasks of the Works Councils, as also the handling of economic questions, and the attainment of socialisation to which every effort must be directed, cannot be effected on the basis of the individual crafts.... For all these reasons the Eleventh Trade Union Congress holds that a fundamental change in the previous Trade Union structure and the statutes based on it is necessary. In the case of great allied industries, e.g. Mining, Smelting and Metals, Building, Printing, Transport, Public Services, Textiles, Leather, Foodstuffs, and Agriculture and Forestry, single Industrial Unions are to be recognised and created. This will be achieved by the amalgamation of the existing Craft Unions. The Congress, basing itself on these con-

---

[1] See above, p. 45.

siderations, instructs the Executive and Committee of the A.D.G.B. to draw up forthwith a scheme for an organic system of Industrial Unions. This scheme is to be laid before the Trade Unions concerned for their further consideration.

Already the preliminary enquiries conducted by the Executive Committee on the lines of the foregoing resolution showed that the difficulties in the way of a radical transformation of the Trade Unions on industrial lines were very great. The powerful Craft Unions in the skilled trades offered a most vigorous and determined opposition to the project, and some of them even threatened to secede from the A.D.G.B. if compulsory measures were adopted. The negotiations were interrupted by the occupation of the Ruhr and by the problems arising from the collapse and subsequent stabilisation of the currency. When the negotiations were resumed in 1924 it was found that the repugnance of the Craft Unions to any enforced scheme of amalgamation was unabated. Accordingly, at the Twelfth Congress, held in Breslau in September 1925,[1] a resolution was put forward by the Executive Committee and adopted by a large majority of the Congress, in which, while recognising the superiority of Industrial Unionism as a form of organisation under modern conditions, it was agreed that this process should only take place by the voluntary agreement and co-operation of the Unions concerned. All the Unions were enjoined to do their utmost to facilitate and further the movement towards amalgamation by industries and, in the meantime, were required to enter into mutual agreements (*Kartellverträge*) to pursue a common policy in questions affecting more than one Union. The Congress also inserted a new section into the Statutes of the A.D.G.B. requiring every constituent Union to admit unskilled workers and women into their ranks.

While the Craft Unions were thus successful in warding off the application of compulsion in this matter, they found themselves constrained to make the important admission of the superiority of the Industrial Union as a form of organisation, and to pledge themselves, not merely not to hinder, but actively to

[1] *Protokoll...des zwölften Kongresses der Gewerkschaften Deutschlands,* pp. 301–324.

support the movement towards amalgamation on industrial as opposed to craft lines.

It must be borne in mind, however, that the above resolution has no bearing on the policy of the non-socialist Unions, of which the "Christian" Unions, in particular, are exceedingly determined upholders of the Craft Union. They object to the Industrial Union on principle as being a mere fighting organisation based on the doctrine of class warfare, in contrast to their own conception of the spirit of Trade Unionism, which they hold should serve to bring about an identification of interest and ideal between the craftsman and the craft or "calling" in which he is engaged in the service of the community.

In conclusion, it may be said that in the numerically preponderant socialist Unions the principle of Industrial Unionism has received a far-reaching recognition, and it is significant that the leaders of this movement, the Metal Workers' Union, have throughout attributed to the Works Councils a position of the greatest importance in the organisation of labour, and have expressly based their advocacy of the Industrial Union in part on the need for a correlative organisation of the Trade Unions, in order to secure the most complete and effective co-operation between both systems of labour representation.

THE PROBLEM OF LEADERSHIP IN THE LABOUR MOVEMENT

The general tendency of the Trade Union movement in Germany has been for many years in the direction of an ever-increasing centralisation. This tendency was intensified during and shortly after the War, when the Trade Unions became one of the strongest economic and political forces in the country. The leaders, who, before the War, had merely been concerned with the internal organisation of their Unions and with the struggle against the employers for higher wages and better conditions, became identified with the machinery of government and administration. After the Revolution many Trade Union leaders were for a time members of the Government, and had to think and act as statesmen, not as agitators and representatives of a particular social class or interest.

It is well known that the extravagant hopes, which had been based on the conquest of political power by the working classes in Germany, were not realised in practice. The Commissions appointed to draw up schemes for the socialisation of industry were unable to come to any practical conclusions. Moreover, the shattered forces of capital were not long in consolidating their strength anew, and offered a stubborn and increasingly successful resistance to the claims and pretensions of organised labour. The very magnitude of the hopes which had been aroused was the measure of the subsequent disappointment, and the workers turned fiercely on their leaders, demanding a reckoning and an account of their stewardship.

Together with a vast increase in the membership of the Trade Unions there went an extension of the salaried personnel of the Unions. The unsuccessful candidates for such posts were loud in their condemnation of the "mandarins" of the Unions. As in Great Britain just after the War, the more radical elements in the German labour movement sought in every way to undermine the influence of the official leaders of the Unions, who were accused of being mere bureaucrats and timid reformists out of touch with the real needs of the situation.

The Works Councils have played a considerable rôle in the revolt against the official leadership of the Unions. Although the revolutionaries failed to capture the Works Councils machinery as a whole or to divert it from the control of the Unions, they have been able to make great use of the Councils to extend the scope of their agitation amongst the workers. The legal recognition of Collective Agreements, and the powers given to the Federal Ministry of Labour to declare such agreements to be universally binding, have necessarily preserved to the Unions their dominating influence in the joint determination of wage rates, etc., with the employers. But the situation has been very different in regard to those important matters which come within the sphere of operation of the Works Councils, and even to matters which should lie outside their sphere, such as the calling of strikes. Here the loss of membership of the Unions and the lack of unity and disruption within them have temporarily weakened their control over the Councils. The Works

Councils, by the nature of their composition and the mode of their election, are more open to demagogic influence than the Unions; moreover, the method of proportional representation enables relatively small groups to send one or two members to the Councils. Hence the extreme sections of labour are often able to obtain representation in a degree far exceeding their numerical importance. Early in 1924, Robert Dissmann, one of the leaders of the Metal Workers' Union, declared[1] that in a large number of firms in Berlin less than 40 per cent. of those employed were members of the Union, while in the Hamburg dockyards not more than 25 per cent. of the employees were organised. At the Thyssen Works in Hamborn, out of 13,500 employees, only 3500 were organised in Trade Unions. The old-established Unions thus temporarily lost control of many of the Works Councils on which their members were in a minority. The extremists were in a position to make a strong appeal to the discontented element and to those who had forsaken the Unions in disgust at their powerlessness to stop the great reaction which accompanied the stabilisation of the mark and the resulting industrial depression. One consequence of this was a renewal of "wild" or unauthorised strikes led by the radical Works Councils. Thus in a strike of metal workers in Düsseldorf in 1924 the Union was completely ignored. The strikers issued a pamphlet stating that:[2]

In a great number of towns the Trade Unions have adhered to the general strike proclaimed by the Works Councils. Where this has not yet taken place the workers must force them to join the movement. The leaders of the Unions who refuse must be ejected from their offices.

The Unions sometimes found themselves compelled to recognise strikes which they had not countenanced and about which they had not been consulted. Where this occurred their prestige suffered from the loss of initiative, and often from the subsequent failure of the strike, while the Councils were able to boast of their success in forcing the hands of the Union leaders.

---

[1] *Protokoll des sechszehnten Verbandstages des Deutschen Metallarbeiter-Verbandes*, 1924, pp. 177–178.
[2] *Ibid.* p. 178.

The Works Councillors enjoy certain advantages over the officials of the Union. They are in much closer direct touch with the rank and file of the workers, their sense of responsibility is necessarily less, and they are more open to the immediate influence of those whom they represent. Being more often the led than leading, they appear to be less bureaucratic and to have greater sympathy with the desires and aspirations of the workers. They are not permanent salaried officials, but for the most part work side by side with their fellows and share their conditions. Even where a member of a Works Council is a Trade Unionist he is apt to ignore advice and to regard his chief duty as being towards those who have elected him rather than towards his Union. In any democracy the masses are always impatient and distrustful of leadership. Having no grasp of the wider factors which lie outside their own immediate surroundings, they cannot comprehend the why and the wherefore of policies based on considerations beyond their ken. In the labour movement the problem of leadership has always been exceptionally difficult. The strength of class feeling can create a solidarity sufficiently great to bridge over, up to a point, wide divergences of real interests amongst different sections of labour. But this class feeling is founded predominantly on the mere relationship of employment with all its risks and uncertainties. The elected and salaried Trade Union official, being no longer in the same category as the rest of the workers, is liable from that very reason to become suspect, and not altogether without cause. For his larger view and deeper sense of responsibility may combine to make him both timid and lacking in resource and also to regard the organisation which he represents, as an end in itself, so that he becomes "officialised" and loses the capacity of the true leader to induce men to follow him.

An official hierarchy has arisen, many of the members of which are merely place holders, interested chiefly in their own advancement and ignorant alike of the needs and wishes of the workers in general.[1]

These difficulties had already made themselves felt in Germany, as in England, before the War. But they have been much more

[1] Graf, "Arbeiterbewegung und Bildungsproblem", in *Gewerkschaftsarchiv*, May 1924.

acute during the post-war period, when violent political and economic changes have altered the whole aspect of social life and when the minds of the masses have been subjected to the influence of new and disturbing ideas.

It was inevitable that the Works Councils should have afforded an outlet for many active and impatient minds, who, observing the comparative failure of political democracy during the years immediately succeeding the Revolution, turned to direct industrial action as a simpler and more effective method of attaining the goal they desired. With such men the very narrowness of their field of vision is a source of strength, for they can pursue their aims with a single-minded enthusiasm, unfettered by doubts as to the wisdom or practicability of their proposals. Failing in their attempts to revolutionise the Trade Unions they have concentrated their efforts on the Works Councils and used these, partly as a weapon in their struggle against the official heads of the labour movement, and partly as a means of putting their own policies into practice. It is by the success or failure of their policies in the long run that they are inevitably judged by their fellows in the works, and experience hitherto serves to show that it is comparatively seldom that a revolutionary majority is elected to a Works Council two years in succession. Big promises and little achievement, disturbances in the works, unsuccessful strikes, all combine to make them fall out of favour with their electorate. Conversely a moderate Works Council is often succeeded by one of more radical tendencies owing to the discontent stirred up by its critics during its period of office.

Problems of leadership inside the individual establishments have indeed proved as difficult as those within the Trade Unions themselves. Instances are given in Chapters IV and V of the hostility and criticism often met with by Works Councils, which are frequently such as to render the members unwilling to submit themselves for re-election to their office. The salaried official of the Trade Union is paralleled by those members of the Works Council who (in big businesses) are released from work and become in effect salaried functionaries, although they are paid by the employers and not by the workers. The Works

Councillor is perpetually exposed to attack on two fronts: if he is very active in his duties he renders himself obnoxious to his employer, while if he tries to exercise a moderating influence and perhaps to prevent the putting forward of demands which he regards as unwise, he is accused of being in the pocket of the employer. One thing, however, seems to be admitted by all those who have studied the functioning of the Works Councils. The responsibility and experience gained by the tenure of office of Works Councillor have a marked effect on those who hold it. The most fire-eating revolutionary is sobered by his contact, as a rule for the first time, with the realities of industrial life.[1] Although the frequent changes in the composition of the Councils must militate against their working efficiency, there is some compensation to be found in the fact that thereby a large number of persons are enabled to undertake the duties and functions imposed on the Works Councils.

In the course of time the area for the selection of Trade Union officials and leaders will be greatly widened, and there will be far more scope and opportunity for working-class ability to find outlets within the ranks of the labour movement than have ever existed before.[2] The period of operation of the Councils is still too short for marked results in this direction to be observed. Economic conditions also have been abnormal since the War and it is probable that the enormous increase in the membership, and therefore in the numbers of officials, of the Unions, between 1918 and 1922, absorbed many who otherwise would have been influential members of Works Councils.

It seems certain that, just as the institution of Works Councils has reacted upon the structure of Trade Unionism and has contributed to the post-war movement in the direction of Industrial Unionism, so also it will influence the policies and the methods of the Unions.

Although the average Works Councillor has in the past been

[1] See below, pp. 98–9.
[2] Cf. Reports of Factory Inspectors in Prussia for 1921, p. 104: "Many ambitious workers see in the position of a Works Councillor and in the exercise of the functions of that office the beginnings of a rise to a responsible position in the Trade Unions."

very much under the tutelage of the Union official in all matters connected with administrative work, the conduct of negotiations, the knowledge of legal provisions, etc., there is developing, especially in the great combined works, a type of Works Councillor who in turn has much to teach the official of the Union. Those who sit on Works Councils are not merely in closer contact with the feelings and wishes of their fellow-workers, but they have also a direct and immediate knowledge of industrial conditions as they operate in the unit of industry, the individual establishment, whether large or small. Besides this practical experience, which the Union leader often lacks, the Works Councillor has access to much economic information owing to his right to inspect the balance sheet and profit and loss accounts of his firm. Although this information is supposed to be confidential, there is no doubt that a good deal of it does filter through to the Unions. Thus the Works Councils feel that they are in a position to make important contributions to the Unions, and they resent the endeavours of the latter to exclude them as far as possible from the preliminary discussions, at which the general lines of policy in regard to wages, hours of work, etc., are worked out and determined.[1] In general, the Councils, with their still active leaven of extremists, are prone to be in favour of a more vigorous forward policy than would commend itself to the Unions by themselves, and the necessity of bearing this in mind is certainly not without influence on the policy of the Unions. The Trade Unions by their schools are giving a training to considerable numbers of men in the theory and strategy of the labour movement, which previously had been confined to those who were already officials. This knowledge is being deepened and extended by a type of practical experience which in the long run must be of great educative value, though it must be remembered that this process is retarded by the instability of the membership of the Councils. It is clear, however, that the emergence of this new type of labour leader is giving rise to important problems as to the division of functions

---

[1] In some cases Works Councillors do serve on the expert Committees of the Trade Unions which are engaged in drawing up the Union case, but they are excluded from the actual negotiations with the employers.

and inter-relations between the Councils and the Unions—problems which so far do not appear to have been faced by the latter.

THE WORKS COUNCILS AND WORKERS' EDUCATION

One of the outstanding features of the labour movement in Germany since the War has been the growth of interest in working-class education. The chief stimulus to this development has come from the Works Councils, and from the partial transformation of the aims of organised labour away from mass opposition to and conflict with the employers over questions of wages, hours of work, etc., towards a voice in the wider problems of industrial structure and policy.

It has been estimated that at the end of 1922 there were more than 200,000 Works Councillors and Works Stewards in Germany, the great majority of whom were by no means properly equipped to undertake the functions imposed on them by the law. The mere comprehension of the terms of the 106 sections comprising the Works Councils Act involves considerable capacity to understand the precise meaning and significance of words, while for a proper execution of the rights and duties of a Works Council an extensive knowledge of the vast body of German labour legislation, as well as of accountancy and of economic reasoning and practice, are required. A very short experience of the actual practice of the Works Councils, coupled with the unmistakeable failure of the early political Workers' Councils, convinced many of the workers of this fact and led to a demand for instruction which was on a much greater scale than anything known before the War. The type of instruction needed was also different. Neither the pre-war type of classes for Trade Union officials, nor the short courses of general lectures given to large bodies of unselected or ill-assorted workers, was adequate for the new situation.

The A.D.G.B. and, in general, the central organisations of the Trade Unions found themselves, at first at least, unable to provide the facilities needed to satisfy this newly arisen demand for education. In the first place, the ever-increasing inflation diminished their funds and lessened their power to finance a big educational campaign; secondly, they were so fully occupied with the big problems they had to face that they were unable to devote much attention to this matter; thirdly, the strength of the early Works Councils movement lay in its decentralised character and opposition was expressed to any attempt to "capture" the Works Councils Schools or to conduct them on centrally run lines. Hence the bulk of the courses were provided locally by the individual Trade Unions, though they were assisted by contributions from the central organisations and from the Reich, which in 1920 devoted 1,000,000 marks and in 1922 3,000,000 marks to the education of the workers. A certain number of schools also sprang spontaneously from the ranks of the workers themselves to meet the need which was so urgently felt.

The greatest diversity prevailed at first in different parts of the country in regard both to the method and type of teaching and to the composition of the classes; sometimes as many as 700 listeners were brought together in a single hall and treated to lectures on economic or social subjects, with results which were inevitably unsatisfactory. Many of those attending the courses over-estimated their own capacities, and cherished the confident expectation that, at the end of a short course, they would be capable of turning out their employers and managing their undertakings on socialist lines.[1] Others, finding an extensive pabulum set before them, selected courses whose titles sounded attractive, but for the understanding of which they lacked sufficient background.[2] A common experience of the courses, therefore, was the loss of a considerable proportion of those attending them, before their conclusion. Great difficulty was experienced in obtaining teachers with the proper qualifications, and although many University lecturers in the different centres willingly offered their services, their academic methods of lecturing were often the reverse of successful when applied to working-class audiences.

[1] Fricke, "Betriebsräteschulung", in *Betriebsrätezeitung des A.D.G.B.*, June 1923.

[2] Ellert, "Lehrberatung in Betriebsräteschulen", in *Betriebsrätezeitschrift des Metallarbeiter-Verbandes*, December 23, 1922.

Some of these difficulties it has been possible in the course of time to overcome, but some still remain, with others to be mentioned later.

As has been stated, the majority of the courses intended for the instruction of Works Councillors have been organised by the Trade Unions and, as a rule, the three great groups of Unions have gone to work separately. The "Christian" Unions in particular have carried out an intensive and very efficient educational campaign amongst their members, but have been very determined in their refusal to co-operate with the Socialist Unions, in view of the Class War sympathies of the latter.

Most of the Works Councils Schools are what the Germans call *Zweckschulen*, i.e. schools intended to cater for a special purpose or object, in contrast with those giving a wide and general higher education. They are, however, differentiated from the former type of Trade Union Schools, in that they are more closely concerned with broad economic questions and with problems of business management. Where possible the classes are kept small and confined to from 25 to 30 members.

In the "Free" Trade Union Schools the teaching of economics is generally coloured by the Marxian standpoint, though in many cases courses are also given by academic lecturers and others who are not adherents of the Class War.

The courses given are mostly concerned with elementary economics, mainly realistic and descriptive; labour legislation; trade unionism; and social policy, including questions of hygiene.[1] There are naturally wide variations both in the quality and extent of the teaching, depending largely on the teaching resources at the disposal of the Unions. In very small localities the teaching is often done entirely by a local Union official, with the help perhaps of one or two salaried employees. But elsewhere the teachers are commonly drawn from very diverse classes —e.g. high school teachers, engineers, journalists, teachers in trade and continuation schools, etc. As a rule and where possible they are paid for their work by the Trade Unions.

Besides the special Works Councils Schools of the Trade Unions, the members of these bodies have also taken advantage

[1] Gumpert, *Die Bildungsbestrebungen der freien Gewerkschaften*, p. 135.

of other educational facilities, such as the State-provided People's High Schools, the ordinary Trade Union Schools for their officials, etc. In some of the Unions travelling teachers have been appointed (e.g. the Boot-makers' Union) who have a wide area assigned to them in which they travel about and instruct the Works Councils.

All this type of teaching is designed for the ordinary Works Councillor to assist him in the carrying out of his duties, and the classes referred to are held in the evenings and attended by workers who are engaged at their normal work during the day. There are, however, a number of institutions which draw their hearers from a wide area and which give a considerably more advanced type of teaching. Such institutions are the Akademie der Arbeit at Frankfurt; the socialist residential school at Schloss Tinz near Gera; the special courses instituted by the University of Münster; the "Free" Trade Union Seminar at Cologne; the State Technical Schools in Berlin and Düsseldorf, etc. All these are used by the Trade Unions, partly as a means of broadening the outlook and increasing the capacity of their officials, and partly to train teachers for their Works Councils Schools. It is exceedingly difficult, as well as expensive, to arrange for the long holidays necessary to allow members of Works Councils who are in actual employment to attend such courses. Nevertheless, at University towns in different parts of the country short courses have in many cases been arranged, which are specially designed for the Works Councillor and arrangements are made which will enable him to attend them.[1] In the Ruhr and the Rhineland the Miners' Union hold special courses for Works Councillors who are members of the Boards of Control of the mines.

The volume of educational activity initiated or participated in by the Trade Unions is thus very considerable, although it has undoubtedly suffered in quality and usefulness from its sporadic and disconnected character, and the lack of central co-ordination. It is unfortunately impossible to obtain any general figures of the extent to which advantage has been taken of the facilities available. In the case of the Berlin Works

[1] Cf. Gumpert, *loc. cit.* pp. 136–143.

Councils School and the Berlin Trade Union School the total attendances from 1921 to the end of the first part of 1924 were approximately 13,000—not an overwhelming achievement for a city of nearly 4,000,000 inhabitants. Taking the country as a whole the early enthusiasm, which drove considerable numbers of Works Councillors to the schools in 1920 and 1921, gradually waned as the first ardour and keenness for the new movement wore off. Then came the climax of the currency inflation in 1923 followed by the hardships of the stabilisation period. Many Works Councils Schools all over the country had to shut down and the attendances at those which remained open dwindled to a very small figure.

The following statement showing the number of courses given and the attendances at the Works Councils courses held at the Socialist Union centre in Dresden is instructive:

1920	54 courses	2765 students
1921	15 „	867 „
1922	14 „	431 „
1923	13 „	493 „
1924	12 „	331 „

Since the latter part of 1924, however, with the improvement in the financial position of the Unions and some decrease in unemployment, most of the schools have been reopened and courses have been better attended again. Thus the Report of the Factory Inspectors for Saxony for the year 1925 refers to the establishment of a new Works Councils School in Dresden which provided courses for Works Councillors, extending over two years, with which were associated visits to new and up-to-date factories in the neighbourhood. Ninety-eight lectures were also given on economic and labour questions, which were attended by 6500 persons. The Report goes on to say:

The conviction is expressed that this educational work, which has been carried on now for five years in Dresden by the Trade Unions, has not merely enabled large numbers of Works Councillors to have a proper understanding of their own duties and functions, but has been of important service to the economic life of the district, including the employers. There are already said to be signs that the employers' organisations are adopting a less antagonistic attitude towards the

Works Councils Act, and are participating hopefully in the education of Works Councillors.[1]

It has been well said[2] that it is idle to talk of a mass demand for higher education on the part of the mass of the workers; the total number attending such courses is small and would be much smaller were it not for the considerable moral pressure exercised by the Unions on their members to attend such schools when they have been elected to the Works Councils on the Trade Union ticket.[3] The Unions rightly feel that it is vital to their interests that the Works Councillors should receive instruction to fit them for their duties, not only because they realise that the only hope of a successful reconstruction of industrial organisation lies in an educated and disciplined body of workers in each unit of industry and commerce, but also because they know that if they can control effectively the education of the Works Councils they will thereby gain command of the whole movement and keep it within the bounds they desire. Above all, the Trade Unions dread the possibilities of syndicalism to which the Works Councils type of organisation is peculiarly exposed. Hence the great emphasis they lay in all their teaching on the importance of the Unions as the bodies controlling the broad policies of the workers, while the Works Councils are to regard themselves as merely the outposts of the Unions in the individual establishments. The lack of discipline and dissensions within the Unions during the post-revolution years have made a deep impression on the leaders and have convinced them that the only remedy lies in a more thorough and more general infiltration of Trade Union ideas into the masses. Finally, the hope is cherished that the new class of Works Councillors, trained in the practical experience of every-day industrial life and taught to regard their own activities and surroundings as part of a more comprehensive whole, may form a *corps d'élite* of German labour, which will bring to the Unions themselves new blood and fruitful ideas.

[1] Report of Factory Inspectors for Saxony, 1925, p. 25.
[2] Fricke, "Die Berliner Gewerkschaftsschule", in *Gewerkschaftsarchiv*, September 1924.
[3] Seidel, *Die Betriebsräteschule*, p. 18.

The chief obstacles in the way of the education of members of Works Councils have been found to be—firstly, the fluctuating personnel of the Councils as a result of the constant changes in their membership; secondly, the great strain imposed on the Works Councillor in attending evening classes after a hard day's work in addition to the execution of his duties, many of which have to be carried out after working hours; thirdly, the inadequacy of the elementary education of the average worker; fourthly, the teaching in many of the special schools, which has been designed more to pump facts and knowledge into the listeners than to give them a critical faculty and a power of reasoning for themselves; fifthly, the indifference of many of the workers to the need for further education. That the quantitative success of the Works Councils should not have been overwhelming is scarcely to be wondered at, nevertheless it is great in comparison with that of pre-war days and, above all, two hundred thousand Works Councillors are gaining, by virtue merely of their office, an insight into the problems and difficulties of business management and of the working relations between employers and employees, the ultimate value and influence of which it would be difficult to over-estimate.

There remains one further instrument in the hands of the Trade Unions, by means of which they can exercise a powerful influence over the training and development of the Works Councils—the special Works Councils newspapers edited and produced by the Unions. The number of such journals was very considerable during the active period from 1920 to the middle of 1923, but most of them disappeared under the financial difficulties accompanying the climax of the currency inflation. The important *Betriebsrätezeitung*, brought out jointly by the A.D.G.B. and the Afa, ceased publication towards the end of 1923 and has not since been resumed. Articles of special interest to the Works Councils are now published from time to time in the ordinary *Gewerkschaftszeitung* of the A.D.G.B., but the extent of such information is relatively small. On the other hand, many of the individual Trade Unions have renewed the issue of their Works Councils journals. The outstanding publication of this type is the *Betriebsrätezeitschrift* of the Metal Workers' Union, which appears every fortnight and contains 30 or more pages. The articles deal partly with general economic problems, such as types of industrial organisation in the metal or other industries, commercial policy, currency questions, etc., and partly with matters directly affecting the activities of the Works Councils, including legal decisions and awards of Arbitration Boards, etc. The quality of the articles maintains an astonishingly high level, and testifies to the relatively high intellectual standard of those for whom the paper is written. Most of the other journals intended for the Works Councils are on a much less ambitious scale, but they contain a great deal of useful practical information for their readers and, as a whole, are edited with a marked sense of responsibility and absence of extremist views.

At the periodical Congresses of the individual Unions the editing of these periodicals is subjected generally to severe criticism from the radical members of the Unions, on the ground that they preach too much moderation and endeavour to damp down the revolutionary ardour. In practice, while emphasising the imperfections of the Works Councils Act from the labour point of view, the editors and contributors to the Works Councils journals urge on their readers the necessity both of knowing the exact terms and scope of the Act and of keeping within them. They are never tired of emphasising the need of loyalty to the Trade Unions and of warning their members against making Works Agreements with the employers, without the consent of their Union leaders. They do good work in drawing attention to the duties of the Councils in regard to such matters as works hygiene, the prevention of accidents, and other duties incumbent on them under the Act. In these and other ways the Works Councils journals contribute to the task of enlightening the members of the Councils and assisting them in carrying out their duties efficiently and conscientiously, while at the same time they strengthen and consolidate the influence of the Trade Unions on the Works Councils.

CHAPTER IV

The Effects of the Works Councils on Industrial Relations

The years which have succeeded the passing of the Works Councils Act have been in many ways abnormal and the experience of the practical working of the Act can only be understood in its relation to the economic conditions, which have been in a state of continual flux throughout this time.

MARCH 1920 TO MARCH 1921

The first 18 months after the end of the War were a period of upheaval and violent revolutionary ferment. The factory Committees, which had been set up in 1916 by the Auxiliary Service Act, were converted in many cases into Councils of Workers whose aims were mainly political. These Councils were frequently able to destroy all semblance of factory discipline; they practically took over the administration of the concerns in which they were working, and employers who sought to assert their authority were maltreated and sometimes killed. No employee could be dismissed, whatever the reason might be, without an immediate strike and industrial conditions over a large part of Germany were reduced to a state of chaos. At the same time it was realised by most reasonable people, and especially by the responsible leaders of the Trade Unions, that Germany could only be saved from complete disaster by a rapid turn-over of industry from war-time to peace production and by a large increase in the output of industry and agriculture. The left wing of German labour was nearly as much anti-Trade Union as it was anti-capitalist and when, therefore, the struggle for the control of labour was settled in favour of the Trade Unions, the reaction on the relations between the workers in general and the employers was very marked.

By the passing of the Works Councils Act in February 1920 the representation of the workers in each establishment was crystallised in a form which was as definite as the intricate and frequently obscure provisions of the Act made possible. This had the great advantage of setting legal limits to the scope and activities of the Councils, with the result that the employers knew more or less where they stood. The Act provided for the immediate dissolution of all committees or councils of workers already in existence and for their replacement by the new statutory Works Councils. Although it only lays down minimum conditions and the functions of the Councils can be extended by joint agreement with the employers, the latter naturally, both then and since, tended to fall back upon the exact letter of the law. During the first year of operation a vast number of disputes arose over the question of the interpretation of the Act. As has been already pointed out, a large section of the workers was exceedingly disappointed with the limitations imposed by the Act on the scope of the Councils and many attempts were made, sometimes with a considerable degree of success, to secure better terms from the employers. When the latter resisted, strikes and serious conflicts broke out. The Independent Socialists and Communists conducted an active propaganda amongst their members, urging them not to be content with the restricted powers given to the Councils but to seize the rights to which they considered they were entitled. This tendency was intensified by the fact that, in practice, many of the earlier committees set up prior to the passing of the Act had enjoyed powers which they had wrested from the employers in favourable times and which considerably exceeded those given to the new statutory bodies. These powers they were not prepared to relinquish without a struggle. On the other hand, a large section of the employers was at first utterly opposed to the Act. They regarded the Works Councils constituted under it with an extravagant fear and dread and set out to resist them tooth and nail. Special commentaries were prepared under the auspices of the employers' organisations showing how the pretensions of the Works Councils could best be resisted and, in general, everything was done to whittle down the practical powers of the Councils to a minimum. In the face of these opposing tendencies it is not surprising that the operation of the Act during the first few months was marked by strikes and unrest and that many of the new bodies had a stormy and troubled career.

The chief work of interpreting the Act down to the end of 1923 was in the hands of the Conciliation Boards set up by the Order of December 23, 1918. These bodies, which are described in detail elsewhere,[1] were immediately inundated with an enormous number of appeals, both from the employers and from the Councils. The Act itself, as has already been observed, is a very long and complicated measure drawn up in typical legal phraseology. Some of the numerous obscure passages are no doubt attributable to this, but some expressions appear to be deliberately ambiguous, being the results of a compromise amongst the parties at the time the Act was being drafted. In a number of cases a form of words was adopted the meaning of which was open to doubt, but the drafting was accepted by both parties, each hoping that when it came to the administration of the Act the interpretation which it put upon the clause in question would prevail. Hence the Conciliation Boards, besides having to deal with obvious infringements of the Act by the workers or by the employers and with the mass of ordinary appeals on which a decision had to be given in accordance with its terms, had also to give rulings as to the meaning of a large number of doubtful provisions. As the Act did not provide for any central judicial body to which appeals could be made from the decisions of Conciliation Boards, each of which had unrestricted competence in its own area, conflicting decisions were naturally given in many cases. Thus for a time there was a great deal of confusion and uncertainty. At first, moreover, the Conciliation Boards were new to their work and it took time to expand the machinery to deal with the volume of appeals pouring in on all sides. Inevitably there was a great deal of delay. An employer might have a perfectly good case against his Works Council for actions constituting " gross misfeasance of duty ". But it might be many weeks before he could secure the compulsory dissolution of the offending Council and, in the meanwhile, the conduct of his business could be made practically impossible. One of the obscure points of the Act is the question whether, when a Works

[1] See above, pp. 23–6.

Council has been compulsorily dissolved, the identical members can be re-elected. The general consensus of legal opinion and the usual practice of the Conciliation Boards has answered this question in the negative. But at first, at least, this was not invariably so and in any case the workers could go on strike and refuse to return to work until the old Works Council had been accepted by the employer. If the position of the workers was strong he could easily be compelled to agree. Throughout a considerable part of 1920 the communist element was active in parts of Germany, especially in and around Berlin; a communist Works Council, determined to make use of its position to obstruct the authority of the employer in every possible way, could cause a vast deal of disturbance and unrest in a factory, without necessarily carrying matters to such a pitch that an order for compulsory dissolution could be obtained against it.

One of the chief complaints of the employers in the early days of the Act was that the Works Councils insisted on holding their meetings during working-hours and also often called meetings of the Works Assembly—i.e. of the whole body of workers. Although the Act requires that meetings of the Council shall be held "normally" outside working-hours and that meetings of the Works Assembly shall only be held in working-hours if the consent of the employer has been obtained, these provisions were often infringed. In gross cases the Works Council was dissolved on appeal to the Conciliation Board, but the loss of time before this could take place frequently involved a big decline in output and in most cases during this period any action taken by the employer against the Works Council led to a strike.

While the Act was new the very novelty of it led to an immense amount of interest being taken in its operation by the employees. The Council members took up their offices often with more zeal than discretion, wishing to justify themselves in the eyes of their electors, who hoped for great improvements in their conditions as a result of this new form of representation. Hence the tendency was to lay exclusive stress on those parts of the Act in which the Works Council is regarded as the organ for defending the interests of the workers against the employer. This led, for one thing, to the excessive frequency of meetings referred to above, and to an immense amount of talk and discussion throughout the works and consequent loss of time. Moreover, although the employer cannot be compelled to attend meetings of the Works Council, to which he is invited, it is often undesirable and impolitic from his point of view to refuse to be present and, except in large concerns, there may be no suitable person to whom he can delegate the work of representing him. A very active Works Council can thus occupy a great deal of the employer's time at the expense of his other activities. The employers had also a good deal of cause for complaint during this period owing to the practice of many Councils of taking every single case of dismissal to the Conciliation Board, even though the dismissal was clearly justified. This always involved the attendance of either the employer or his representative and the Conciliation Board had the power to compel the appearance of the employer himself if it wished. The Board was often unable to decide a case at a single hearing and would adjourn it, perhaps for further witnesses or more documents. If at the next hearing the witnesses did not put in an appearance or the documents were not forthcoming, the case was again adjourned.

As the Conciliation Board could be invoked not merely for cases of dismissals but for practically all disputes arising out of the interpretation of any of the 100 or more sections of the Act, the aggregate amount of time spent in this way could easily become a matter of serious moment to the employer.

Another very fruitful source of friction between the employer and the Works Council was the provision requiring all statutory works rules (*Arbeitsordnung*) to be drawn up by agreement between the employer and the Council. If they failed to agree the matter had to be referred to the Conciliation Board whose decision was binding on both parties.

The foregoing summary of some of the chief instances of friction between employers and employees during the first year of operation of the Act shows that these were due, in many cases, either to the novelty of the Act and to unfamiliarity with its working on the part of all concerned, or to the very troubled conditions, both political and industrial, which were the immediate legacy of the War and the Revolution. Some of these causes of friction, on the other hand, were inherent in the working of the Act and have manifested themselves to a greater or less extent ever since.

It must not, however, be imagined that, even during this first period, there were no off-setting effects to be put to the credit of the Works Councils. The strength of the Communists and Independent Socialists varied greatly in different parts of the country and wherever their influence was small or non-existent the course of the Works Councils was far more peaceful and orderly. Moreover, by degrees, as the Trade Unions strengthened their control over the machinery of the Works Councils and incorporated the latter within their organisation, they were able to diminish the number of "wild strikes" and to instil moderation into the members of the Councils. Instances were to be found in which the Works Councils used their influence against that of agitators within the works and strove to preserve peaceful relations between the employers and the body of employees.

It is also the considered view of many observers, both of employers and of others holding no special brief for the Works Councils, that the trouble and unrest which characterised this early period were the direct consequence of the revolutionary wave which swept over the country at the end of the War. While it is true that many people of extreme views were elected to sit on the Works Councils, these men would in any case have created disturbances, and there is good ground for the belief that the existence of a statutory constitution for these bodies, with a right of appeal to the Conciliation Board on the part of the employers as well as of the employees, exercised a restraining and moderating influence in preventing excesses and keeping the workers within certain bounds. One of the chief features of this period was the revolt of the rank and file against the Trade Unions, and there can be no doubt that the Conciliation Boards interpreted both wisely and firmly those provisions of the Act which were designed to prevent the Works Councils from ousting the Trade Unions from their position as the real and effective leaders of labour in wage disputes and major questions of policy.

MARCH TO DECEMBER 1921

By the end of 1920 the revolutionary ferment in Germany had to a large extent subsided and the communist element in German labour had lost much of its influence. The Trade Unions had been fairly successful in reasserting discipline within their ranks, while on the other hand the employers were settled firmly in the saddle again and were presenting a solid front to the claims of labour. The Conciliation Boards had got into their stride and were accomplishing their difficult and arduous task with a good deal of success, as may be judged by the complaints of many employers that their decisions were unduly favourable to the Councils, and of many of the workers that these Boards were strongly biased in favour of the employers. Rulings by the Federal Minister of Labour had provisionally settled a number of disputed points, for in most cases his rulings were adopted by the Conciliation Boards, and there had grown up a large body of decisions on important questions arising out of the Act. Both the employers and the workers had now some experience of the practical operation of the Act and, in particular, of the policy pursued by the Conciliation Boards in its interpretation.

The most comprehensive source of information as to the activities of the Works Councils all over the country is to be found in the Reports of the Factory Inspectors of the different States. It has already been pointed out that the Factory Inspectors in Germany have much wider functions than in this country, for they are not merely concerned with questions of hygiene, accidents, etc., but are required to supervise the execution of the greater part of the very extensive protective labour legislation. The Works Councils are expressly instructed by the Act to co-operate with the Factory Inspectors in preventing accidents and remedying conditions injurious to the health of the workers and, in practice, the Inspectors usually get in touch with the Works Councils when making their visits of inspection. As the Chief Factory Inspector of each district (*Gewerberat*) was, down to the end of 1923, in most States responsible for decisions in disputes arising out of the elections and the procedure of the Works Councils, his subordinate

officials were brought into very close contact with the operation
of the Act, and were often able, by giving advice on points of law,
etc., to enlighten both the Councils and the employers on many
matters relating to the functions and legal rights of the Councils.

The verdict of most of the Factory Inspectors on the functioning of the Works Councils, so far as the relation between employers and workers in 1921 was concerned, was fairly favourable.
There was general agreement that conditions in this respect
were much better in 1921 than in 1920. In particular, there were
far fewer attempts on the part of the Councils to extend their
functions beyond the limits set by the Act, though such attempts
had by no means disappeared. Many disputes still arose owing
to the insufficient acquaintance of the workers, and sometimes
also of the employers, with the provisions of the Act. In some
cases the employers were at fault for adopting an unduly narrow
and rigid interpretation of the functions of the Councils.

The procedure of the Works Council still gave rise to considerable difficulties, disputes being frequent over the indemni-
fication of members of the Council for time lost and for expenses
incurred in the execution of their official duties under the Act.
In most large concerns the employers found that it paid them to
release one or more members of the Council from all productive
work, rather than to put up with the continual friction and waste
of time involved in deciding on its merits every claim for time
alleged to have been spent by a member in the course of his
duties. In the district of Merseburg it was reported that in the
largest works in the district employing 15,364 workers, four
wage-earning and two salaried employees; in a dye factory
employing 4107 workers, four wage-earning and one salaried
employee; and, in a film factory employing 3117 workers, three
wage-earning and one salaried employee, were entirely freed
from work, their normal earnings being paid to them by their
employer. In the same Report it is stated that, in the larger
concerns, the Council was provided with a special room with
furniture, telephone, typewriter, journals, copies of laws, etc.,
in accordance with the size of the concern. In some cases
the demands of the Works Councils for facilities were altogether
unreasonable, and were rejected on appeal to the Chief Factory

Inspector. The number of hours set aside each week, in working-time, for interviews between the Council and the employees, also gave rise to dispute on occasion, though the arrangement was welcomed by some employers, as employees were otherwise prone to leave their work and to remain for a long time in the Works Council's room.

Few of the employers appear to have complained of the direct cost of maintaining the Works Councils, except where an appreciable number of members of the Council had to be exempted from work. In a large group of electrical works in Berlin under a single management employing 31,000 wage-earning and 14,000 salaried employees, the costs occasioned by the Works Councils amounted to 950,000[1] marks in the year. In this group there were 25 Works Councils, 21 Wage-earners' Councils and 20 Salaried-employees' Councils. Payment for loss of time was the chief item in most cases. Thus in a big works in the Cologne district, with a Council of 21 members, it was reckoned that 50,000 labour hours had to be paid for during the year, which had been employed on Works Council business.

In the large industrial concerns in the Province of Upper Silesia an agreement was come to between the employers' organisation and the Trade Unions, whereby each member of a Works Council received a flat sum of 80 marks per month to cover normal expenditure. As a rule, however, the practice was for the Works Council to hand to the employer a statement of actual expenses incurred and, not unnaturally, a good many extravagant claims were made. It is scarcely surprising that the claim of a Works Council for the refund of the amount spent on food and drinks when a meeting had been held on Sunday in an inn, was rejected by the employer, or that the standpoint of the latter was upheld on appeal.

The number of meetings held by the Works Councils and the Sectional Councils varied very greatly according to the conditions prevailing in the concern in question. In general, the meetings of the whole Works Council were not very frequent, most of the business being despatched by the Sectional Councils, and the Works Council being only summoned together on special

[1] About £2000 at the average rate of exchange for 1921.

occasions. In a concern with 21 Works Council members, seventy-five meetings were held in the year; in another with 11 members the Works Council held eight, the Wage-earners' Council thirty-two, and the Salaried-employees' Council seven meetings. In a mining district it was usual for meetings of the Works Council to be held once a month. The Report for the district of Cologne gives the following picture of the procedure of the Works Council of a large cable factory:

The various duties of the Works Council are entrusted to Committees of three or four members, whose Chairmen are available for interviews at a stated time on certain week-days outside working-hours; thus the Council has the following Committees: a Welfare Committee, a Food Committee, a Tax Committee (for the deduction of taxation, deductions from wages and the pledging of wages), a Social Committee (for works hygiene and the prevention of accidents), and a Complaints Committee which also deals with the care of those disabled in war or by accidents, while the Salaried-employees' Council has a Wage Committee.

Meetings of the Works Assembly only took place on rare occasions, as for example when the Council wished to cover itself by obtaining the agreement of the body of workers to certain important proposals. Cases still occurred, though much more rarely than in 1920, where friction arose with the employer owing to meetings of the Works Assembly being held in working hours in defiance of the wishes of the employer. The latter, however, by refusing to pay for the time spent in such meetings, even if he consented to their being held, could discourage them fairly effectually.

The provision of the Works Councils Act requiring all the existing statutory works rules to be reconsidered and agreed with the Works Council, gave rise to a great many disputes. The chief difficulties arose over the prohibition of smoking, over the fixing of fines and wage deductions for damage, and over the search of the persons of the workers on leaving the factory. The objection of the Works Councils, in both the latter cases, was on the ground that such measures constituted an unjustifiable humiliation of the workers. On the other hand, many employers offered a determined opposition to Section 80, Paragraph 2, of the Act, which empowers Works Councils to co-operate in the fixing of fines in each individual case and sought to embody provisions in the rules of employment which restricted this right. Hence, from one side or the other, appeals to the Conciliation Boards were repeatedly made and the decisions, which were binding on both parties, were by no means always in favour of the employers. It was noteworthy that, in a number of cases, the Councils were willing to accept provisions for the levying of fines provided that the objectionable word *Geldstrafe* (fine) was replaced by some colourless term such as *Lohnabzug* (wage-deduction). In some cases the dispute over the prohibition of smoking during working-hours, to which the employers attached great importance, was settled by a compromise, by which workers over 18 years of age were allowed to smoke pipes, but cigars and cigarettes were forbidden. In the majority of industries, works rules were drawn up in the form of a Collective Agreement between the Trade Unions on the one hand and the employers' organisations on the other, but the signature of the Sectional Council concerned in each of the individual establishments was still necessary. When, as not infrequently occurred, the Council refused to attach its signature, appeal was made to the Conciliation Board, which as a rule made use of its powers under the Works Councils Act to declare the rules binding on both parties.

The views of the Factory Inspectors as to the manner in which the Works Councils carried out their functions in 1921 show that there was a remarkable lack of uniformity. Even in the same district conditions appear to have varied widely from one firm to another.

Many of the Reports speak of the Councils as having "settled down" and taken their place as a useful piece of machinery in the relations between employers and employed. The complexity of the Act and the difficulties arising out of its interpretation are cited as frequent causes of disputes. The chief factor, however, in determining the relations between the Councils and the employer was the composition and personal characteristics of the members of the Council, on the one hand, and the character of the employer, on the other hand.

Where the Council consisted of the younger workers, especially if they were of the communist persuasion, there was always a great deal of trouble, but if the older and more moderate men had the control there was sometimes a great deal of genuine co-operation with the employer. In many cases, however, the chief difficulty lay, not with the Works Council itself, but with the body of workers and the Council found itself powerless, because it lacked the support of the workers. Not infrequently the Council stood in the position, either of having to resign or to put forward demands which it knew to be unjustified. Sometimes the members of the Council, under these conditions, would give way and become the mouthpiece of the workers, while in other cases they would resign and refuse to stand for re-election. Several of the Reports criticise the Councils for excessive timidity and unwillingness to oppose unjustifiable demands of the workers, in the face of the almost invariable accusation of having been bought over by the employer. In general, the more conscientiously they sought to carry out their duties the greater was the opposition and discontent on the part of their electors.

On the other hand, the Reports bring out clearly that the attitude of the employer was often primarily to blame for unsatisfactory relations with the Works Council. Many of the employers were hostile to the whole principle of the Act, and resented the power of the Council to interfere in questions of the internal management of the works. Hence they contested every action of the Council, with the result that appeals had continually to be made to the Conciliation Board and the establishment was kept in a state of unrest and ferment. When the employers accepted the Act and gave the Councils their legal powers with a good grace they were generally able to get on well together.

Perhaps the most common criticism of the Works Councils made by the Factory Inspectors was that they regarded their functions as comprising exclusively the representation of the economic and other interests of the workers, and ignored those provisions of the Act which required them to support the employer in increasing the productivity of the concern. But this criticism was tempered in some of the Reports by the observation that it must necessarily take time, and a much longer experience of the working of the Act, before the Councils could be expected to put the provisions contained in Section 66 into operation, and that the rapid depreciation of the currency had inevitably diverted all their attention and energies to the defence of their economic position. In most cases, the Trade Unions were referred to as exercising a moderating influence on the Works Councils, and drawing their attention, by the institution of Works Councils Schools and in other ways, to the responsibilities of their office and their duty to the community. On the other hand, some Councils were prone to adopt a purely Trade Union policy in the works; in particular, cases of interference with the freedom of association of the workers were numerous and widespread.

The following extracts from the Reports of the Inspectors for a number of important districts, including Berlin and Düsseldorf, give an indication of some of the general conclusions arrived at as a result of the operation of the Works Councils during 1921:

A comprehensive verdict on what has been achieved by the Works Councils Act can only be pronounced provisionally and with reserve; so far as can be seen the favourable effects are preponderant, and these will become more marked as it becomes possible to get rid of mutual distrust, as the knowledge of the Act becomes deeper, and when the interpretation of the Act has been put on a firm basis.[1]

Mutual relations have beyond doubt markedly improved. On both sides a spirit of conciliation can be observed: on the side of the employer, because he has gradually come to accept the notion of a certain right of co-operation of the workers in the business and has further recognised that the existence of a legal representation of the workers with defined powers can only be of advantage to him, especially in negotiation with the workers; on the side of the employees, because they have realised that it is also in their interest to elect serious and peaceable persons to the Works Council. It can therefore be expected that, with a peaceful development of the Works Councils, they will become a means of promoting industrial peace.[2]

In the majority of cases the employers credited the Works Councils with a reasonable and often a beneficial attitude; these appeared of especial value in that, often owing to their existence and the possibility of their intervention, both sides refrained from unreasonable claims and measures and the employees had the feeling that at least the possibility existed, in the event of dismissals or the issue of works rules, of having proper consideration given to their point of view.[3]

[1] Report for Berlin, 1921, p. 107.   [2] Report for Breslau, 1921, pp. 178–179.
[3] Report for Hanover, 1921, p. 334.

In practice most of the Works Councils paid little attention to the carrying out of the duties imposed on them of preserving the establishment from disturbances and of helping to secure the highest possible standard of production and the maximum degree of working efficiency, and the Trade Unions often drew the attention of the Works Councils to their duty in this respect. Very many believe that they have fulfilled their chief functions when they put forward complaints of the employees and take care that in wage negotiations the highest possible wages are secured.[1]

The experience in the carrying out of the Works Councils Act cannot be regarded as particularly satisfactory. The Works Councils are only rarely able to free themselves from the consciousness of dependence on their electors. In particular, in carrying out the duties imposed on them by Clauses 1, 3, 6 and 8, of Section 66 of the Act, they are often influenced by this feeling of dependence, with the result that they adopt a one-sided attitude against the management and in favour of the employees.[2]

JANUARY TO DECEMBER 1922

The Reports for the year 1922 were much shorter than for 1921 and correspondingly less space was devoted to the activities of the Works Councils. On the whole the tenor of the Reports in regard to these institutions was very much the same as in the previous year. Although a few of the Inspectors still adopted an unfavourable view, the majority noted a considerable further improvement on 1921. Cases of abuse and of the exceeding of their proper functions by the Councils were fewer, and the co-operation between the Councils and the managements of most concerns was more satisfactory. It was repeatedly stated that they worked together for the most part without friction.

Two favourable judgements and one unfavourable may be quoted here:

By far the greater number of Works Councils deserve approbation in that they endeavoured successfully to encourage and maintain good relations between employees and employers and also to settle differences of opinion amongst their fellow-workers.[3]

In general, the co-operation between management and Works Council seems to be developing more favourably all the time, as can be seen from the example of a large machine works in which the

[1] Report for Lüneburg, 1921, p. 364.
[2] Report for Dortmund, 1921, p. 792.
[3] Report for Liegnitz, 1922, p. 122.

relation in earlier years was not very satisfactory, but in which in the year covered by this Report, the Works Council gave powerful support to the management, especially in the supervision of juvenile workers and apprentices; it was also partly due to its influence that working-time was better employed by the workers.[1]

That the Works Councils have exerted a favourable influence upon the establishments and upon the relation between the workers and the employer can hardly be claimed. It is only in a few works where the management and the Council work hand in hand that this in-fluence can be observed.[2]

That disputes over the interpretation of the Act were still a cause of friction can be seen from the following statement:

The Factory Inspectors have been much occupied in clearing up and settling differences of opinion between Works Councils and works managements which have arisen over the operation of the Works Councils Act. Disputes frequently originated over unimportant points, but were then extended to a conflict over the fundamental rights and duties of the Councils, which threatened to cause a stoppage of work.[3]

In general it must be borne in mind that the year 1922 was one of considerable industrial prosperity throughout Germany. Unemployment was considerably smaller than in 1921, and smaller even than in 1913, while the progress of inflation had not yet proceeded so far as to impoverish utterly the bulk of the population. The cessation of all saving and the increase in the rapidity of circulation of money stimulated the temporary demand for goods in the home market, which had not yet been able to make good the deficiencies of nearly five years of war and blockade. The manufacturers found themselves full up with orders and hampered only by shortage of coal and by difficulties with labour.

Under these circumstances, the Works Councils, supported as they were by the Trade Unions which had been joined by the mass of the workers during the years immediately following the War, found themselves in a very strong position. In 1922, and indeed throughout the first four years after the War, the Coun-cils were often able to extract concessions from the employers by virtue of their bargaining strength and of that of organised

[1] Report for Düsseldorf, 1922, p. 330.
[2] Report for Halle, 1922, p. 403.
[3] Report for Arnsberg, 1922, p. 274.

labour in general. Prices were rising continuously, trade was brisk and while, on the one hand, a strike meant a considerable sacrifice of profits, on the other, the inflationary process lessened the importance of elements of cost which would have bulked much larger in the eyes of the employers in a period of industrial depression. During this period also, and still more during the greater part of 1923, the demand for clerical labour was enormous. There had been a great expansion in the organisation of salaried employees, especially so far as socialist Trade Unions were concerned and in many cases these employees were at least as class-conscious as the wage-earners; hence their members on the Works Councils backed up the wage-earners in the demands that the latter put forward to the employers. Especially in the Ruhr, it was common for one of the technical employees to be elected Chairman of the Council, and in such cases the employer found himself faced with a formidable body which could not easily be either browbeaten or ignored.

The greater orderliness of the Works Councils movement in 1922 was by no means solely due to the activity of trade and industry and to the capacity of the Councils to wring concessions from the employers. In a large measure it was due to a growing sense of responsibility on the part of those elected to serve on these bodies. The decline of the communist agitation as a mass phenomenon has already been mentioned, and with it went also a change in the attitude of the workers in many establishments towards individuals of extreme views. The loss of employment and the dislocation caused by "wild strikes" became apparent and recoiled on the heads of the instigators. When the new elections came round, people of more moderate disposition were commonly elected, though in some cases the reverse operation also took place. The educational activities of the Trade Unions were in full swing and the special Works Councils Schools were deepening and extending the knowledge of the Act and of the correct interpretation of its provisions.

The following extract from a statement made by the Chairman of the Works Council of a large locomotive factory in Cassel gives an indication of one factor at least in the return to more peaceful industrial relations:

There is no better school of instruction in the intricate problems of industry and economics than the practical co-operation and daily negotiations which take place between the Works Councils and the heads of firms. This fact has without a doubt had the result that thousands of influential radical Works Councillors, who at one time regarded the director, employer and higher official merely as superfluous parasites, have, through their Works Council activities, come to realise what an enormous measure of energy, intelligence and hard work are necessary in order to run a large-scale industrial enterprise and to secure its success.

Thus the Works Councils, through greater understanding, have to a marked extent substituted in the Works Assemblies practical discussions for political catchwords and phrases and, through their permeating influence, have helped to extract the German labour movement from its domination by radical politics, thus contributing greatly to industrial peace.[1]

A somewhat similar tribute to the calming influence of the Works Councils is also to be found in an article by a writer in *Der Deutsche*, an organ of the "Christian" Trade Unions:

Who would have believed in 1920 that it would be possible in so short a time to surmount the period of wildest ferment? Assuredly the Trade Unions as a whole have had a great share in this return to sanity. But this work could never have succeeded had it not been that thousands of responsible workers in the little works parliaments had set their faces in favour of law and order.[2]

Two further elements in the situation deserve mention, both of which were operative to a greater or less extent during the early years of the Works Councils.

Firstly, many employers were quick to learn that the Councils might in many ways be turned to their advantage. For example, the new tax laws had imposed heavy burdens on the employers in connection with the deduction of taxes from wages. Some of them found that they could avoid the expense of setting up and staffing a special department to deal with this work, by the simple expedient of handing it over to the Works Councils to do for them. Many of these were anxious to have some practical work to do in addition to mere talking, and were not sufficiently experienced in such matters to look the gift horse in the mouth. From the employers' point of view it was an admirable expedient:

[1] Karl Asterott, in *Soziale Praxis*, September 12, 1922.
[2] *Der Deutsche*, March 10, 1923.

it saved them money and kept the Works Councillors too busy to attend to their proper jobs. Another very common variant of the same device was for the employer to encourage the Council to undertake welfare work on behalf of the body of the employees. The employer would place the necessary funds at the disposal of the Council, with the aid of which the latter would purchase potatoes, lard and other foodstuffs and distribute them to the employees—a much-appreciated service in those times of ever-rising prices, great shortage of supplies, and food queues. These and similar activities had the advantage of making the workers more contented and providing a harmless outlet for the energies of the Works Council, while the employer was left free to manage his business without interference. From the first, however, the Trade Unions set their faces against such an interpretation of the functions of the Works Councils. Their more radical members were wont to refer satirically to those Councillors who devoted their period of office to this work as *Schmalz-spartakisten* (literally "lard-Spartacists").[1] By degrees the running of canteens and the distribution of food came to be regarded as outside the proper scope of the Works Councils and the practice fell increasingly into disrepute. This result was hastened by the fact that, in a number of cases, the Councils bought supplies on their own account and at their own risk. Sometimes they made a profit, which in turn laid them open to serious imputations on the part of their fellows, but often they discovered to their cost that the business of the trader is not invariably an easy one, and had their fingers badly burnt in the process. An indication that this practice has not entirely disappeared is afforded by a commercial advertisement which appeared in a German newspaper in 1925:

Works Councils! Remunerative opening for wide-awake active factory workers by taking over the representation of a firm selling wearing apparel to employees on the instalment system. Suitable for the Chairman of a Works Council of a large factory who is in touch with the Works Councils of other firms. Good prospects of obtaining additional earnings of 100 marks per month and upwards.[2]

[1] The Spartacists were the group of extremists who in 1919 sought by armed revolt to bring about the dictatorship of the proletariat.
[2] Quoted with indignation in the *Zentralblatt der Christlichen Gewerkschaften Deutschlands*, May 11, 1925.

A good many Works Councils also were, from the socialist point of view, only too eager to respond to the blandishments of the employers on questions affecting productivity, so long as they concerned other matters than wages or hours or conditions of work. When an employer, for example, who was working for export found difficulties in obtaining the necessary export license, he would discuss the matter with his Works Council. The Chairman and one or two members of the Council would get their fares paid to Berlin and would descend upon the Government Department in question, prepared to cajole and threaten until their demands had been granted. Or, again, contracts would fall off and the factory be faced with working short time or turning off employees. The Works Council would scour the country for new orders, often with considerable success. One of the great difficulties in the way of continuous employment at this time was the shortage and intermittent delivery of coal. Works Council deputations actually used to be sent to the coal mines of the Ruhr and other districts to parley with the miners, and to induce them to work extra shifts, at a time when the miners' Trade Unions were strenuously engaged in contesting any extension of the normal working-day. It is recorded that the miners frequently yielded to the appeals of the Councils and, in the face of the opposition of their Unions, conceded voluntarily that which no amount of pressure on the part of the employers would have induced them to grant.

The Works Councils were also not always free from what is expressively called in German *Betriebsegoismus*, i.e. from joining with their employers in what was in effect extortion at the expense of the rest of the community, thus affording a proof of the syndicalist dangers to which any decentralised control of production by the workers immediately concerned, would be exposed.

A second element to be considered is the degree to which some employers were able, by means of corruption, to win over the Works Councils or their most influential members. That cases of this type existed is beyond doubt, but it is naturally impossible to obtain any idea as to their extent or importance. The writer was assured by Trade Union leaders that such cases

101

were few and far between, but from other sources the impression was gained that their number was not inappreciable, particularly during the first two or three years, when many "wild men" were elected to the Councils. For it is an instructive fact that it was the extremists and the windy demagogues who proved to be the most unstable in practice and who succumbed the most readily to the wiles of the employer. It has been found not infrequently that an employer will be more anxious to get rid of an upright and conscientious Works Councillor who knows his duty and is determined, while observing the limitations of the Act, to secure the measure of the legal rights to which the Councils are entitled, than of the most irresponsible agitator who finds it convenient for the moment to label himself as a Communist. While the former endeavours to exercise a real measure of co-determination in questions of the management and internal organisation of the factory, the latter neither knows nor cares anything in regard to such matters and is likely, if he is given sufficient rope, to discredit both himself and those who agree with him, by putting forward demands which are palpably fantastic and unreasonable.

Corruption may take many forms, varying from open bribery to more subtle hints of the possibility of promotion or of other favours to come. One opportunity for this is given by the expenses claim, sent in periodically to the employer; for the latter may allow it to be understood that he will not scrutinise too closely the individual items on the claim so long as the Council is behaving itself—from his point of view. Or again, the following case has occurred: the Chairman of the Council (and as a rule it is the Chairman who is the most important person to win over to the side of the employer) goes into the employer's room for an interview on some matter. The employer says: "My dear Mr X, your clothes are very shabby; a person in an important position like yours should be better dressed. Order yourself a new suit of clothes and send the bill in to me". The *quid pro quo* is not expressed, but is certainly understood.

In a case which came to the writer's knowledge, in the early days of the Works Councils, the Council of an important factory in the suburbs of Berlin applied to the employer for the refund of money spent on tram fares to and from the factory. The employer professed to be surprised at learning that the Works Council adopted such a humble and dilatory method of going to work and offered instead to place motor-cars at the disposal of its members for this purpose. On the first day, when they arrived in state, the employees all turned out to gape and to admire. On the second day there were murmurs of dissatisfaction, and on the third day the Council were stoned. The employer rejoiced, knowing that henceforward the influence of that particular Council was destroyed irretrievably.

Some of the more subtle forms of blandishment are well described in the article by the writer in *Der Deutsche* referred to above:[1]

The materialistic standpoint of many of the employers is shown by the extraordinarily skilful tactics which they employed to transform the Works Councils into willing tools in their hands. Outwardly they appeared to make large concessions to the Councils in all negotiations. Well-furnished rooms, release from productive work, and special subventions constituted the first stage; emancipation from the Trade Unions the second stage. In the place of upright, far-seeing Trade Unionists, whose chief field of operation should be the economic problems of the Works Councils Act, there have grown up in many cases bodies of works police. The co-operation of the Councils in the management of the works has degenerated in practice into the management of canteens. The auditing of lard and potato transactions has taken the place of the auditing of the balance sheet and profit and loss accounts, while the control of the works has manifested itself in the supervision and correction of their own fellow-workers.

On the whole it is probable that cases of open bribery were not at any time very numerous, but the use of more indirect methods of persuasion, at a time when the Works Councils had still a good deal of real power, was quite common and often by no means ineffective.

Finally, a proportion of employers sought to disarm the Works Councils by the display of a very conciliatory attitude and by making far-reaching concessions, even at times going beyond what was necessary under a liberal interpretation of the Act. The members of the Works Council would be treated with an almost exaggerated respect, telephones and typists and office

[1] See p. 99.

furniture on a generous scale would be put at their disposal, Works Councillors would be largely released from productive work, and the co-operation of the Council invited at every opportunity.

In some cases this attitude was dictated purely by tactical reasons and the privileges granted were largely withdrawn as soon as changing economic conditions shifted the balance of power in favour of the employers. In others, however, there was a genuine desire to assimilate this new body, which had been interpolated between the management and its employees. It was realised that, by constituting a sort of non-commissioned officers' corps in the undertaking, a Works Council might fulfil valuable functions, especially when it could be encouraged to give a lead to the employees and to exercise a restraining and educating influence on them. The expression is fairly frequently to be found in the Reports of the Factory Inspectors that the relations between the Works Councils and the employers were "exemplary", and though this might be due to a variety of causes, in part at least it may be attributed to the fact that, once the Works Councils Act was on the statute books, many employers acquiesced in the existence of these bodies and sought to make use of them as a means of preserving harmonious relations and increasing efficiency.

With this policy of assimilation, which was widely pursued with varying degrees of success in different parts of Germany, may be contrasted what has been termed by a recent writer[1] the "paralysation policy" of the employers. Where the employers refused from the outset on general grounds to recognise the rights of the Works Councils to restrict their autocratic rule, or where the Works Council proved impossible to work with, countervailing measures were adopted soon after the passing of the Act to frustrate the Councils and to paralyse their activities.

The most general and effective of these measures, especially in large undertakings, was the constitution by the employers of a special department within the works whose task it was to deal with relations with labour and especially with the Works Council. To some extent this was intended to relieve the management proper from the enormous demands on its time and energies

[1] Brigl-Matthiaz, *Das Betriebsräteproblem* (1926), p. 125.

caused by the Councils in their early period, when appeals were being made to Conciliation Boards at every opportunity, and when consultations and meetings were being held daily. But the main purpose was to set up an expert department to fight the pretensions of the Councils and repel their interference as far as possible. The members of these departments were usually lawyers, who employed their training and ability to check every attempt of the Works Councils to exceed their statutory authority and who endeavoured, by interpreting every section of the Act in the narrowest possible way, to reduce the Councils to comparative impotence. Their activities were bitterly resented by the Councils, which complained that thereby they were deprived of that direct personal contact with the management, which it was one of the intentions of the Act to foster. It also had the disadvantage, from their point of view, that the official with whom they negotiated could always fall back on higher authority, by ruling that he was not empowered to deal with the question at issue until he had referred it back to the Directors. While there can be no doubt that these departments often proved too clever for uneducated Works Councillors, with the result that their legitimate activities were hampered, it is also true that extremist influences amongst the Councils were largely responsible for driving the employers to adopt repressive measures. In the larger undertakings these Labour Departments have continued to function, notwithstanding the subsequent decline in the bargaining power of the Councils, for they have proved of great practical value in maintaining continuity of policy in labour matters, and in securing uniform conditions of employment in all branches of the undertaking.

In other ways also employers could fight the Works Councils, as, for example, by playing off one body of employees against another—the members of the socialist Trade Unions against those belonging to the "Christian" Unions, the unorganised against the organised, even the Communists against the rest. *Divide et impera* proved in many cases a very effective policy, for it led the Councils to waste their strength and energies in internecine squabbles and hindered them from presenting a united front to the employer, based on the general support of the employees.

The employers also had always the weapon of an appeal to the Conciliation Board for the dissolution of the Council or the compulsory retirement of a particular member for "gross misfeasance of duty", and in not a few cases it was ignorance of the law or inadvertence rather than wilful intent which gave the employer the opportunity he had been looking for. By deliberate provocation it was sometimes possible to provoke a Works Councillor till he lost control of himself and laid himself open to dismissal without notice. Finally, in extreme cases an excuse could be found for closing the whole works and, on reopening, the members of the Works Council would be refused readmission. Where the employer was in a strong position he could, in this and similar ways, either make every one afraid to undertake the office of Works Councillor, or constrain the Council to lead a purely nominal existence.

So long as trade was good and the Trade Unions were well organised and powerful, there were limits to the extent to which this policy of paralysing the Councils could be adopted and even when it was successful, the ill-will that it created amongst the employees was detrimental to the peaceful and orderly conduct of the undertaking. But later on, especially in 1924, the employers found themselves with much freer hands and were often able, if they wished, to disregard the Works Councils almost completely.

Many of the aspects described in the foregoing pages of the relations between the Works Councils and the employers in 1921 and 1922 are of permanent importance, because they afford an idea of the way in which these bodies may be expected to function during the upward trend of a trade cycle; but the situation in these years was still by no means normal, owing to the continuance of inflation on a great scale; to the very short experience which all parties then had of the operation of the Works Councils Act; and to the fact that considerable sections of German labour were still under the influence of the Revolution.

The first eleven months of 1923 were the period of the most colossal inflation that the world has ever seen. The cost of living, which in January was 1120 (1913–14=1), rose to 630,908 in August and reached its highest point on November 26 with 1,535,000,000,000. The pace was altogether too giddy for any sort of rational existence; every side of life and every institution fell into the background before the elementary struggle, merely to keep alive and to preserve some measure of sanity in the face of what at the time appeared to be the complete collapse of a civilisation. The accumulated funds of the Trade Unions were swept away and they were forced to economise in every direction possible. Most of the Works Councils newspapers were stopped and the special schools for Works Councils were closed, partly for lack of funds and partly because hardly anyone could afford the time and the expenditure on fares, etc., in order to attend the courses. The Councils, which ever since their inception had been compelled to devote most of their time and energies to wage adjustments, were now more than ever forced to supervise the more and more rapid changes in wage rates as they moved upward with the rising prices. Collective Agreements had to be negotiated anew at ever shorter intervals and, with each change, a great deal of work devolved on the Councils in seeing to the detailed application of the new tariffs and explaining their meaning and operation to the employees. Despite all the efforts of the Unions and the employers' associations it became increasingly difficult to make the necessary adjustments in time, with the result that many employers broke away from their associations and preferred to negotiate direct with their employees, i.e. with the Works Councils representing the latter.

While the chief preoccupation of the Councils during this period was with wage problems, which were necessarily the centre of interest of the whole body of workers, they had also a great deal to do with questions of hours, especially in regard to the working of overtime, in so far as this was not regulated by Collective Agreements. While bursts of great activity were common in some industries and some undertakings, short time and the partial or complete closing-down of works were even more prevalent, owing to the dislocation caused by the occupation of the Ruhr and the consequent shortage of coal. Here also the Councils were called upon to perform a useful and important rôle in co-operating with the management in the selection of those workers who could with the least hardship be the first to be dismissed. At the same time, there was still plenty of scope and opportunity for the Councils to exercise a moderating influence in regard to ordinary dismissals not arising out of trade slackness, and their powers of protecting the workers from wrongful dismissal remained one of the most practical and valued of their functions.

Apart from the activities here mentioned the Works Councils appear to have accomplished little during this period.

NOVEMBER 1923 TO DECEMBER 1924

The stabilisation of the currency in November 1923 brought to a sudden stop the great crescendo of inflation which had characterised the preceding years ever since the end of the War. The reversal of conditions was dramatic in its completeness. All the feverish activity based on incessantly rising prices came to an abrupt stop and industry and commerce were plunged into acute depression. The number of unemployed in receipt of benefit (only a fraction of the total number out of work) rose from 248,600 in September 1923 to 1,592,000 in February 1924, and though it fell within two months to not more than half the February figure, it remained at a very high level throughout 1924.

It has been previously pointed out in Chapter III that the sudden devaluation of the mark brought to a head the dissatisfaction of many of the millions of new adherents to the Trade Union movement since the War. Internal dissensions and conflicts of policy; the burden of the weekly contributions; the powerlessness of the Unions in the face of a reaction which enabled the employers to lower wages and extend hours with impunity; the desire of many to obtain work under any conditions offered them—these and other causes led to an efflux from the Trade Unions on a gigantic scale. June 1924 represented perhaps the nadir of the practical importance and influence of the

Unions; from then onwards conditions improved slowly, but both numerically and in other respects the Unions had suffered such severe losses that for the time being they were almost impotent.

The reaction of these conditions on the position of the Works Councils was very great:

(a) The temporary collapse of the Trade Unions as an effective force deprived the Councils of one of their main supports in dealing with the employers. The Councils were driven in many cases to adopt Works Agreements which ran counter to the terms of the Collective Agreement.[1] They came then to realise what had been so often urged on them by the Union leaders, that Works Councils in the absence of strong Trade Unions might become a source of weakness rather than of strength to the workers in their industrial relations with the employers.

(b) The disruption of the Unions left many undertakings, even the large ones, with a majority of unorganised employees, some of whom inclined to syndicalist or communist ideas and others to an ultra-friendly alliance with the employer, resembling the "Yellow" Unionism of pre-war days. The resulting Works Councils were hopelessly divided amongst themselves and had no broad basis of authority and agreed policy on which to rely, in contrast to the earlier position when the majority both of the employees and of the members of the Councils were Unionists, and acted, as a rule, in accordance with the instructions of the local Union officials. It was common under these conditions for a Council, which had arrived at an agreement with the employer over works rules or other conditions of employment, to find the agreement repudiated by the employees. If then a Works Assembly was held to enable the Council to defend its action, the meeting was occupied, more often than not, with unprofitable recriminations between employees and members of the Council and between one member and another, ending frequently with the resignation of some or all of the Council.

(c) For the first time since the end of the War a widespread wave of unemployment swept over the country and placed the employers in a position of unqualified strength within the factory

[1] See above pp. 57–63.

and the business undertaking. The Works Councils found themselves forced to remain strictly on the defensive, and became in fact far more concerned with the question whether they themselves would join the unemployed and have to subsist on the mere pittance given in the form of unemployment benefit, than with the stalwart upholding of their rights and privileges. The special protection given to members of the Councils by the Act was of no avail in the face of the wholesale closing-down of factories and the dismissal of all employees. When they were reopened, the Works Councillors were often not re-engaged and their successors had a drastic warning of their own probable fate should they make themselves obnoxious to their employers. Black-lists were common and work very hard to find. Hence the Works Councils were driven to adopt a policy of inactivity in regard to all questions where their intervention was not welcome to the employer. Hardly anything was heard of the statutory quarterly reports or of the inspection of balance sheets, and many Councils sought safety by remaining so completely in the background that their existence was completely forgotten.

Not merely were there many good reasons for the Works Councils to adopt a cautious and retiring attitude in their dealings with the employers, but some of their most important functions in the past fell into the background or were taken from them during this period. Owing to currency stabilisation the Councils ceased to have nearly so much to do with wage adjustments. Moreover, the Hours of Work Order of December 21, 1923, transferred wholly to the Trade Unions the power of negotiating with the employers over extensions of working-time. Even where there is no Collective Agreement the Works Council has now no power to conclude a Works Agreement with the employer for lengthening the normal working-day, though it can still conclude such an agreement in respect of a reduction of working-hours or the determination of the beginning and end of the working-day. Further, the prevalence of unemployment led to a great decrease in the effectiveness of the intervention of the Councils to prevent dismissals of employees. Dismissals were now no longer isolated occurrences but took place wholesale and, being occasioned by the partial or complete closing-down of

actories, fell outside the powers of the Councils. The only
function left to them in this matter was the difficult and thank-
less duty of selecting employees for prior dismissal in such a way
as to minimise hardship. There is a good deal of evidence in the
Reports of the Factory Inspectors to show that the Councils
performed this work conscientiously and well, but it is natural
that it should have made them many enemies.

(d) Just as during the inflation period the support of the
salaried members of the Councils had been very valuable, where
it had been accorded to the wage-earning members, so the withdrawal of that support after the end of 1923 weakened the position of the Councils. The salaried employees as a whole were
even worse hit by the trade depression than the wage-earners.
Stabilisation of the currency immediately rendered superfluous
the work of tens of thousands of clerical employees in banks and
all commercial and industrial undertakings, and unemployment
increased among their numbers to an enormous extent. Hence
very few of those who were sufficiently fortunate to retain their
posts were willing to run the risk of incurring the displeasure of
their employer by taking an active part on the Works Council,
or even, in many cases, of permitting themselves to be elected
at all. The wage-earners, therefore, lost a measure of counsel and
moral support which had often been of great value and assistance
to them in the past.

(e) During the early years of the Works Councils the practice
had grown up amongst employers of releasing a number of the
Works Councillors, in some cases the whole Council, from productive work. The practice was naturally commonest in the big
undertakings, but was also adopted to a greater or less extent
in medium-sized works. This was partly intended as a concession
to the Councils and, partly because less interruption to the
organisation of work was caused by the complete release of some
or all of the Councillors than by the repeated breaks arising out
of the exercise of their legal functions during working-time.

In the course of time this procedure proved to have serious
disadvantages. The "freed" Works Councillor lost the benefit
of close contact with his fellows at the working-bench and became a mere official sitting at a desk—a transformation entirely

contrary to the whole idea of works representation. Not merely was there the same risk as in the case of the Trade Union official, that he would get out of touch with the practical problems of the daily working life of his fellows, but also he tended to lose his influence over them and to become a target for all kinds of envious and malicious attacks.

On the other side, apart from the cost to the employer of keeping a number of men on full wages without getting any work in return, it was found that these men often had not got enough to do to keep them fully occupied. In some cases that led to the moral deterioration of the man in question, who, at the end of his time of office, was so uprooted from his normal working existence, that he could not return to it and had to be discharged, as he could no longer do his work properly. In other cases the "freed" Works Councillor would devote his energies to creating something to do, and thus become a source of agitation and unrest in the undertaking.

Thus a reaction against this widespread release of Works Councillors from all productive work was inevitable. To a slight extent it had set in already in 1922 and 1923, helped on by the fact that many of the Trade Union leaders were opposed to the practice on general principles, but it was chiefly in 1924 that this privilege came to be withdrawn or curtailed in great measure. With the decrease in the practical functions of many of the Works Councils it became less necessary for them to devote the whole of their time to their official duties and, at the same time, the employers were now strong enough to take back rights which they had formerly granted under pressure. In some industries and districts the whole question was regulated on uniform lines by a Collective Agreement. Thus, in Upper Silesia, a Conciliation Board gave an award, which was made binding by the Federal Labour Minister, according to which, in works employing from 601 to 1500 workers, one member of the Works Committee, and in larger works two members, were released from work for one hour daily on each of the first five working-days of the week.[1] In very large undertakings the Chairman of the Council is often the only man released from all work, while the remainder are

[1] Report of Factory Inspectors for Upper Silesia, 1923/1924, p. 208.

allowed collectively an aggregate of so many hours free in the week, the distribution of which is left to the Council itself.

Although, as has been noted, this development is one which has been in general accord with the policy of Trade Union leaders, it was not at all popular with the Works Councillors themselves and contributed markedly to enhance the arduousness and unpopularity of the office.

(*f*) For all the above reasons there developed an ever-increasing unwillingness on the part of those who had had experience of serving on Works Councils to stand for election or to allow themselves to be re-elected.[1] Resignations were numerous, and the number of establishments in which no Council at all was appointed became large. With the increase in the power of the employers and the growing risk of unemployment, the attractiveness of the office of Works Councillor was greatly diminished, while the attendant drawbacks and inconveniences loomed much larger.

No separate Reports for the year 1923 were issued by the Factory Inspectors and it was not until 1925 that the Reports for the two years 1923 and 1924 were issued in a single volume. The information contained in them relates chiefly to 1924 and represents as usual the fruits of a great deal of valuable first-hand observation. The general tenor of the Reports can be seen from the following extracts:

In negotiations over the closing-down of establishments the Works Councils, in consequence of their greater practical knowledge, often showed themselves more successful and possessed of greater understanding than the representatives of the Trade Unions who also took part in the negotiations. The manager of a large concern expressed the view that, after the removal of radical elements from the Works Council owing to a strike, the activity of the workers markedly increased; output and therefore piece-wages of almost all sections rose by about 25 per cent. since there was no longer organised restriction of output; the number of working-hours engrossed by the Council fell from 70 to 12 per week, while the number of disputes fought out in the Courts or Conciliation Boards sank to one-tenth of their former number.[2]

The views of employers concerning the necessity and value of works representative bodies continue to be very diverse. Some hold

---

[1] See below, pp. 126–9.   [2] Report for Berlin, 1923/1924, pp. 72–73.

that co-operation with the Works Council has been "admirable in every way"; that the Council "has represented the interests of the firm as well as those of the employees and has never opposed the just demands of the management"; that it "not only has endeavoured to prevent accidents but has also urged every man to do his duty and fulfil his obligations". Others take the view that the Councils have grievously neglected their duty and have abused their position to interfere unwarrantably with the conduct of the business, relying upon their statutory protection against dismissal.[1]

The Works Councils have in general lost in importance, partly because the many points of friction which a few years ago disturbed the relations between employers and employees have become less; partly because of the fear of the workers, in the prevailing unemployment, of losing their jobs, and partly because the attitude of the radical elements, whose excessive demands were bitterly opposed by the employers, induced the more peaceable workers to have as little as possible to do with matters affecting the Works Councils. There is much truth in the assertion of an old Trade Unionist that the communist agitation in the individual works has brought the whole question of works representation into disrepute.[2]

Not a few employers—even in large works—still look with an unfavourable eye on the institution of the Works Council. In one case it was reported that the employer had threatened with dismissal every employee whose name stood on a list of candidates for election to the Works Council, and similar action is reported from the district of Dresden....But there are also, especially in the larger works, a number of employers and managers who would no longer like to be without a properly constituted Works Council...and it was noteworthy, in a conference with employers' and employees' representatives to hear, from the mouth of the influential manager of one of the greatest textile works in Saxony, the view that the introduction of Works Councils represented a real achievement of the post-war period.[3]

Practically without exception all the Factory Inspectors are agreed that, during the year of industrial depression following the stabilisation of the currency, the Works Councils had lost very heavily in prestige and practical significance and that the employers had completely recovered the upper hand in their relations with the employees and the Works Councils, which to some extent they had lost during the years of inflation and artificial prosperity. They also all emphasise the decline in the

[1] Report for Lüneburg, 1923/1924, p. 329.
[2] Report for Osnabrück and Aurich, 1923/1924, p. 355.
[3] Report for Saxony, 1923/1924, p. 29.

numbers of the Councils and the growing reluctance of employees to be elected to serve on them.

The difficulty of securing first-hand information as to the attitude of employers in Germany towards the institution of the Works Councils is naturally very great. It is unsafe to generalise from individual enquiries, and conditions have always varied greatly, not only from one part of the country to another, but from industry to industry and from one establishment to another within an industry. For one important area, the Ruhr District, there exist however some valuable data, which, when the necessary qualifications have been made, do afford some evidence of the practical experience of a large number of employers in dealing with Works Councils. Towards the end of 1924 an industrial journal of high standing, the *Deutsche Bergwerks-Zeitung*, circulated a questionnaire concerning the activities of the Works Councils to almost all works throughout the Ruhr District. A very large number of answers was received, which were then summarised and published in the columns of the journal. This questionnaire, together with the summarised answers, is printed in Appendix v of this volume and will be found to throw a good deal of light on the attitude of this group of employers in Germany towards the institution of the Works Councils.

JANUARY 1925 TO JUNE 1926

The economic situation in 1925 remained unfavourable, being subject to the same general influences as had been operative during 1924. The shortage and costliness of credit dominated the whole situation. Bankruptcies were numerous and manufacturers were afraid to sell against credit, but demanded payment on or within a few days of delivery—terms with which the merchants were unable to comply. Hence stocks accumulated in the manufacturers' warehouses, orders were scarce, and unemployment continued to be very considerable. In addition to widespread unemployment for these reasons, there was a very heavy turn-over of labour owing to the reorganisation of industry which was proceeding actively during this whole period. Much of the industrial grouping which had taken place during the inflation years had to be broken up, and there supervened an intensive process of amalgamation on horizontal lines involving the shutting down or re-adaptation of many plants. Moreover, in all industry, there was a widespread demand for "rationalisation"—a Teutonic version of scientific management *plus* "Fordism", but also comprising every sort of measure that could lead to reduced costs of production and greater industrial efficiency.

This severe trade depression, combined with a high degree of instability of employment in most industries, inevitably militated against any marked recovery of bargaining power on the part of labour. Nevertheless, the Trade Unions were much more effective in 1925 than 1924, for although they did not regain many of their lost members, they were able to replenish their funds and consolidate their organisation. Discipline in their ranks improved greatly and their officials became once more the real leaders of labour throughout most of the country.

The position of the Works Councils was a far more difficult one, for their members, unlike Trade Union officials, were dependent in large measure on the goodwill of the employers for their livelihood; the latter may be likened to the Staff behind the lines, while the former were in the front trenches.

The Unions could give general support and encouragement to the Councils but they were often quite unable to prevent considerable casualties from occurring amongst these "outposts of the Trade Union movement", as the Works Councils are often described. Victimisation was a very real peril and, as in 1923, the dread of it exercised a restraining influence on the Works Councils, often preventing the election of Councils or reducing their activities till they led a merely nominal existence.

The Reports of the Factory Inspectors for 1925 show a remarkable uniformity of opinion in regard to the evolution of the Works Councils. The Reports are agreed that the influence and prestige of the Councils showed a further decline during this year, partly as a result of the economic situation and the fear of dismissal and, partly owing to the prevalence of abuse and criticism of the Works Councillors by their fellow-employees.[1] To some extent this latter factor was also a consequence of the former,

[1] Cf. Report for Berlin, p. 84.

because the dissatisfaction of the workers with their representatives was due in part to their powerlessness to extract concessions from the employers. The number of Works Councils elected in the smaller industrial undertakings still further declined, while in many districts Councils had almost disappeared in commercial establishments, apart from banks and insurance companies.[1] On the other hand, there was general agreement that the Works Councils continued to exist and to function in the larger industrial undertakings throughout the country and that in these cases they had done valuable work, especially in connection with negotiations over the closing-down of factories.[2] In the large works also the relations between the employers and the Councils are reported to have been good. Several of the Reports emphasise the importance, for the status and bargaining power of the Works Councils, of support on the part of Trade Unions.[3]

[1] Cf. Report for Magdeburg, p. 249.
[2] Cf. Report for Arnsberg, p. 445.
[3] Cf. Report for Hessen, p. 71, and for Liegnitz, p. 198.

CHAPTER V

The Works Councils and Industrial Self-Government

THE SCOPE AND POSITION OF THE WORKS COUNCILS

The Works Councils Act applies, in whole or in part, with but few exceptions, to all industrial and commercial establishments which employ five or more persons and to all agricultural units in which not less than ten permanent workers are normally employed. To this fact a great deal of the interest and importance of the Act is due. The most diverse and disparate undertakings come within its scope and the experience of its operation is correspondingly varied. It is unfortunately not possible to give recent figures showing the number of establishments in present-day Germany, as the last Industrial Census was taken as long ago as 1907. Some idea of the scope of the Act can, however, be obtained from the following figures, which relate to the number of establishments and of persons employed therein in industry, commerce and agriculture in 1907:

	Number of establishments employing					
	6 to 10 persons		11 to 20 persons		Over 20 persons	
	Establish-ments	Persons	Establish-ments	Persons	Establish-ments	Perso
Industrial and Commercial	149,259	1,104,600	71,456	1,022,800	81,549	6,915,
Agricultural	383,194	2,684,600	55,791	750,900	27,240	1,463,
Total	532,453	3,789,200	127,247	1,773,700	108,789	8,379,

Certain figures recently drawn up by the Ministry of Labour on the basis of the Reports of the Factory Inspectors,[1] while not directly comparable, go to show that, for the same areas, there has been no very great change in the total figures of establishments and of numbers employed. On general grounds, however, it is to be expected that the proportion of the large establishments and of persons employed in them is greater now

[1] *Reichsarbeitsblatt*, No. 19, 1924.

than in 1907. On the basis of the 1907 figures Works Councils
or Works Stewards could have been elected (under the present
Act) in 302,264 industrial and commercial establishments employing 9,043,000 persons, provided that these establishments
contained a sufficient number of persons eligible for election.

On the other hand, the number of persons totally excluded
from the operation of the Act is also very great, as is indicated
in the following table which likewise relates to 1907:

	Number of Establishments				Number of Employees			
	Industrial		Commercial		Industrial		Commercial	
	Total	% of Total	Total	% of Total	Total	% of Total	Total	% of Total
Small Establish-ments (1 to 5 employees)	1,870,000	89·6	1,205,000	93·8	3,200,000	29·5	2,057,000	61·6
Medium Estab-lishments (6 to 50 employees)	187,000	9·0	76,400	6·0	2,715,000	25·0	889,000	26·6
Large Establish-ments (over 50 employees)	29,000	1·4	2,800	0·2	4,938,000	45·5	395,000	11·8

From this table it would appear that by far the larger number
of all establishments (even allowing for the fact that Works
Stewards can be elected where five persons are employed) fall
completely outside the scope of the Works Councils Act. This
admittedly represents a serious limitation of the principles of
co-operation between employers and employed, adopted in
Article 165 of the German Constitution. The omission of such
great numbers from the operation of the Act is to be explained
on two grounds. In the first place, the Act is a very large and
complicated measure and the administrative difficulties which
would arise from its application to the great mass of tiny concerns would be enormous. Secondly, in such "dwarf" concerns,
as they are termed in Germany, the relations between the employer and his employees are so close and intimate that it may
be claimed that the latter hardly stand in any need of a special
representative organ. It is at least arguable that their interests
can be better defended by the Trade Unions (where such exist)
than by any extension of the representative system within the
concerns themselves. Such explanations do not, however, apply

to the exclusion of these workers, as also of all those employed in establishments with fewer than 20 employees (i.e. those represented by a Works Steward), from the very important provisions of the Act which accord a measure of protection against unjustified dismissals.

No official figures are available which show the numbers or distribution of Works Councils in Germany to-day. An estimate, which must necessarily be very rough, was made by the Central Works Councils Bureau for the "Free" Trade Unions, according to which there were about 250,000[1] Works Councillors and Works Stewards at the end of 1922, of whom from seventy-five per cent. to eighty per cent. were said to be organised within the "Free" Trade Unions.

In the metal industries, which have the largest number of organised workers in Germany, there were, in 1922, in 11,557 establishments, 32,565 wage-earning and 7219 salaried employees who were members of Works Councils or Works Stewards. In the textile industries in the same year there were 25,239 Works Councillors in 7219 establishments. Since that time the numbers have diminished, owing to causes which are discussed below and which are partly of a temporary character.

At the time when the Councils movement was at its height after the War, much play was made with the notion of economic self-government and it seems clear that the framers of Article 165 of the Constitution of Weimar[2] conceived of the Works Councils as the lowest stage in a general system of industrial representation. That Article provided *inter alia* for the creation of Regional Workers' Councils and a Federal Workers' Council, which, in association with representatives of the employers and other sections of the community, should form Regional Economic Councils and a Federal Economic Council. To these bodies very extensive powers of initiation of economic measures into the Reichstag, and of criticism of such measures brought forward

---

[1] This was probably a considerable over-estimate, even at the time when it was made.
[2] See above, p. 9.

by the Government, were to be given and the view was also widely held that they would make possible an important degree of devolution of administration in economic matters, by transferring this from the Central Government to new organs which would be better fitted for such tasks than a politically elected Parliament.

Although seven years have elapsed since the adoption of the Weimar Constitution, the Regional Economic Councils have not yet been established, while, although a Provisional Federal Economic Council has been in existence since May 1920, it differs, widely, both in composition and powers from the lines laid down in Article 165 of the Constitution.

The chief obstacles in the way of the establishment of the Regional Economic Councils have been the controversy over their precise composition and functions and over their relation to existing economic organisations. There have long been in existence in Germany important bodies representing different economic interests—in particular, the Chambers of Commerce, the Chambers of Handicrafts, and the Chambers of Agriculture. Common to all of these bodies was the fact that they were official, that they were based on legal provisions, that they were composed wholly of employers and that they provided an important measure of occupational representation. When legislation affecting any branch of industrial or commercial activity is under consideration, the Chambers in question are asked to report and considerable weight and importance are normally attached to their views. Everywhere they are officially recognised and entrusted with duties which make of them semi-public institutions, while in the Hanseatic Cities the Chambers of Commerce are given regulating and controlling functions and are in effect a part of the general administrative machine. In addition, they do important work in providing and disseminating information among their members and in protecting their general interests in relation both to the State and to the public.

During the last few years a violent controversy has raged over the position of these bodies in the final scheme of industrial representation. The Trade Unions, as representing the labour

121

movement, are practically unanimous in demanding that all the Chambers of Commerce, Handicrafts and Agriculture shall be reconstructed as joint bodies composed of equal numbers of representatives of labour and of the employers. The insistence on this demand is stimulated by the knowledge of the great mass of documentation on all matters of industry and commerce which is at the disposal of these Chambers and to which labour wishes to have access. Further, the workers wish to have an equal voice in the drafting of reports to the Government on important questions, referred by it to the Chambers, which constitutes one of the most important of their functions. Equal participation in the work of such Chambers would at last give labour a footing within the industrial camp and would enable it, both to influence the formation of economic policy and to gain valuable experience of the problems associated with the control of industry.

On the other hand, the employers have strenuously and, hitherto successfully, opposed these pretensions of labour. They contend that the greater part of the practical work of the Chambers is concerned with problems of industrial and commercial policy and with technical questions of all kinds. With none of these matters are the workers as such directly concerned and to their discussion they can bring neither practical experience nor trained intelligence. The employers are, however, quite willing that to each Chamber should be attached a representative body of employees who would, in conjunction with the employers, consider and report on all questions directly affecting the labour contract and the position of the workers in industry. This solution is rejected by the Unions on the grounds, firstly, that, being proposed by the employers themselves, it is quite certain to be valueless to the workers; secondly, that these separate Chambers of Labour, lacking the far-flung organisation of the employers, would find it impossible to collect the necessary material and would, in practice, find themselves impotent; and, thirdly, that it is precisely in the general questions of economic policy that the workers wish to have that voice which was promised to them by Article 165 of the Constitution. Various proposals have been put forward both by the Government and by the Provisional

Federal Economic Council which incline more to the views of the employers than to those of the employees, but none of these has yet been officially adopted or put into a final form.

All the proposals which have been made are agreed in regarding the Chambers of Commerce, Handicrafts and Agriculture, enlarged by some form of labour representation, as the lowest stage of the new structure of industrial self-government. The middle stage is to be formed by the Regional Economic Councils which, according to a scheme drawn up by the Provisional Federal Economic Council, should be composed partly of members of the Chambers of Commerce, etc., partly of representatives of the economic organisations of employers and employees and, partly of representatives of municipalities, the professions, officials, and co-operative societies. No details have yet been worked out as to the functions of these Councils. The whole question of the formation of Regional Economic Councils has, indeed, been thrown rather into the background by the strife over the composition of the Chambers of Commerce, Handicrafts and Agriculture. In fact, during the course of negotiations with the Government, the Trade Union leaders stated clearly that they attached comparatively little importance to the formation of these Councils, provided that they attained their desires in regard to the Chambers[1]—a view which seems to be dictated by considerations of immediate tactical advantage and neglects the more important ultimate interests of labour.

The employers, on the other hand, having lost their initial enthusiasm for the notion of self-governing economic provinces, are now inclined to regard unfavourably the prospect of the formation of Regional Economic Councils, on the ground that they would overlap with the existing Chambers and would tend in the long run, either to supplant the latter, which they would regard as a misfortune, or to become a superfluous and unnecessary piece of organisation. For the present, at least, the question of their formation appears to have been postponed indefinitely.

The Federal Economic Council constitutes the apex of the

[1] Wissell, "Wirtschaftsräte in Deutschland", in *Gewerkschaftsarchiv*, November 1924, p. 351.

whole system. According to a scheme drawn up by the Provisional Federal Economic Council, some of the members should be nominated by the Regional Economic Councils, some by the organisations of employers and employees and some by representatives of other interests. The Government however have recently prepared a draft Bill on quite different lines. The future Council is to have 144 members in place of the 326 members of the existing Provisional Federal Economic Council. The Council is to be composed of three equal sections[1]—Section 1, employers' representatives; Section 2, employees' representatives; Section 3, representatives of co-operative societies, municipalities and other public bodies, and persons nominated by the Federal Government. Plenary meetings of the Council will only rarely be held and most of the work will be done in the main Committees and in the sub-committees. There will be three main Committees—a Committee on Social Policy, a Committee on Financial Policy and a Committee on Economic Policy.

It is contended by the Trade Unions that this scheme contravenes the principles of Article 165 of the German Constitution; for labour, instead of having an equal voice in the Council with the employers, will only constitute one out of three sections and the experience of the Provisional Federal Economic Council shows that the representatives of the Communes and those nominated by the Government support, as a rule, the interests of the employers rather than of the workers. The Trade Unions hold that all the representatives of the other classes must be regarded as employers, against whom must be offset an equal number of employees.

It will have been observed that, in none of the schemes outlined above, is there any proposal to link up with the system of occupational representation the Workers' Councils, provided for in Article 165 of the Constitution, or the statutory Works Councils. The reason for this, so far as the Workers' Councils are

[1] The employers' and employees' representatives are not to be elected but nominated by the organisations concerned on to a panel from which the members to serve on the Council are appointed by the Government. The District Economic Councils (if they are eventually constituted) will thus have no direct voice in the selection of the personnel of the Federal Economic Council.

concerned, is that these Workers' Councils constitute the most distinctive residue of the original Council or Soviet idea to be found in the German Constitution. But the historical development of Germany since 1919 has been further and further away from the realisation of this idea, to which the bulk of the Trade Unions are as much opposed as the employers. There is in fact a disposition on the part of the Trade Unions to let the Workers' Councils drop out altogether, on the ground that, as the latter would presumably have to be elected by the vote of the whole body of employees, they would in fact constitute an independent type of labour organisation which would run a very serious risk of coming in conflict with the Trade Unions. The attitude of the Unions is that they and they only are the properly constituted leaders of the labour movement, and that there is no room in it for any rival or alternative bodies. It can be readily understood that the Unions, which have fought and overcome the Soviet principle in the Works Councils, have no desire to see it return in the almost equally dangerous guise of Regional and Federal Workers' Councils.

So far as the Works Councils are concerned, the Trade Unions are quite determined to keep in their hands the nomination of the employees' representatives on to any regional or central bodies. Moreover, for technical reasons, the Works Councils would not make satisfactory electoral bodies. In the first place, this form of representation (including the Works Stewards) does not exist in any of the small establishments normally employing less than five persons; secondly, owing to the method of composition of the Works Councils smaller establishments would be favoured in contrast with the larger ones; thirdly, the personnel of these Councils is constantly fluctuating; and, fourthly, this method of election would be unlikely to produce the men who would be most competent to sit on the higher Councils.

Thus it is probable that the Works Councils as such will be restricted, in the future as in the past, to their functions and duties in the individual establishments, without acting, as was hoped by the original supporters of the Councils movement, as the basis of a grandiose scheme of control over industry and commerce, exercised by the workers directly engaged in the productive process.[1] It is inevitable that this should be so if the Trade Unions are to preserve their effective leadership over the forces of labour. It will, however, be greatly to the advantage both of the Works Councils and of the Unions, if care is taken to see that the ablest members of the Councils are selected in sufficient numbers to serve on the Regional Workers' Councils and on similar joint bodies. The wider the view that these men can get of the complexities and inter-relations of the productive process as a whole, the more valuable will be their counsels and experience within their own sphere of operation as Works Councillors. Although, under existing conditions, an organic connection between the Works Councils and the rest of the nexus of occupational representation appears to be impossible, there is no reason why sufficient contact should not be maintained, with the aid of the Trade Unions, to enable the Works Councils to realise their place in the economic system and their true relation to the community.

THE REPRESENTATIVE CHARACTER OF THE WORKS COUNCILS

(a) *Elections.* In view of the widespread demand in Germany, as in other industrial countries, that labour should have a greater share in the control of working-conditions, a good deal of importance attaches to the question how far advantage has been taken by German workers of their legal right to elect Works Councils in the various industrial and commercial undertakings throughout the country. In the absence, for the most part, of official figures, the chief information on this subject is given in the Reports of the Factory Inspectors since 1920.

An outstanding feature of these Reports is the emphasis laid on the growing unwillingness of the employees to elect Works Councils and, in particular, of individual members to allow themselves to be elected or re-elected to serve on the Councils. Already in 1921, only a year after the passing of the Act, many cases are noted in which no Councils had been elected. Often the reason given by the workers was that their relations with

[1] Cf. Feig, "Betriebsräte und Wirtschaftsräte", in *Die sozialen Probleme des Betriebes* (1925), p. 201.

their employer were excellent and that they stood in no need of a Works Council. Sometimes the Collective Agreements in force were so comprehensive that a Works Council appeared to be superfluous. In other instances so little interest was taken in the Act that no one troubled to put forward a list of candidates. In the smaller firms it was not uncommon for the very elaborate and complicated procedure laid down in the Act, for the election of the Council by the system of proportional representation, to be ignored, and for the Council or the Works Steward to be elected openly by a simple show of hands. Unless the employer or any of the workers entered a formal protest against this, the Factory Inspectors did not, as a rule, interfere. In the smaller firms, again, an important cause of the non-appointment of Works Councils was the lack of sufficient candidates who satisfied the necessary conditions for election, in particular the age requirement (24 years). It was observed in some districts that the employers took care to keep the numbers of regular employees below 20 in order to prevent the formation of a Works Council,[1] while firms employing nearly 300 workers restricted the number so as not to exceed 300, and were thus able to prevent the Councils from acquiring the right to have access to the balance sheet and profit and loss account of their firm.

Conditions during 1922 were not markedly different from 1921, but the difficulty of finding members of Councils willing to accept re-election was becoming more pronounced and was commented on in many of the Reports. It is observed in the Report for the very important industrial district of Düsseldorf that: "Although for the time being the number of establishments without a Works Council is still relatively small it would seem that a certain indifference and weariness in regard to the Works Council system is extending amongst the employees ".

The years 1923 and 1924 saw great changes in general economic conditions in Germany. The extreme inflationist period of 1923 provided a good deal of work for the Councils to do, in the form of adjustments of piece-wages to changes in the basic

---

[1] A Works Council, which must have a minimum of three members, has also the power to appeal against the dismissal of employees, a power which is not given to the Works Steward.

rates which moved on a sliding scale with prices. But in 1924 and 1925 the stabilisation of the currency removed the necessity of this work. The Councils were powerless to prevent the mass dismissals of employees which resulted from the trade depression and were merely left with the invidious task of selecting those to be turned off. The fear of unemployment made the post of Works Councillor still more unattractive. By this time, all the novelty and the greater part of the original enthusiasm for the Works Councils had disappeared; on the other hand the disadvantages of office had become startlingly apparent.

The chief causes of the frequent refusal to stand for election are stated in the Reports to be: (1) general indifference; (2) fear of the employer; (3) the attitude of the employees towards their elected representatives. The following extracts from the Reports are typical of the conditions observed by the Factory Inspectors:

In 1924 an end was put to the complete release of Works Councillors from productive work....As a result the interests of many Councillors in their office waned; at the same time the interest of the employees as a whole in the Councils declined and their importance decreased more and more....In several cases the Election Committee, appointed in accordance with Section 23 of the Act, absolutely refused to conduct an election, giving as a reason the lack of interest of the employees.[1]

The interest of the employees in the small and medium-sized establishments seems to be vanishing. The cases in which there was no re-election, or where no one was found willing to assume the difficult post of Chairman, are on the increase. Even the managements of works which lay stress on the value of having a Works Council have often failed to induce the employees to carry out an election.[2]

The institution of Works Councils has not been strengthened during the period under review; in fact in many works their prestige and effectiveness have suffered greatly. The inflation period of 1923, the stabilisation crisis of 1924, and a number of strikes were almost as disastrous for many Works Councils as for the undertakings. In numerous cases works were shut down and the whole of the employees dismissed. When they were reopened the employers often deliberately refrained from re-engaging the former Works Councillors.

[1] Report for Upper Silesia, 1923/1924, p. 208.
[2] Report for Magdeburg, 1923/1924, p. 232.

There was naturally little inclination amongst the re-employed workers to take up the dangerous and thorny office of Works Councillor. Thus great undertakings were for a period without any Works Council and the Council which was ultimately formed was often only a sham.[1]

In the administrative district of Chemnitz in Saxony, a representative body was lacking in 228 establishments in 1923: in 1924 this number had increased to 603. In the district of Dresden, out of 102 artificial-flower factories, there were only 88 in which there was a Works Council or Works Steward. In the districts of Leipzig and Zwickau there was no representative body in 348 and 647 industrial establishments respectively. In the district of Leipzig, in concerns with only salaried employees, there were Works Councils or Stewards in 23 per cent. of those inspected in 1923 and in only 12 per cent. in 1924, while in industrial concerns the corresponding figures were 53 per cent. in 1923 and 50 per cent. in 1924.[2] The Reports of the Factory Inspectors for 1925 show no improvement in this respect, a further decline in the number of Works Councils being noted in every district save one.

In a Works Councils Conference in June 1925 it was stated that, whereas in 1923 there were 26,000 Works Councillors in 6991 establishments in the German textile industry, in 1924 there were only 17,040 Works Councillors in 3954 establishments, though as the figures for 1924 were not quite complete it is probable that the total number was rather higher than is indicated for that year.[3]

When all the available evidence is taken into account, it would appear that the absence of statutory representative bodies is relatively common in the smaller works in all industries and exceedingly common in commercial undertakings of every sort where only salaried employees are engaged. Practically no advantage has been taken of the provisions of the Act empowering the formation of special Works Councils for those engaged in out-work for an employer (*Hausgewerbetreibende*). On the other hand, Works Councils are still to be found in almost

---

[1] Report for Erfurt, 1923/1924, p. 282.
[2] Report for Saxony, 1923/1924, pp. 28–29.
[3] *Protokoll über die Konferenz der...Betriebsräte der Textilindustrie*, 1925, p. 49.

all large industrial works, in which contact between employer and employee is more remote and difficult than in small firms.

(b) *Women*. In the Reports of the Factory Inspectors for the years 1923 and 1924, a special study was made of the position of women in relation to the representation of employees on Works Councils. There was a general consensus of opinion that, with very few exceptions, women were not represented on the Councils in proportion to their numerical strength. Thus in 374 businesses of all kinds, inspected in Berlin, employing 165,633 men and 116,564 women, the total number of Works Councillors and Works Stewards was 3417. Of this number 2669 were men and only 748 women. Similarly, in the district of Merseburg, in 74 businesses employing 45,354 men and 12,315 women, there were 558 men and 80 women Councillors. In 44 textile factories in Krefeld, employing 1300 men and 2900 women, the Works Councils were composed of 114 men and 14 women. The Chairmanship of the Council was occupied by men in 29 businesses and by women in 15. A more favourable proportion was found in the Chemnitz textile industry, where the female worker constituted 70 per cent. of the employees and had 63 per cent. of the representation on the Works Councils, while in 162 out of 332 businesses a woman was the Chairman of the Council.

Not merely was the numerical representation of women inadequate, having regard to their numbers, but in most cases the women Councillors were found to be playing a very subordinate rôle to the men and, even where women were exclusively employed, they were seldom able to elect competent and efficient representatives. The following are the chief reasons given by the Factory Inspectors for the inferior position of women on the Works Councils:

1. The youth of many of the women workers disqualifies them from voting and still more from being elected as members of the Councils.

2. The older women are mostly married and their free time is fully occupied with household duties, while the young and unmarried ones have other interests and do not expect to remain permanently in industry.

3. Trade Unionism being much less developed amongst the

women than amongst the men, there are fewer of the former who are familiar with the kind of problems with which Works Councils have to deal.

4. Where both men and women are employed it is common for the women to consider that their interests will be more effectively represented by a man than by a woman, as the latter is apt to yield too easily to the opposition of the employer.

5. Women who assume the office of Works Councillor seem specially exposed to the enmity and jealousy of their fellow-workers and this renders their office burdensome and unattractive. They are often afraid, also, of the publicity and prominence involved.

6. In some cases men have refused to co-operate and work side by side with women on the Councils.

The picture presented in the Reports is, however, by no means uniformly unfavourable so far as women are concerned, and a number of striking instances is recorded where they have accomplished excellent work. Here too it must be borne in mind that economic conditions have latterly been such as to damp the ardour of the workers for all forms of labour organisation, and the women are as much subject as the men to the influence of the fear of unemployment.

(c) *The Salaried Employee.* One of the distinctive features of the German Works Councils Act is the division of the Works Council into two bodies—a Wage-earners' Council and a Salaried-employees'[1] Council—each elected separately by the members

---

[1] Salaried employees are defined by the Works Councils Act as comprising "all persons who work for remuneration in any of the occupations specified in Section 1 of the Insurance Act for Salaried Employees, even if they are not compulsorily insured". The latter Act makes the following classification of employees who come within its scope: (a) salaried employees in positions of authority; (b) works officials, foremen and other higher employees; (c) commercial employees (clerical workers, shop assistants, etc.); (d) members of orchestral and theatrical undertakings; (e) school teachers and instructors. For the purposes of the Works Councils Act the term "salaried employees" (*Angestellten*) is extended to apprentices in the occupations referred to, and also to all clerical workers engaged on work of a subordinate and routine character. It is noteworthy that even the higher officials and employees of businesses are ranked among the salaried employees and are therefore eligible to vote and to be elected on the Councils. Only directors and those exercising managerial functions or those who hold a power of attorney (*Prokura*) are excluded from the category of salaried employees.

of its own group and each with largely distinct functions. This is in conformity with a similar division of the Trade Union Movement, in which the salaried employees have for many years been organised separately from the wage-earners. It has long been one of the aspirations of the socialist movement to unify the organisations of wage-earning and salaried employees and, though this has proved impossible, a good deal of progress in this direction has been made in recent years by the large increase in the membership of Unions of salaried employees grouped under the Afa and affiliated to the Socialist Unions of the wage-earners, whose policy is that of the Class War.

When the Works Councils Bill was in preparation, the representatives of the salaried employees held out for separate representation on the Works Councils and, though there was much discussion as to the definition of the term, there was general agreement over the necessity for distinguishing between the two groups.

Under the Works Councils Act the salaried employees are entitled to representation on the Councils in proportion to their numerical strength, in the same manner as in the case of the wage-earners, and the representatives of each group are normally elected by the votes of the members of their group exclusively. Whereas, however, the wage-earning employees comprise the relatively homogeneous body of manual workers, the salaried-employees' group embraces many distinct and diverse categories. Thus the foreman in a factory, the clerk in an office, the shop assistant, the musician in an orchestra, the waiter in a restaurant, the head book-keeper in a large business, the engineer or chemist in a works—all these are regarded as salaried employees and are consequently entitled to vote for, and to be elected to serve on, a Works Council. It is clear that, not merely do the interests of different classes of salaried employees vary widely, but their working relations both to the employer and to the wage-earners with whom they may be employed are by no means uniform with those of the wage-earners amongst one another or *vis-à-vis* the employer. It is for this reason that the Act provides for the formation of two Sectional Councils within the Works Council, to each of which is given, in the first instance, exclusive competence to negotiate with the employer as to all conditions of wages and employment affecting solely the group it represents. It is only in questions which concern the whole body of employees, or in the event of negotiations having broken down between the employer and the Sectional Council, that the Works Council as a whole becomes the competent body to deal with the matter.

It is desirable to distinguish between conditions where, as in banks or shops, the salaried employees are in an overwhelming majority, and the state of affairs in an industrial undertaking where the wage-earners constitute the main body of the employees. In the former case there is no question of a conflicting interest between the wage-earning and the salaried employees. There still remains, however, the fact that amongst the employees who are eligible to vote and to be elected some are the superiors in the business of others, a fact which renders their position in relation to their employer and to their fellow-employees a difficult one. The resulting problem can be more conveniently discussed in connection with the second case referred to above. In the early and turbulent days of the Works Councils it was notorious that the Salaried-employees' Councils, especially in the large banks, were in many cases more radical and extreme than the Wage-earners' Councils in most industrial undertakings. But this phase was of relatively short duration. The inflationist period had led to an altogether abnormal demand for clerical workers in every branch of industry and commerce, and the ensuing stabilisation wrought even greater havoc amongst the ranks of these employees than in the general body of workers. Hence the fear of dismissal proved a potent factor not merely in discouraging possible excesses on the part of the Councils, but, in general, in rendering people unwilling to submit their names as candidates for office. An instance recorded by the Factory Inspectors in the Berlin district, although probably exceptional, is none the less noteworthy. In a large insurance firm there was no election to the Works Council because the management had promised an increase of salaries in the event of the employees refraining from the exercise of their rights to elect a Council.[1]

[1] Report of the Factory Inspectors for Berlin, 1923/1924, p. 71.

In medium-sized shops and similar businesses it is rare to find a Works Council in being and those which are elected lead for the most part a purely nominal existence. In most banks and other large commercial undertakings Councils are still elected, but they rarely meet the employer more than once or twice in the year and, under present conditions, are frequently devoid of influence.

In industrial undertakings the co-operation between the two groups of employees, though sometimes satisfactory, as a whole leaves much to be desired.[1] The wage-earner is apt to have a profound mistrust of the salaried employee, whom he by no means regards from the outset as a brother in arms or a comrade in the common cause of withstanding the employer. In their normal working relations, the salaried employee (when he is a foreman or engineer or holds a post of responsibility in the works) is the superior of the wage-earner, who must obey the former's orders as the representative of the employer. To secure promotion, and even to keep his post, the foreman must maintain discipline and try to secure the greatest possible working efficiency. His interests therefore often appear identified with those of the employer rather than with those of the workpeople. As a speaker in a Conference of Works Councils in the metal industries expressed it: "The economic standpoint and outlook of the salaried employee are in large measure capitalistic".[2]

In the practical work of the Councils the salaried employees, in industry at least, find themselves in a minority and are therefore easily outvoted. They have to put up with the crude and often forcible expressions of their wage-earning colleagues on the Council, who are not inclined to mince matters when their views are opposed and who are always apt to suspect ulterior motives on the part of those who do not see eye to eye with them. On the other hand, the salaried employees, in many cases, regard themselves as having a higher social standing and as being better educated, and naturally give great offence when they allow this

---

[1] Cf. "Die Bedeutung der Zusammenarbeit von Arbeitern und Angestellten im Betriebsrat", by Bernhard Letterhaus, in *Betriebsrätepost*, October 1924.
[2] *Protokoll der Konferenz...der Betriebsräte...der Metallindustrie*, December 1924, p. 11.

to become apparent. Thus the relations between the representatives of the two sections on the Council are often the reverse of harmonious. The salaried employee becomes discouraged, vacates his seat on the Council and thankfully retires to his ordinary activities where he is not perpetually exposed to abuse and suspicion. The attitude of members of this section towards the Councils is further influenced by the fact that they normally stand in a much closer relation to the employer than the wage-earners. On the one hand, they have much more ready access to him and therefore have less need of a special system of representation and, on the other, they are in a position of even greater dependence on the goodwill of the employer. It is harder for them to find a new post if they lose their employment than for the average wage-earner and their prospects of promotion, on which their whole future depends, are likely to be jeopardised if they incur the resentment of the employer. The risk of arbitrary dismissal—one of the chief inducements for the formation of a Council—is also less serious in their case.

From the standpoint of the employer, the Salaried-employees' Council is in many ways more to be feared than the Wage-earners' Council. For it must be remembered that the part of the Works Councils Act, which is most distasteful to the employers, is the so-called advisory functions given to the Works Councils and the correlative right of access to confidential information as to the financial position of the undertaking and other problems of management. While a body composed of ordinary wage-earners is very unlikely to make much out of a balance sheet, it is a different matter when the Council contains salaried employees also and when the head book-keeper, for example, may be a member. The employer is therefore specially sensitive to awkward questions put by such employees and is able to give very practical effect to his displeasure, in ways which cannot be challenged before a Labour Court. A speaker at the above-mentioned Conference of Works Councils in the metal industries complained that the salaried employees did not venture, for fear of the employer, to open their mouths in criticism or to ask for explanations of the balance sheet when it was put before the Council. Other speakers protested against the tendency, which they described as common, for wage-earning members of the Councils to be promoted by the employer and turned into salaried employees, some of their best men being thus lost to the Works Councils movement.

It is not surprising that it is becoming increasingly common to find industrial undertakings in which there is no Salaried-employees' Council, either because no one is to be found who is willing to submit his name as a candidate for election, or because there is no demand for representation. In such cases the Works Council consists of the wage-earners alone. There is, however, a general consensus of opinion amongst almost all observers in Germany that the division of the Works Council into two sectional bodies, representing wage-earning and salaried employees respectively, has been justified and there is no agitation for a reform of the system in the direction of a single elected body responsible for safeguarding the interests of all employees.

(d) *The Works Assembly*. The Works Assembly is a meeting of all the employees in an establishment (including persons not entitled to vote for the election of the Council, e.g. employees below 18 years of age, foreign nationals, etc.). It is within the discretion of the Chairman to convene it at any time, though a meeting must not be held within working hours except with the consent of the employer. The Chairman must call a meeting of the Assembly to discuss questions of policy under consideration by the Works Council, on the demand of the employer or at the wish of one-fourth of the employees. In addition to the Assembly of all the employees, separate Assemblies may be called of wage-earners and of salaried employees. In very large works employing thousands of men, a Works Assembly of all the employees is clearly not a practical method of consultation and it is more common for each of the departments in the works to appoint a delegate to represent their wishes and interests. The Works Assembly is then in practice replaced by a joint meeting between the Council and the body of delegates.

The outstanding feature of the Works Assembly is its powerlessness to dictate to the Council once the latter has been elected. In the original Bill drawn up by the Government and laid before the National Assembly a provision was included, enabling the

136

Works Assembly to revoke the mandate either of the whole of the Council or of any of its individual members, provided that a resolution to this effect was passed by more than a two-thirds majority of the Assembly, voting by secret ballot. The power of recall at any time, of elected representatives by a vote of no-confidence on the part of their electors, appeared for the first time in the French Commune in 1871, and had later a very important place (in theory) in the Constitution of the Russian Soviet State. The German Socialists, who took their lead from Moscow and who therefore had a profound distrust of the ordinary forms of political democracy, were keenly in favour of extending the right of recall to the employees in the case of Works Councils. On the other side, it was urged that the period of election was short (only one year), that all feeling of responsibility would be removed from the members of the Council if they were made completely dependent on the wishes of the body of employees and that, in practice, a vote of censure, even though it could not be immediately enforced, would have a powerful effect on the Council. This latter view was adopted by the majority of the National Assembly and the Government proposal was dropped. Under the Act, the Works Assembly has only the right to present requests and proposals to the Works Council on matters which fall within the general competence of the Council; it has no power to enforce its wishes until the statutory mandate of the Council expires, when it can elect a new Council.

The employer has no right to be represented at meetings of the Works Assembly, except in cases where the meeting has been called at his instance. In practice this is somewhat rare, though occasions may arise when the employer is in dispute with the Works Council and desires to test the strength of feeling of the body of employees and perhaps to put pressure through them on the Council. The Assembly has, of course, the right to invite the employer to be present at any meeting held.

The only persons not actually employed in the establishment, who are entitled to be present at a Works Assembly, are one representative from each of the Trade Unions to which any of the employees belong. The admission of Trade Union representatives is not made dependent on a vote of the employees, but is a right which can be exercised without let or hindrance.

The conduct of the business of a Works Assembly is in the hands of the Chairman of the Works Council, who alone is entitled to convene a meeting; hence any sporadic gathering of the employees is not a statutory Works Assembly. The employer is responsible for the costs of a Works Assembly—as a rule limited to the provision of the room in which the Assembly is held. But this obligation exists only where the meeting was necessary, i.e. where its object could not have been attained in any other way and where the agenda was confined to matters which lay within its proper scope. The room provided must be suitable and must, if necessary, be lighted and heated. If the employer has no room of sufficient size available, or if he refuses to put a room at the disposal of the Chairman for the meeting of the Assembly, a suitable room may be hired outside and the cost charged to the employer. The only defence of the employer then lies in an appeal to the Labour Court and the submission of evidence showing that the action of the Chairman was not justified by the circumstances of the case.

The main purpose of the institution of the Works Assembly is to preserve a close connection between the Works Council and the body of employees, so that, on the one hand, the former may be strengthened by the support of the latter and, on the other, that the employees can bring suggestions and grievances to the notice of the Council which it can then discuss with the employer. When works rules are agreed between the Council and the employer and are countersigned by the Chairman of the Council, the prestige of the Council is involved and it has a responsibility, which it cannot escape, for securing the maintenance of the rules. It is exceedingly repugnant to a conscientious Works Council to be taunted by the employer with its powerlessness to enforce the recognition of agreements which it has concluded. When this is the state of affairs, the hands of the Council are doubly weakened, both in regard to the employer in any future negotiation and in regard to the workpeople, who are ignoring the decisions and counsel of their own representatives. Hence, if the Works Council wishes to avoid possible trouble, it will endeavour to secure the consent of the employees before taking any decision of real importance to which they might object. It frequently has the difficult task of enlightening the employees as to the actual facts and as to the motives leading to a proposed change; in so doing it is likely to come up against much ignorance and prejudice. The opportunity to state its case, in a meeting with a recognised Chairman and subject to rules of procedure, is afforded by the Works Assembly, which thus fulfils an indispensable function in the system of works representation. Although, as has already been stated, there is no legal power of recall, it is common, though not invariable, for a vote of no-confidence in the Council on a matter of importance to be followed by the resignation of the Council.

A meeting of the Works Assembly is often by no means an agreeable ordeal for the Works Council, for it gives the other employees a means of ventilating grievances and animadverting on the performances and records of some or all of the members of the Council. It affords an ideal opportunity for any extremist agitator to inveigh against the weakness or incompetence of his elected representatives and, with an eye on the next election, to gain a cheap popularity by dangling almost unlimited hopes before his fellows if only the proposals of himself and his friends are adopted. One of the commonest accusations and one that is most difficult to disprove, is that of corruption against any members of the Council who have sought to exercise a moderating and restraining influence on the more extreme elements. Any Councillor who has the courage to support an unwelcome proposal or to refuse a request, on the ground that his duty compels him to do so, is liable to be termed a traitor to his class and to be accused of having been bought by the employer.

In view of the very exposed position of the Council, standing as it does midway between the employer and the body of employees, it is not surprising that a common complaint against the Councils and one to be found in numerous passages in the Reports of the Factory Inspectors, is that they completely abdicate from any real position of leadership and become merely the mouthpiece of their electors. Afraid to reject any

resolution of the Assembly, however extravagant, they find themselves forced to support, before the employer, proposals which
they are unable to defend against his arguments. In such
cases they shelter themselves behind the body of the employees
by declaring to the employer that they are powerless to oppose
the wishes of the majority of those employed. If, as is probable,
their representations meet with no success, this is apt to be
attributed to their lack of vigour in handling the matter,
while at the same time the relations between the employer and
the employees are further strained. It must not be imagined,
however, that the Works Councils are always found wanting in
this respect, or that there are not many instances where they
have successfully exerted their authority and have opposed unreasonable demands of the employees. In this they are often
helped by the representatives of the Trade Unions, who are
present at meetings of the Works Assembly.

The presence of Trade Union officials also gives opportunity
for campaigning speeches to be made with a view to attracting
as many as possible of the employees to become organised in
this or that Union, though this is likely to lead to disorder
unless the great majority are already members of one Union
or Federation of Unions. The same observation holds good of the
utilisation of the Works Assembly for political debates, which
played so great a rôle in the years immediately following the
coming into force of the Works Councils Act. The very wide and
deep divisions within the ranks of the workers on political
questions have contributed greatly, both to unrest and disturbances in the works and, in many cases, to the practical
impotence of the Works Councils to pursue an orderly and con-
sistent policy based on the support of the main body of employees.

During the first two years after the passing of the Act, the
Works Assemblies were an exceedingly active and, on the whole,
disturbing element in the new system. They were held with the
utmost frequency and, wherever possible, permission was ex-
torted from the employers for them to be held during working-
hours. A refusal to grant this was often met by an immediate
strike and employers complained, with reason, of the immense
amount of time wasted while agitators were making fiery

speeches in denunciation of the capitalist system. As the revolutionary tide ebbed, however, Works Assemblies came to be held much more rarely, until now it would appear that, in many cases, meetings of the Assembly are not held sufficiently often to maintain proper contact between the Council and its electors.

THE SUPERVISORY FUNCTIONS OF WORKS COUNCILS

(a) *General Labour Legislation.* The Works Council is entrusted by the Act (Section 78 (1)) with duties which make it virtually a part of the State machinery of inspection. It is required to supervise the carrying out of all legal provisions for the benefit of employees. The volume of labour legislation in Germany is enormous and highly intricate, as can be seen from the single example of the Works Councils Act. It has, moreover, been in a state of flux since the War owing to the effort of the legislature to give effect to Article 157 of the new Constitution, which provides for the creation of a unified Labour Code. Many new measures have been passed, others are still in course of preparation, and even the fundamental legal principles at the basis of such legislation appear to be undergoing a change.[1] Hence the ordinary untutored employee who is elected to a Works Council finds himself pledged to the execution of functions which would tax the knowledge and competence of a skilled lawyer.

In many cases, having his hands full with more immediate and pressing matters and with neither the capacity nor, it may be, the inclination to acquire a mastery of the innumerable provisions by which the labour contract is hedged round and protected, the Works Councillor selects the easier path of doing only as much as is required from him by his fellow-workers. It is, however, one of the merits of the Trade Unions that, by their schools, their press and the personal influence of their officials, they have done their utmost to prevail on the Works Councils to take their duties seriously in this and other respects, and to fit themselves for the many and varied responsibilities of their

[1] Cf. Sinzheimer, *Grundzüge des Arbeitsrechts*, and Potthoff, *Wesen und Ziel des Arbeitsrechts*.

office. It is characteristic of the *Pflichtgefühl*, or sense of duty of the German worker, that instances have occurred where precisely the most conscientious members of a Works Council have resigned their office, owing to a feeling of helplessness in the face of the duties imposed on them and to a consciousness of their lack of the education and training necessary to cope with them properly.

In large undertakings it is a usual practice for the Works Council to nominate a small committee of two or three of its members to supervise the execution of labour legislation, while in smaller concerns this duty is often entrusted to a single member, the selection being determined, where possible, by the possession of special qualifications. Here, as in other parts of the Act, the efficiency of its operation in practice is lessened by the short (annual) tenure of the office and the frequent changes in the personnel of the Works Council.

Amongst the most important matters with which the Works Council is concerned, both in its supervisory capacity and, to some extent, in a more active manner, is the question of the hours of work. On the one hand, it has to see that the normal hours of work laid down in the Collective Agreement are observed. Only in the absence of such an Agreement can it directly negotiate with the employer in regard to the length of the working-day. Further, although it has a voice in the determination of the provisions of the *Arbeitsordnung*, or works rules relating to the beginning and end of the working-day, the duration and period of intervals for rest and meals, etc., once the rules have been adopted the functions of the Works Council is purely supervisory. On the other hand, the Council plays an important rôle in all deviations from the normal working-day, except in so far as these are established by Collective Agreements. Since the Hours of Work Order of December 21, 1923, the Works Council has merely the right to be heard before any extension of the working-day, which proceeds from a decision of the employer or is based on official sanction. If the Works Council refuses its assent it cannot prevent the extension from being operative, but it can greatly hinder the employer in the practical execution of his legal right to work longer hours. As a rule the whole weight of the influence of the Trade Unions is used to persuade the Councils not to agree to longer hours, so as to support the Union policy of a rigid eight-hour day. Often they are successful and the Councils are able to reinforce to an important extent the fight of the Trade Unions against the extension of hours of work. The Factory Inspectors repeatedly complain that the Works Councils have opposed, on principle, a blank negative to any proposals for working overtime, without regard to the necessities of the economic situation or to their statutory duty to further the efficiency and productivity of the establishment in which they are employed. This attitude, however, is by no means universal and many instances are to be found where Works Councils have acquiesced in the working of overtime, to the great dissatisfaction of the Trade Unions, and have confined themselves to securing as high rates of pay as possible for the extra hours.

(b) *The Prevention of Accidents and the Promotion of Works Hygiene.* Of all the duties entrusted to the Works Council one of the most important and most practical is that of endeavouring to prevent accidents and injury to health arising out of employment in the works.

Whenever an accident takes place, a member of the Works Council must be called in to take part in any enquiry as to its nature and causes. It is the duty of the Council to report to the Factory Inspector any infringement of factory regulations concerning safety, health, etc., to see that the employees themselves carry out all the necessary regulations, and to use its influence to convince them of the importance of taking proper precautions against accident and illness.

In the nature of things, it is impossible to obtain conclusive evidence as to the extent to which Works Councils in general have carried out these duties. In many of the large works there is a sub-committee of the Council which specialises in this question and sometimes produces good results. The most trustworthy and comprehensive information on this matter is to be found in the Reports of the Factory Inspectors. In the Reports for 1921, the complaint was general that many Works Councils took exceedingly little interest in this side of their duties; not infrequently they actually put obstacles in the way of the

Factory Inspectors: in other cases they were either ignorant of or indifferent to their obligation to assist in the prevention of accidents. On the other hand, a considerable number of instances were given in which valuable suggestions had been made by the Councils. The Reports for subsequent years tell substantially the same tale.

It must be borne in mind that the progressive depreciation of the mark caused the time of the Works Councils to be mainly occupied with wage adjustments and similar matters, and that their other functions fell very much into the background. Now, however, that wages are relatively stable, greater attention is able to be given to the prevention of accidents. The following extracts from the Factory Inspectors' Reports illustrate the conditions in different parts of the country:

From the observations made it seems quite possible that, with continuous and organised instruction by the Inspectors, some of the Works Councillors will be trained to give material assistance in carrying out measures for the prevention of accidents. In any case, there is no doubt that the workers are more ready to pay heed to advice to make proper use of protective installations when it comes from the mouth of a member of a Works Council who owes his post to the confidence of his fellows, than when the foreman issues corresponding orders.[1]

At the request of the Works Council of a large undertaking belonging to the iron industry at Bielefeld the Factory Inspector gave a two-hours' lecture on the subject of works hygiene and the prevention of accidents to an attentive audience of about 1000 persons. Requests to give similar lectures at other works show how satisfactorily the interest of the workers in the prevention of accident and illness, which before was often lacking, has been awakened since the coming into force of the Works Councils Act.[2]

Most of the Works Councillors lack not only the necessary training for the special task but also goodwill and proper understanding. The chief cause of this is that the representatives of the workers are chiefly selected for their oratorical gifts and devote most of their attention to the wage question. Further, they are often shy of putting themselves in opposition to their fellows, who pay little heed to protective measures or even set them aside altogether.[3]

A committee of the Works Councils of several shipping yards drew up a report on measures to be taken to prevent accidents in the con-

[1] Report for Frankfurt, 1921, p. 84.
[2] Report for Minden, 1921, p. 430.
[3] Report for Wiesbaden, 1921, p. 502.

struction of scaffolding for ships, and placed it before the Factory Inspectors. The proposals were well-thought-out and were subsequently used as a basis for the issue of new regulations, which were agreed with representatives of the joint association of employers and workers for the prevention of accidents.[1]

Works Councillors took part regularly in accident investigations; their suggestions in this field were not of much value.[2]

While the Works Councils devoted their chief attention during the period of daily currency depreciation to the economic cares of the workers...the stabilisation of the currency gave rise to a growing interest in other duties, especially in the field of labour protection.[3]

Unfortunately measures for the prevention of accidents often met with insufficient support from the Works Councils....It is only latterly that an improvement is observable in some cases. It is reported from the Bautzen district that a large number of the Works Councillors had no knowledge of the accident regulations and that, even of those present at a lecture on accident prevention, about 40 had never read the regulations.[4]

The Works Councils, almost without exception, have failed to co-operate in the prevention of accidents.[5]

Taking the Reports of the Factory Inspectors as a whole from 1921 to 1925, it is impossible to detect any appreciable progress in the activities of the Works Councils in this field. The later Reports are no more encouraging than the earlier. In many cases no reference whatever is made to the Works Councils in this connection and, where they are referred to, it is generally with the remark that little or no assistance had been received from them. The favourable instances quoted above are unfortunately exceptional and cannot be regarded as typical of the great majority of Councils, though this does not deprive them of their value as showing what might be accomplished.

It is worthy of note that a number of the Reports emphasise the fact that the Works Councils have been more active and more successful in dealing with questions of hygiene than with the prevention of accidents. Improvements in matters such as lighting, heating, air supply and dust, and the provision of

---

[1] Report for Hamburg, 1922.
[2] Report for Liegnitz, 1922, p. 128.
[3] Report for Potsdam, 1923/1924, p. 32.
[4] Report for Saxony, 1923/1924, p. 157.
[5] Report for Liegnitz, 1925, p. 199.

washing facilities, cloak rooms, etc., have not infrequently been due to suggestions put forward by the Councils. Even in this field, however, their achievements as a whole have been at best inadequate.

The Trade Union leaders, not unnaturally, are sensitive to the accusation that workers' representatives are neglectful of duties which are not only of great practical importance, but are amongst the few in the whole Act concerning which there is no dispute. They are, therefore, constantly at pains to remind the latter of their duties in this respect. Articles dealing with the subject are to be found in the current Trade Union and Works Councils Press and increasing attention is being given to courses of lectures at Works Councils Schools by experts on the prevention of accidents and the promotion of works hygiene.

The comparative failure of the Works Councils to carry out these functions in a satisfactory way is indisputable, but a number of factors must be taken into account:

(1) During the first few years, when the Councils were new, they were overwhelmed with work, much of which had little bearing on their proper functions. Apart from disputes, dismissals, etc., their time was mainly taken up by wage adjustments, made necessary by the progressive depreciation of the currency. Although the stabilisation of the mark has lessened their work in this respect, conditions since then have been abnormal, because the depression of trade and unemployment have often made the Councils afraid to make suggestions, which might be unacceptable to the employers.

(2) It is well known that many workers, especially the younger ones, commonly under-estimate the dangers of their work and are reluctant to use safety devices, which almost always involve a little more trouble or a slightly lower rate of output per unit of effort. Hence the endeavours and well-meant advice of the Works Councillor have to a large extent fallen on unreceptive soil—he has been told to mind his own business and get on with the job for which he was elected, instead of interfering with the actions of his fellow-workers. Moreover, where the Works Council has succeeded in convincing the employer of the necessity of some new installation for the benefit

of the workers, the latter have felt affronted in their innate con-
servatism and have condemned the Council and refused to make
use of the improvement. The Council then feels humiliated and
also weakened in the eyes of the employer. Strong and conscientious Works Councils have often taken severe measures
against workers who have flagrantly endangered the lives or
health of their fellow-workers and have in many cases secured
the dismissal of the offenders. This action, necessary though it
may have been, is naturally unpopular with the body of the
workers and increases the difficulties of the position of the
Council. Thus it is not surprising that the line of least resistance
is often chosen and, after one or two rebuffs, the Council decides
to let things drift.

(3) The task of preventing accidents and promoting factory
hygiene is highly technical and few of the members of Works
Councils have the knowledge and experience necessary to make
useful and practical suggestions.[1] As has been mentioned above,
the Unions are trying to remedy this by providing special courses
of instruction in these matters, but progress is inevitably slow
and the changing composition of the Councils makes continuity
difficult.

(4) Although, in theory, the employers are in agreement with
the exercise by the Works Councils of their supervisory functions,
in practice they sometimes put difficulties in the way. In the
mining industry, in particular, it is complained that members of
the Council are prevented from making tours of inspection of
the mine during working-time.

(5) Many Works Councillors are still not alive to the importance of functions which involve peaceful co-operation with
the employer, rather than conflict and the representation of the
divergent interests of the employed. When, as in recent times,
owing to the weakness of organised labour, the exercise of the
latter functions becomes difficult or impossible, the former are
commonly ignored and neglected in the general atmosphere of
disillusionment and ineffectiveness.

The picture presented is not a very encouraging one, but the
fact that some of the Councils have done good work in this field

[1] Cf. Report of Factory Inspectors for Stettin and Stralsund, 1921, p. 148.

affords some ground for hope that, in the course of time and with the progress of education, the rôle of the Councils as protectors of the safety and health of the worker will become increasingly effective.

(c) *The Execution of Collective Agreements.* If, in so far as the execution of legal enactments is concerned, the Works Councils are in a measure incorporated into the general administrative machinery of the State, they are also constituted the local agents in each establishment of the Trade Unions, in the sense that they are required to see that the ruling Collective Agreements are properly observed. It has been shown above[1] that such Agreements can arise, either as the result of a freely concluded bargain between a Trade Union and one or more employers, or of an arbitration award recognised by both parties, or, lastly, as the result of an award which has been declared officially binding on both parties. A Collective Agreement has in some respects the force of law, for any worker who is paid below the ruling rates can sue his employer in the Labour Courts and can obtain the ruling rate, but whether it would pay him to do so would depend largely on current economic conditions and on the relative bargaining strength of the employer and the Trade Union. In practice, a group of workers may be faced by the alternative of unemployment or the acceptance of a smaller wage than that established in the Collective Agreement and, rather than be unemployed when trade is bad, they will often prefer to accept the latter alternative and say nothing about it. Since the end of 1923 such infractions have been even commoner where hours of work are concerned than in respect of wages.

During the period of inflation, the Works Councils were able to render important services to the Trade Unions by reporting cases of infringement and by opposing a stubborn resistance to attempts of the employers, especially in the smaller establishments, to modify conditions to the detriment of the employees. In this endeavour they were normally supported by the labour tribunals.

In the subsequent depression, the Councils were in many cases unable to withstand the pressure of the employers and were

[1] pp. 37-8.

constrained to accept their conditions. Nor were the Councils always unwilling, because employers were sometimes able to strike a bargain which was not wholly unfavourable to the employees, although it might conflict in some important respect with the terms of a Collective Agreement and with the policy of the Trade Unions. Some account has been given in Chapter III of the opportunities for the conclusion of "Works Agreements" which were afforded by the existence of Works Councils, and it was there pointed out that, under certain conditions, a Works Agreement might have the legal effect of a Collective Agreement. In general, however, experience has shown that the great majority of Councils have, throughout the whole period, regarded themselves as the responsible agents of the Trade Unions and have fought and often suffered dismissal on behalf of the maintenance of the terms laid down by Collective Agreements. It is probable that in the absence of Works Councils the extent to which Collective bargains were infringed during 1924 and 1925 would have been greater than was actually the case. There certainly can be no doubt that in times of good trade the Councils have in fact carried out their functions as the watch-dogs of the Unions, with the result that the power of the latter has been strengthened.

The Works Councils themselves gain by being entrusted with specific duties which are direct and positive and which bring them into close contact with the Unions. In regard to wages, in particular, the Works Council has facilities which are denied to the Trade Unions, for the Council has the statutory right to investigate the wages books of its firm and to demand any other information necessary to ascertain whether or not a Collective Agreement is being observed in all its details.

THE DETERMINATION OF WAGE RATES

The Works Councils are expressly excluded by the Act from any right to co-operate in the determination of wage rates, wherever such rates are the subject of negotiation between Trade Unions and the employer or association of employers—i.e. wherever there is a Collective Agreement. In the absence, however, of a Collective Agreement, the Works Council becomes the competent body and, in the event of disagreement, it can, like the Trade Union, appeal to a Conciliation Board. In this case, in the absence of official intervention, the award of the Conciliation Board is not mandatory; it is only a recommendation, not a binding decision.

Owing to the great expansion in recent years in the scope and sphere of operation of Collective Agreements, the rôle of the Works Councils in the direct determination of wages is normally not large. Nevertheless, in the frequent intervals between the lapse of one Agreement and the conclusion of another, the Works Councils are called upon to act on behalf of the employees and to negotiate interim settlements with their employers. This situation arose repeatedly in 1924 and 1925, and there is a good deal of evidence to show that in such cases both sides benefited by the existence of a responsible and recognised body representing the employees. That this duty is not always welcomed by the Councils can be seen from the following extract from a report written in 1925 by the Chairman of the Works Council of a large undertaking employing 11,000 men:

As a general collective wage agreement for the Berlin metal industries is no longer in operation...the chief activity of the Works Councils consists in the settlement of wage disputes....I see a certain danger for the Works Councils in the assumption by them of the leadership in wage movements. But circumstances are often stronger than the best intentions and force us to intervene.

While it is only under exceptional circumstances that the Works Councils are directly concerned with the establishment of basic wage rates, the position is very different in regard to the fixing and modification of systems of piece wages and to the introduction of new methods of wage payment in general. Many Collective Agreements do not contain detailed piece-work rates for each branch of industry and each factory in accordance with its special conditions. Here the Works Council, under Section 78 (2) of the Act, has the duty of co-operating with the employer—a co-operation which, it is true, does not imply the power to veto the proposals of the employer, but which does entitle the Works Council to demand to be consulted and to express the wishes and attitude of the employees. In many cases, through ignorance or apathy, or a desire to stand well with the employer, the Works Councils do not take any steps in this matter. But often and, especially, in the larger undertakings in the metal and other industries, the Councils have played a very active part in the application of piece-work rates. On more than one occasion leading German industrialists have told the author that the Works Councils were of very great value during the inflation period, when wages and all other conditions were incessantly changing, both in agreeing to modifications with the management and in explaining the nature and mode of operation and, often, the necessity of the changes to the rest of the employees. In such cases the consent and approval of the Works Council to alterations in piece-work rates gave, on the one hand, a certain guarantee to the employee that he was not being defrauded and, on the other hand, smoothed the way for the employer and lessened the friction caused by the change. It has been found that, where there is a strong and efficient Works Council, the common objection to piece wages, based on the fear of rate-cutting, is less in evidence than where the employer alone is responsible, without any check, for the fixing of rates.

In addition to the drawing up of piece-work lists and their detailed application, the Works Council is concerned with the grouping of the workers in the system of wage classification. If it can induce the employer to move men up from a lower to a higher wage class it will have succeeded in improving their position without altering the wages fixed in the Collective Agreement.

One of the most practical of the functions of the Works Council, and one which plays a very large part in its daily routine, is that of acting as a mediator in individual disputes as to the proper rate of wages to be paid to a worker. Anyone who believes that he is not receiving his proper pay may complain to the Works Council, which can then take the matter up with the management, if it considers that the complaint is in any degree justified. It is thus often able to rectify minor injustices which the worker himself would be powerless to redress.[1] How

[1] Cf. the frequent instances to be found in *Aus dem Tagebuch eines Betriebsrats* (1925), which gives an admirable picture of the daily life of an efficient Works Council.

successful such action is depends, as in all other sides of the practical work of the Councils, partly on the tact and the capacity of the Council to discriminate between good and bad cases, and partly on the attitude of the employer towards any intervention by the Council. Where the employer is at loggerheads with his Council he will often rather ostentatiously refuse requests put forward by the Council, while at the same time giving it clearly to be understood that he will be much more sympathetic towards an employee who approaches him directly with an application for higher wages or promotion. It is thus not uncommon for wages and other conditions of work to be fixed for certain groups of employees behind the backs of the Works Council, which knows nothing about the negotiations until it finds out later what has happened.[1]

WORKS WELFARE INSTITUTIONS

By Section 66 (9) the Works Council is given an unconditional right to participate in the administration of works pension funds and workers' dwellings attached to the works and belonging to the employer, but only a restricted right of participation so far as other welfare institutions, such as crèches, sports grounds, baths, reading rooms, etc., are concerned. In the case of the latter institutions, the right of participation may be excluded altogether by the testamentary dispositions of the donor. The right of participation does not affect or restrict the property rights of the employer in any workers' dwellings, etc., which he owns. He is free to sell or otherwise dispose of them without requiring the consent of the Works Council. On the other hand, when, for example, a company sets aside in its balance sheet certain sums for welfare purposes, the Council is entitled to protest if these sums are later transferred without its consent and used for other purposes. Sometimes, as in a recent case which came to the writer's notice, money may be temporarily alienated with the consent of the Works Council. A company got into financial difficulties and, at a meeting of the Control Board, the proposal to raise a foreign loan was discussed. The conditions offered were

---

[1] Cf. *Protokoll über die Konferenz der Arbeiter-Aufsichtsräte...in der Textilindustrie*, June 1925, p. 22.

very arduous, but their acceptance seemed unavoidable if the company was to carry on. The Works Council member of the Board, however, suggested that the company should borrow the sum required from a large welfare fund which had been accumulated out of the profits of past years. This suggestion was adopted and the money was obtained at a very moderate rate of interest.

There is no doubt that the right to participate in the administration of welfare schemes is valued by the workers and that it has often been possible thereby to secure concessions and to make representations to the employer in regard to matters which would otherwise have escaped notice.

The term participate (*mitwirken*) has given rise to much dispute and many divergent rulings in the Courts. The view which seems to have the best foundation is that, for example, in the case of works dwellings, the Works Council has the right to co-operate in the formulation of general rules for the management of the dwellings and their allocation among the workers. But it cannot interfere with the action of the employer in applying the rules to individual cases. In general, the Council has the right to be represented on any managing committee or other body responsible for the administration of the welfare scheme in question. Disputes over the practical operation of these rights are dealt with by the Labour Courts. It should be noted that the legal right of participation under the Works Councils Act is confined to those welfare institutions which are common to all the employees, and does not apply to institutions which are only provided for the benefit of one or other of the sections of employees (wage-earners only or salaried employees only). Where it has been desired to exclude the Works Council altogether, advantage has sometimes been taken of this provision and the statutes have been altered so as to restrict the application of a particular scheme in this way.

In many cases, however, the co-operation of the Councils is welcomed by the employers, especially in regard to such matters as the management of works canteens, etc., which often take up a great deal of time on the part of the Councils and, while giving them something concrete to which to devote their energies, diminish their opportunities of interfering in other less welcome directions.[1]

THE INTERNAL ADMINISTRATION AND DISCIPLINE OF THE FACTORY

The contract of service which an employee makes with his employer is based in law on a mutual obligation—on the side of the employee to perform certain tasks subject to the direction and control of the employer, and on the side of the employer to pay certain agreed wages for the accomplishment of those tasks. There is further an implied obligation on the employee to carry out his work under the conditions and terms laid down by the employer. In most large English factories these conditions are embodied in works rules, which are drawn up by the employer alone, without as a rule any consultation or discussion with the workers and he is solely responsible for their interpretation in practice.

In Germany, since 1891, the State has intervened and has regulated to some extent this vital side of the labour contract, by compelling all industrial and most commercial undertakings employing 20 or more persons to draw up a code of works rules (*Arbeitsordnung*). While the actual content of these rules is not defined by law there are certain statutory provisions which are obligatory. The *Arbeitsordnung* must contain provisions relating to:

1. The beginning and end of the normal working-day, together with the pauses laid down for adult workers.

2. The time and method of the payment of wages, with the condition that the normal wage payment must not take place on Sunday.

3. The period of notice to terminate the contract of service, and the reasons for which dismissal without notice may take place.

4. In so far as provision is made for fines or punishments, the method of their determination and, if they are fixed in money, the way in which they are to be levied and the purpose for which they are to be expended.

[1] See above, p. 100.

5. In so far as provision is made for wages to be withheld owing to breach of contract (cessation of work without proper notice), the use to be made of the sums withheld.[1]

No punishments may be imposed which would offend against decency or public morals and, wherever fines are levied, they must be devoted to the welfare of the employees in the works. Fines imposed for breach of the *Arbeitsordnung* must not exceed one day's normal earnings of the employee concerned.

Prior to 1920 the employer was alone responsible for the issue of the *Arbeitsordnung*, and the employees had no say in determining any of its provisions. The only control to which it was subjected was that of the administrative authorities—as a rule the Factory Inspectors—to whom a copy had to be sent for examination to see whether it was in conformity with the law. Since the passing of the Works Councils Act in 1920 the employer is compelled, in all establishments in which, by virtue of the Industrial Code an *Arbeitsordnung* is obligatory, to circulate a draft to the Works Council. If the Council objects to any of the provisions it must negotiate with the employer and endeavour to reach a settlement by agreement. In the event of a failure to secure agreement, either party may appeal to the Conciliation Board, whose decision is final on all matters except those relating to the length of the working-day. The employer is also powerless to alter any of the provisions of the *Arbeitsordnung* without going through the same procedure and, either obtaining the consent of the Works Council, or, failing that, the decision of the Conciliation Board. The powers of the Works Council in this respect extend not merely to the statutory *Arbeitsordnung* but also to all other working rules issued by the employer. There are, however, two important distinctions, firstly, that the employer is not bound by law to do more than issue the *Arbeitsordnung*. The Works Council cannot compel him to draw up working rules of a more comprehensive character, though in practice, in most large and medium-sized undertakings, it is to the interest of the employer to do so, and the Works Council then gets the opportunity of discussing them and perhaps of securing

[1] The amount thus withheld may not exceed a week's wages. The employer, however, retains the right to sue for damages due to breach of contract.

155

their amendment. Secondly, decisions of the Conciliation Boards are held not to be binding on both parties in the case of working rules which go beyond the statutory provisions of the *Arbeitsordnung.*

The Works Councils Act refers specifically to the important question of the imposition of punishments and fines, and states that "The determination of penalties provided for in Section 184 *b* (4) of the Industrial Code shall be carried out by the employer jointly with the Council of Wage-earning or of Salaried Employees. In the event of dispute the Conciliation Board shall decide". The bulk of legal opinion, as well as of decisions of the Conciliation Boards, has interpreted this paragraph to mean that the Sectional Council concerned has the right to be consulted in every individual case in which a penalty is imposed and, if it disagrees, to appeal to the Conciliation Board. The employers have always maintained, sometimes successfully, that the Council has only the right to be consulted in regard to the general principles governing the imposition of fines, etc., and that the practical application of these principles is in the hands of the employer without interference from the Council. However, as a rule, as has been stated, the Conciliation Boards have not upheld the employers' contention. Since the new Conciliation Order of October 30, 1923, this question has been definitely settled. The Councils are now entitled to intervene whenever an individual fine or penalty is imposed and, in the event of disagreement, the issue can be carried to the Labour Court for an award.[1]

The framers of the Works Councils Act, in drafting the provisions relating to the agreement of working rules between the employer and the Works Council, were careful not to interfere with the growing tendency in recent times for such rules to be fixed by Collective Agreements between Trade Unions and employers. Hence it is laid down that the Works Council is only competent to deal with those matters which are not regulated by Collective Agreement. Although the direct influence and control of the Councils over working conditions is thereby con-

[1] Cf. Flatow and Joachim, *Die Schlichtungsordnung vom 30. Oktober 1923,* p. 63.

siderably weakened, the right of the workers as a whole to a voice in the determination of the conditions under which they carry out their work is not impaired, but is merely transferred to another and, in many ways, more efficient type of labour organisation—the Trade Union. Moreover, in most Collective Agreements, many rules are not stated absolutely, but are left to be applied in agreement or with the co-operation of the Works Council. It is also impossible to frame rules which can apply in every detail to the different conditions of every factory or works, and the Council has then full power to negotiate with the employer and, if necessary, to call in the Conciliation Board when additional rules are proposed by the employer. In particular, the beginning and end of the working-day and the pauses for meal-times, etc., are commonly left to be agreed between the employer and the Council.

The Trade Unions have also endeavoured in many industries to secure uniformity, by agreeing with the employers' associations upon a *Musterarbeitsordnung*, or normal form of working rules for use throughout an industry. This has not the legal effects of a Collective Agreement, in that its provisions may be modified by local agreement, but the organisations on both sides recommend their members to accept it as the *Arbeitsordnung* for each individual works and this is done in the majority of cases. It is also of importance wherever either side wishes to insert rules which diverge from those in the *Musterarbeitsordnung* and which are objected to by the other side. If the dispute is taken to the Conciliation Board, the latter as a rule decides along the lines of the normal rules agreed for the whole industry. Some idea of the comprehensiveness of these rules may be obtained from the table of contents of the *Arbeitsordnung* agreed in 1920 between the Trade Unions and employers' associations in the Rhenish-Westphalian Iron and Steel Industry.[1]

Works Rules form, in a sense, the written constitution of the works and are binding not merely on the workers but also on the employer. The power given to the Works Council to agree to these rules with the employer, in so far as they are not determined by a Collective Agreement, represents a very real and vital extension

[1] Appendix VI.

of the principle of industrial democracy within the factory. Further, in the event of a disagreement between the employer and the Works Council over the formulation of the rules, either side can appeal to an external body, the Conciliation Board, which sits with an impartial Chairman and hears the case and is empowered to give a decision binding on both parties. Thus the one-sided autocracy of the employer, in the matter of discipline and the control of labour in the works, has been abrogated in no small measure and the workers are given an appreciable voice in their working-conditions. It is true, of course, that discipline must be preserved in a modern factory, based as it is on intensive division and combination of labour, and the employer therefore remains solely responsible for the executive handling and execution of the working rules. But in the important questions of penalties and fines and also of dismissal, the consent and co-operation of the Works Council is required by law, subject to the right of appeal to the Labour Courts. If there is a dispute over the interpretation by the employer, in practice, of any of the rules, the Works Council can take the matter to the Conciliation Board and obtain a ruling, or, if it refuses to intervene, the individual worker who feels aggrieved can take his case to the Labour Court for decision.

THE ENGAGEMENT AND DISMISSAL OF EMPLOYEES

(a) *Engagements*. The Works Councils Act gives only a scanty measure of co-operation to the Councils in the task of engaging employees. Under Section 75 (8) the Sectional Councils are empowered to agree with the employer on general principles governing the engagement of the employees in their groups (wage-earners and salaried employees). In the event of disagreement, either side may appeal to the Conciliation Board, whose award, however, has no binding power. If it is impossible to arrive at an agreement on the principles to be adopted, the employer has a completely free hand, but if an agreement is concluded, the employer becomes bound by the general principles laid down. Although his executive power in regard to engagements is not thereby diminished, the Works Council can appeal to the Labour Court against any particular engagement on the ground that it has infringed the principles agreed on. If the Court regards the appeal as justified it is empowered to declare the engagement null and void and, therefore, to require the dismissal of the employee concerned. It may, however, content itself merely with recording the fact that the engagement was in contravention of the general principles, without giving any ruling as to the dismissal of the employee. It might happen, for instance, that an employer had engaged an extra apprentice in addition to the number permitted under the agreement and that, before the case was decided, one of the other apprentices had left his employment; in such an event the Court could decide to take no action.

The Act requires that, wherever general principles governing engagements are agreed upon between the employer and the Sectional Council, they must include a proviso that the engagement of an employee shall not be dependent upon his political, military, religious or trade union activities, nor upon his membership or non-membership of any organisation engaged in such activities, nor upon any sex discrimination.

In practice, the statutory rights given to Works Councils in regard to engagements have proved relatively unimportant and not many Councils have troubled to draw up general principles in agreements with the employer, or, where they have desired to do so, have succeeded in gaining the consent of the employer. Where principles are agreed on they are concerned as a rule with such matters as the following: the number or proportion of apprentices to be engaged; the employment of married or unmarried persons; the engagement of foreigners; the relative numbers of skilled and unskilled workers, etc.

(b) *Dismissals.* It has long been recognised that the uncertainty and lack of continuity of the labour contract constitutes one of the chief disadvantages of the present industrial system from the standpoint of the wage-earner. To some extent this uncertainty is unavoidable, having regard both to the continual and largely unforeseen changes in economic conditions and also to the necessity for a reasonable degree of liberty on the part of either side to terminate a contract entered into. That loss of employment, which results from economic changes, can

159

be met, partly by the organisation of the labour market and of the industrial system generally and, partly by the maintenance of the worker during the period of unemployment. With this aspect of the problem we are not here concerned. There is, however, another aspect, which arises from the liability of the individual employee to be dismissed arbitrarily at any time, for reasons which may have nothing to do with his conduct while working or with the efficiency of his work. Even if he is dismissed on grounds of unsatisfactory behaviour or incompetence, it may well be that he has been the victim of prejudice or merely of faulty evidence. That gross injustices are often perpetrated, as a result of the unfettered exercise of the power of dismissal, is undoubted, and the knowledge that every worker is exposed to this danger and that there is no redress has always been one of the most potent causes of industrial unrest and discontent.

It is here that the Works Councils Act has intervened in an effective and practical manner, by introducing restrictions on the right of dismissal. Before discussing the nature and operation of these provisions, it is necessary to describe the legal position in Germany in regard to dismissals before the passing of the Act.

Under the German Civil Code (*Bürgerliches Gesetzbuch*) there are two forms of dismissal—according to whether notice is given, or whether the dismissal takes effect immediately without notice. In the former case the legal term of notice depends on the mode of remuneration of the employee. If he is remunerated by the day, then notice can be given on one day to take effect on the following day; if it is by the week, a week's notice must be given; and if it is by the month, a month's notice, and so on. In practice, the great majority of all employees in Germany fall under the Industrial Code (*Gewerbeordnung*), which requires a notice of 14 days to be given normally, unless (which is often the case) other conditions in regard to the period of notice are determined by Collective Agreement. During the period of notice, the worker is bound to carry out the work given him by his employer and the employer is bound to pay him his full wages.

Under certain circumstances, however, the employee may be dismissed without notice, namely, where, in the words of the

Civil Code, there is "an important reason". What is "an important reason" is not defined in the Civil Code, but the following are some of the cases which, according to the Industrial Code, are to be regarded as sufficient grounds for instant dismissal:

(1) falsification of the work books or other documents shown to the employer at the time of engagement;

(2) theft or misappropriation;

(3) unauthorised leaving of work, or repeated refusal to carry out the obligations imposed under the labour contract;

(4) carelessness with fire in the face of warnings;

(5) assaulting or offering gross insults to the employer or his representatives or members of his family;

(6) wilful damage of the property of the employer or a fellow-worker.

Further provisions are often contained in Collective Agreements and in the works rules.

Prior to the Works Councils Act, there was no check whatever on dismissals which were given with the proper notice, but in the case of dismissals without notice, the employee had the right to appeal to a Labour Court (*Gewerbegericht* or *Kaufmannsgericht*) and to have an investigation made into the causes of his dismissal. If the Court found that the dismissal without notice was unjustified, the employee was entitled to the usual number of days' notice and to wages for the corresponding period. In such cases the decision was based on a very rigid and exact interpretation of the terms of the Industrial Code and the employer had to prove that the particular case fell within the scope of its provisions.

The Works Councils Act has not modified or abated any of the legal provisions, in the Civil and Industrial Codes, relating to dismissals. But it has superimposed a new and important series of provisions, designed to protect the worker against arbitrary and unjust dismissal *even when due notice has been given*.

Under the Act[1], an employee who is dismissed with the ordinary legal notice may, within five days after the date of dismissal, enter a protest by appealing to his Sectional Council.

[1] Sections 84–90.

There are four grounds recognised on which such an appeal may be based:

(1) If there is ground for suspecting that notice of dismissal was given on account of the sex of the person concerned, or on account of his political, military, religious or trade union activities, or of his membership or non-membership of any political, religious, or trade union society or military organisation.

(2) If the notice was given without any reasons being stated.

(3) If the notice was consequent on the employee's refusal to undertake regularly some work other than that agreed upon at the time of his engagement.

(4) If the dismissal appears to be unjust and involves hardship which neither the conduct of the employee nor the circumstances of the undertaking can justify.[1]

The right to appeal against dismissal on any of the above grounds does not apply: (a) in the case of the group of undertakings referred to in Section 67 of the Act, wherever the exercise of this right would conflict with the essential aims of such undertakings; (b) in cases of dismissal based upon legal provisions or upon the terms of a Collective Agreement or the award of a Conciliation Board; (c) in cases of dismissal necessitated by the partial or total closing-down of the establishment.

In the special case of instant dismissal without notice, the employee can appeal on the ground of the absence of the necessary legal justification for such action.

When an employee enters a protest with the Sectional Council against dismissal, he must state his reasons and bring forward evidence in support of his case. If the Council considers that the protest is justified, it must first endeavour to bring about an agreement by negotiation with the employer. Failing agreement within a week, the Council or the employee concerned may appeal to the Labour Court within the next five days. Neither protest against dismissal, nor an appeal to the Labour Court, has any effect in postponing the operation of the dismissal. The decision of the Court is final and subject to no appeal.

If the tribunal decides that an appeal is justified and, therefore, that it is a case of wrongful dismissal, the employer is left with two alternatives. Either he can elect to re-employ the

---

[1] Section 84.

162

person concerned or, if he declines to do this, he will be required to pay compensation to the dismissed employee. The extent of the compensation depends upon the number of years during which the worker has been employed in the undertaking, and is calculated at the rate of not more than one-twelfth of the last year's earnings for each year of employment, but may in no case exceed six-twelfths of the total annual earnings. In assessing compensation the tribunal is instructed to give due regard to the economic position of the worker and to the financial capacity of the employer.

Within three days after receiving information that the decision of the tribunal has come into force, the employer has to notify the employee, either verbally or by post, whether he elects to re-employ him or to pay him compensation. If the employer fails to do this, he is deemed to have refused further employment and must pay him the appropriate compensation. If the employer decides to re-employ the dismissed worker, and the latter has already left his employment, he is required to pay him wages for the interval between his dismissal and his re-employment, subject to a deduction for any diminution of expenditure due to the employee being out of work and, also, for any earnings gained from other work on which he may have been engaged. The employer is further entitled to deduct from the sum to be paid to the employee on this account any payments which the latter has received during the interval out of the unemployment or poor relief funds. In this event, the employer must refund the sums in question to the authorities by whom the payments were made.

A worker is entitled to refuse re-employment with his former employer if in the meantime he has entered new employment, but this right lapses if he fails to notify the employer, either verbally or in writing, within a week of being informed of the decision of the tribunal. If he avails himself of the right to refuse re-employment, he is entitled to wages only for the period between the date of his dismissal and that of the coming into force of the decision of the tribunal.

There are certain limitations of a very important character to the scope of the protection, given by the above sections of the

Act, to the workers against unjustified dismissal. In the first place, the procedure here set out only applies to those workers who are represented by a Works Council. In all small concerns, where there is either no representation whatever under the Act or where the employees are represented by a Works Steward, the procedure is not applicable and the workers cannot claim this protection. Cases have been fairly frequent in which employers have deliberately kept the numbers of their employees below 20, i.e. the minimum number required for the formation of a Works Council, in order to prevent a Works Council from being set up.

Secondly, the initiative for appealing to the Labour Court against a dismissal is given only to the Sectional Council concerned. If, therefore, in a given firm, there are both wage-earners and salaried employees, and one or other of these groups has failed to take advantage of its rights under the Act to elect a Sectional Council, the members of that group are powerless to appeal to the other Sectional Council to defend their interests before the Labour Court. The same holds good in the case of employees, who, though entitled to elect a Works Council, have neglected to do so.

Thirdly, if the Sectional Council concerned declines to take up the protest of a dismissed employee, the latter is unable to proceed further or himself to appeal to the Labour Court. That this procedure is open to abuse, in the event of the Council being unfavourably disposed to the particular employee, is obvious.

Fourthly, the power of the Works Council to appeal against dismissals does not apply in the case of dismissals on a large scale, which occur as a result of the partial or complete closing-down of a works or a department of a works, or to dismissals which result from the operation of a Collective Agreement or of statutory provisions. During the recent reduction in the personnel of the German railways and of a number of State undertakings, the right to appeal against dismissals under the Works Councils Act has been taken from the employees concerned.

Fifthly, in the case of the so-called "*Tendenzbetriebe*", i.e.

undertakings which serve political, military, trade union, religious, scientific, artistic or other similar aims, the right to appeal does not apply where "the exercise of this right would conflict with the essential aims of the undertaking".

Subject to these limitations, the employee is afforded a protection against unjustified dismissal, which is regarded by the German workers themselves as being in many ways the most practical and valuable of all the rights given to them by the Works Councils Act. While the security of tenure of the worker is thus improved, the interests of the employer are safeguarded by the provision that an employer, who is unwilling to re-engage an employee in whose favour the Court has decided, can dispense with him on paying compensation based on the number of years during which the employee has been working for him.

There can be no question that this part, at least, of the Works Councils Act has not remained on paper, but has been very effective in practice; in fact it is probable that the number of Works Councils in existence would be far fewer than is actually the case, were it not for the direct and practical advantages to the employees, in the matter of protection against dismissals, which result from the establishment of statutory Works Councils.

Of the four grounds given in Section 84, which can form the basis of an appeal against a dismissal, the most important, because the widest in scope, is the fourth: "If the dismissal appears to be unjust and involves hardship which neither the conduct of the employee nor the circumstances of the undertaking can justify".

It has rightly been observed that every dismissal normally involves hardship and, for purposes of an appeal, it is necessary to prove that this hardship is both unjust in itself and incapable of justification by the conduct of the employee or the circumstances of the undertaking. By far the greatest number of appeals are based on this paragraph of the Act and a very large number of judicial decisions, some of them of great interest, have been given in this connection. A short summary of some of these decisions will convey an idea of the way in which the conception of unjust hardship is interpreted in practice. In all the following cases it was decided that the dismissal, against which appeal was entered, constituted an unjust hardship:

1. Refusal to do work during a strike. (Conciliation Board of Greater Berlin.)
2. Suspected but unproved theft. (Conciliation Board of Bamberg.)
3. Diminished capacity to work, owing to age, after 28 years' service with the firm. (Conciliation Board of Greater Berlin.)
4. Participation in a general strike. (Conciliation Board of Munich.)
5. Dismissal of an employee who had been 23 years with the firm, on the ground that he was in possession of other sources of income. (Conciliation Board of Greater Berlin.)
6. Minor impertinence to the employer or a foreman. (Conciliation Boards of Frankfurt and Rothweil.)
7. Dismissal of a number of workers as a prelude to the offer of a lower wage all round. (Conciliation Board of Greater Berlin.)
8. Dismissal of a woman worker who was the sole support of her husband. (Conciliation Board of Greater Berlin.)
9. Refusal to accept new conditions in addition to those agreed in the works rules. (Industrial Court of Spandau.)
10. Dismissal, owing to shortage of work, of a father of a family when there were unmarried men employed who should have been dismissed first. (Conciliation Board of Königsberg.)
11. Dismissal owing to the discovery that some years previously the employee had been sentenced to imprisonment for theft. (Conciliation Board of Frankfurt.)
12. Dismissal for inadequate reasons is always an unjust hardship. (Conciliation Board of Berlin.)
13. Dismissal owing to temporary interruption of work as a result of a confinement is an unjust hardship—irrespective of whether the child is legitimate or illegitimate. (Conciliation Board of Burg.)
14. Dismissal, without any further reasons, of an unmarried girl about to become a mother. (Commercial Court of Remscheid.)
15. Dismissal of a worker who is unable to work owing to an accident arising from his employment. (Industrial Court of Nürnberg.)
16. Dismissal, owing to falling off of business in the book trade after Christmas, when other employees with shorter periods of employment were kept on. (Industrial Court of Leipzig.)

It will be seen that the Conciliation Boards and Labour Courts have in many cases given a quite broad interpretation of the significance of the phrase "unjust hardship", with the result that the employee enjoys a far greater degree of security of tenure than under the old system of unrestricted right of dismissal.

At the same time there is a great degree of elasticity and the decision in every case is determined on its own merits, without too rigid an adherence to general principles. An illustration of this elasticity is to be found in a decision of the Conciliation Board of Guben, in which it is stated that, in considering dismissals, account must be taken of the general economic situation and the conclusion is drawn that in times of bad trade, when employers are in difficulties, the worker must make out a stronger case against dismissal than when trade is good. This, however, might also operate the other way by intensifying the hardship to the worker as a result of the loss of his employment.

Some indication of the extent to which the workers have availed themselves of the protective sections of the Works Councils Act in relation to dismissals, can be gained from the fact that, in 1924, 45,000 disputes over dismissal were dealt with by the Labour Courts.

In the great majority of cases, when a dismissal has been declared by the Court to be unjustified, the employer has preferred to give compensation in money rather than to take the worker back into his employment. As a rule the compensation fixed by the Court is the maximum allowed under the Act— i.e. one-twelfth of the total earnings of the employee during the past 12 months, for each year of service, with a maximum of six-twelfths. It is only rarely that an employer has been successful in pleading economic necessity as an excuse for a reduction in the amount of compensation due. This is natural enough where it is only a question of an isolated dismissal, but cases of hardship have occurred where a number of employees have been turned off owing to lack of work and the Court, for special reasons, has required compensation to be paid in respect of all of them. The sum then involved may be very considerable.

On the whole, this, the most important practical provision of the Works Councils Act, is also the one to which least objection is taken in principle by the employers. During the earlier years when the Act was in operation, complaints were often heard of the burden on the employer's time and energies, as a consequence of the almost invariable appeal of the Works Council against every dismissal, however clearly justified it might be. But in the last couple of years such complaints have been much rarer, as the Works Councils have become familiarised with the judgements of the Courts and their interpretation of the sections of the Act relating to dismissals. When a Council takes up a case and the decision is unfavourable, it is apt to experience a certain loss of prestige to which, after a little experience, it is unwilling to expose itself. Hence many dismissals are agreed to without demur by the Works Councils, who tend increasingly not to appeal unless they feel they have a good case.

During the years 1923 to 1926 the situation has also undoubtedly been affected by the depression of trade and the large number of dismissals on economic grounds, against which the Works Councils are powerless to intervene.

German law distinguishes sharply between the dismissal of an individual employee and the dismissal of large numbers of employees (*Massenentlassungen*). The latter type of dismissal was very much restricted during what was known as the period of economic demobilisation after the War. Most of these restrictions were removed at the end of 1923, but it is still necessary, in industrial undertakings employing more than 20 persons, for the employer to notify to official quarters his intention to shut down part of his works and to dismiss a relatively large number of workers. If he receives official sanction he can proceed with his dismissals, but if sanction is withheld, he is forced to wait for a period of four weeks before the dismissals become effective, and he may also be compelled during this waiting period to work short time. The legal rôle of the Works Councils in such mass dismissals is not a very important one. By Section 74 of the Act the employer is required to inform the Works Council, as long as possible in advance, of his proposal to dismiss a large number of employees, and to discuss with it the means of avoiding hardship. As no penalties are provided for the breach of this provision, it is often ignored by the employers.[1] On the other hand, many employers find it very convenient to make use of the Works Council to facilitate the carrying out of dismissals, and it is not uncommon for an employer to hand over to the

---

[1] It has, however, been held by some of the Courts that if the employer disregards his obligation to notify the Council, in advance, of his intention to dismiss a large number of employees, the latter can all appeal individually against their dismissal, on the basis of Section 84 (4), i.e. unjust hardship.

Works Council the whole onus of selecting those to be dismissed and those to be kept on. This is a task of which the employer is glad to be rid, and he is often thankful for the co-operation of the Works Council, which is in a position to know the circumstances of the individual cases and to distribute the dismissals in such a way as to cause the least hardship. That there is a certain danger in this of the victimisation of unpopular employees or minority groups cannot be denied, but it seems probable that, on balance, the interests of the employees obtain more recognition by this procedure. The Factory Inspectors in their Reports repeatedly comment on the excellent and valuable work done by the Councils in this matter.

In a number of important decisions it has recently been held that the amalgamation of a number of separate establishments into a single unit for the purpose of securing productive economies, which involves the dismissal of some or all of the employees at the establishments that are shut down, is not a "closing-down" (*Stilllegung*) in the sense of the Works Councils Act.[1] In one such case the salaried employees concerned appealed against their dismissal on these grounds and secured an award to the effect that, subject to a detailed investigation of particular cases, they must be re-employed by the firm in question or else receive compensation. An agreement was then arrived at out of court between the management and the employees' Unions whereby compensation up to 900 marks (£45) was paid to the individual employees. In all, a sum of approximately 30,000 marks (£1500) had to be paid by the firm in order to be finally rid of these employees.

THE PROTECTION OF WORKS COUNCILLORS AGAINST DISMISSAL

Works Councillors and Works Stewards are given special protection against dismissal. When an ordinary worker is dismissed, either with or without notice, the dismissal takes effect in the normal course, regardless of whether a protest has been entered and an appeal lodged with the Labour Court—

[1] Cf. *Reichsarbeitsblatt*, 1925, p. 422.

i.e. there is no postponement of the dismissal. Moreover, even when the Court decides that the dismissal was unjustified, the employer has the option either of choosing re-employment or of paying compensation. In both these respects the Works Councillor or Steward is given a much stronger position. In the case of dismissal with notice, the consent of a majority of the Works Council[1] is necessary for the dismissal to be effective—if this is forthcoming he is of course powerless to take any further action. If, as will normally be the case, the Works Council refuses its consent, the employer can then appeal to the Labour Court for a binding decision. But, should the period of notice have expired before the appeal has been heard, the Councillor is entitled to receive full pay until the decision, though the employer on his side can refuse to give him any work to do. In the event of a decision of the Court in favour of the Councillor, the employer is not given the option of offering the alternative of re-employment or compensation. He *must* re-employ the worker or else continue to pay him his full wages until he has either found acceptable employment elsewhere, or until the termination of the period for which he was elected. The liability of the employer would not necessarily end, even in the latter event, as the Works Councillor might be re-elected for another period of a year, in which case he would be entitled to his normal remuneration for the whole of that period. Moreover, as the worker is not legally dismissed, the employer must allow him entry to the factory in order to enable him to carry out his duties as a Works Councillor. This special protection against dismissal extends also to the transfer of a workers' representative from one establishment (though not one department) of an undertaking to another, and the procedure is identical with that for a dismissal. The decision of the Court in favour of, or against the appeal of the worker, is final and subject to no appeal.

The Act defines three groups of cases in which the consent of the Works Council, or, alternatively, of the Labour Court, is

[1] It is generally accepted that the Works Councillor directly concerned may attend the meeting at which his case is discussed, but should not vote on his own case. Where a Works Steward is concerned, the body whose consent is necessary is composed of the whole of the employees who were his electors.

not necessary for the legal dismissal of a Works Councillor or Steward:

(a) Dismissals based on legal provisions or the award of a Conciliation Board, or arising out of the operation of a Collective Agreement.

(b) Dismissals rendered necessary by the closing-down of an establishment.

(c) Dismissals without notice, for any reason that would make such a dismissal legally valid.

As to (a), this became of great importance after the end of 1923, owing to the drastic steps taken by the Reich to diminish the number of employees in State undertakings and administrative departments, though there is a great deal of uncertainty and difference of opinion as to the practical application of the different Orders in regard to Works Councillors. The view most widely adopted is that, where the department or undertaking concerned has any choice as to who shall be dismissed, the consent of the Works Council must be obtained before a workers' representative is dismissed, or, failing that consent, appeal must be made to the competent Court. But if a whole unit is closed down and the personnel turned off, the Works Councillor must accept his lot equally with the others and has no right of appeal. Dismissals, against which no appeal can be made, may also occur by virtue of a Collective Agreement, as when strike breakers who were engaged during a strike are dismissed under the agreement by which work is resumed. Similarly, when dismissals have to take place owing to lack of work, it may be agreed that the employees shall be dismissed in a regular order, beginning with the last one to be engaged. When the turn of the Works Councillor comes, his position will not save him from dismissal.

(b) The position of the workers' representatives, in the event of the closing-down of an establishment, has been the subject of much dispute and many conflicting decisions. The chief points at issue are, firstly, whether the consent of the Works Council is necessary to the dismissal of a Councillor in the event only of a partial closing-down of an establishment; secondly, whether it is necessary when the closing-down is merely temporary and the motive of the employer is to get rid of his existing employees, including the Works Council, and then reopen with a new body of employees; thirdly, what the position is of the Works Council in the case of a lock-out, where all the employees are dismissed owing to a dispute over wages or other conditions of work, and work is subsequently resumed on new terms. In all these cases a good deal depends on the particular circumstances, but there is at present no uniformity either of legal opinion or of the decisions of the Courts on the fundamental issues involved. During the last two years there have been hundreds of cases where firms have closed down for a time for various reasons and, in practice, the employers have availed themselves of this method, more than of any other, of getting rid of Works Councillors whose activities had displeased them.

(c) In general, a Works Councillor may not be dismissed without notice except for an offence which would render him legally liable, in his capacity as an employee, to be so dismissed. In contrast to an ordinary dismissal with notice, instant dismissal takes immediate effect, even in the case of a Works Councillor, and the employer is therefore entitled to forbid him entry to his premises until the Court has decided as to the legality of the dismissal. If the decision goes in favour of the Councillor, the dismissal is immediately nullified and he can return to his employment and his position as Works Councillor, and can further claim the payment of the wages lost during the period between the date of dismissal and the decision of the Court. One of the most frequent causes of instant dismissal is a "gross insult" offered by the Works Councillor to the employer or to one of his immediate superiors. But the Courts as a rule take into account the special position of the Councillor and investigate the precise circumstances of the insult. If it has been caused mainly by the provocative attitude of the employer, or has perhaps consisted in "giving the lie" to the employer in a moment of excitement during a heated argument, it has repeatedly been held that there was inadequate ground for instant dismissal. The employer is thus required to prove graver causes, in order to justify instant dismissal, in the case of a workers' representative than in that of an ordinary employee.

It is significant that the Act lays down no rules to guide the

172

Courts in deciding whether an ordinary dismissal with notice of a Works Councillor or Steward is justifiable, other than the provision that the Court must not give its consent to a dismissal if it decides that the dismissal constitutes an infringement of the obligation, imposed on the employer by Section 95, not to penalise a workers' representative as a result of the exercise by him of his statutory functions. The onus does not lie on the employee in this case to prove that "unjust hardship" will result from his dismissal; the onus lies instead on the employer, to prove to the satisfaction of the Court that he has sufficient cause for effecting the dismissal. The intention of the legislature was to grant a special protection to the workers' representatives, not merely in their own interests, owing to their peculiar liability to victimisation, but chiefly in the interests of the body of employees in the retention of their own elected representatives for the period of office for which they were elected. This has been frequently, though not universally, recognised by the Courts. In this connection a judgement, issued by the Provincial Court of Elberfeld on November 4, 1924, in an appeal of a Works Councillor against his dismissal, throws an interesting light on the attitude adopted by that Court towards the position and responsibilities of a workers' representative:

The plaintiff, as a member of the Works Council, was under the obligation, in accordance with Section 1 of the Works Councils Act, of safeguarding the common economic interests of the employees in the establishment *vis-à-vis* the employer and, for this purpose, of co-operating in the regulation of conditions which either influenced the contract of employment or, which...might influence it. It is unavoidable that fundamental differences should arise, owing to their different points of view, between employer and employees or members of the Works Council, where their interests clash. To represent, within the provisions of the Works Councils Act, such separate interests of the employees even against the will of the employer, is the imperative duty of the Works Council and of its members. The Works Councillor must not refrain from assuming this duty. In this capacity he confronts the employer, not as a subordinate employee bound to obedience by virtue of a private contract of service, but as a negotiator on an equal footing by virtue of public law. His freedom of action is complete and dictated only by the interests of the employees, but in no way subordinated to the authority of the employer. In view of this legal position and of the facts of the case it is not apparent why the

173

authority of the defendants should suffer if they continue to employ the plaintiff in their business, and thereby demonstrate that they realise the sharp distinction between their relation in public law to the plaintiff as Chairman of the Works Council and their relation to him in private law as his employer: on the contrary, an objective appreciation and handling of the legal and material aspects of the case can only serve to enhance the prestige of the defendants in their works.

Opinions among those directly concerned as to the real efficacy of the protection given to the workers' representatives in factories and businesses are sharply divided. Most of the Trade Union officials and members of Works Councils, with whom the author discussed this matter, took the view that the protection afforded was largely illusory. Experience has shown that there are at least seven different ways by which an employer can get rid of a Works Councillor who is obnoxious to him:

(1) The employer can dismiss a Councillor with the usual legal notice after obtaining the consent of the Works Council. This is by no means always refused if the employer has a good case, or if the Works Councillor is unpopular with the rest of the Council. He may, for instance, belong to a "Christian" Union while the remainder of the Council is composed of "Free" Trade Unionists, or he may be a Communist who has been as much a thorn in the side of his fellow Councillors as in that of the employer. A majority and not a unanimous vote of the Council is necessary for this purpose.

(2) The employer can dismiss him with the usual notice and subsequently obtain the consent of the Labour Court, if the Council refuses to give its approval. He may be a bad time-keeper or in other ways an unsatisfactory worker.

(3) The employer can take advantage of the closing-down of his works for a while, in order to effect the dismissal. This has been one of the most frequent cases during the prolonged period of industrial depression following the stabilisation of the mark. It is a well-established and widely known fact that employers will refuse to re-engage Works Councillors who have shown over-much activity in their office.[1] Hence on the one hand, many em-

[1] Men who become known as having stirred up strife in factories and who are regarded as agitators or as inconvenient people to have on a Works Council are black-listed and refused employment throughout the whole industrial district in which they live.

ployees have declined to submit themselves for election and, on the other hand, those elected have been afraid to put themselves in opposition to the employer. This fact has undoubtedly had much to do with the falling off in the activities of the Works Councils in the last two years.

(4) The employer can dismiss the Works Councillor without notice, provided that he can prove his action to have been legally justified.

(5) The employer can bring an action against him before the Labour Court for his compulsory retirement from office on the ground of gross abuse of his official position and, if successful, then proceed to dismiss him. This assumes that the worker fails in his subsequent appeal to the Labour Court against dismissal. It is a matter of controversy whether an action, which would justify his compulsory retirement from office, *ipso facto* justifies his dismissal. The judgements of the Courts are not uniform on this question, but as a rule the decision depends on the facts of each individual case.

(6) The employer can bring a similar action against the whole Works Council and, if successful, proceed with the dismissal of the Councillor of whom he wishes to be rid.

(7) The employer can come to an agreement with the Works Councillor by which the latter voluntarily leaves his employment. There is nothing to prevent the employer offering a sum of money to the Councillor as an inducement to seek work elsewhere. In a recent case at Heidelberg the Chairman of a Works Council was given notice of dismissal by his employer. When the case came before the Labour Court, the Works Councillor, as frequently happens, was represented by an official from his Trade Union. It was known that the relations between this man and his employer were bad and there was little prospect, if the employer were forced to re-engage him, of peace and harmony in the business. The Court was not asked to give a binding decision, but to help to bring about an agreement which would be to the interests of both parties. Finally, the Chairman of the Council agreed voluntarily to leave his employment in return for the payment to him by the employer of the (quite appreciable) sum of 800 marks (£40).

It will be seen that the employer is by no means without weapons against the members of the Works Council, and that the latter must walk warily in order to benefit by the protection of the Act. It would, however, be going too far to say that the protective provisions of the Act are merely illusory. The decisions of the Courts in thousands of cases prove that this is not the case. Moreover, employers, when asked about this matter, declare that it has often been found impossible to secure the dismissal of a Works Councillor even where he was a poor workman, or where his activities were detrimental to the efficient conduct of the works and to good relations between employers and employed.

In practice, everything turns on the relative strength of employers on the one hand and of organised labour on the other. During 1924 and 1925, the evidence of the intimidation and victimisation of Works Councillors is so widespread, that it is quite plain that legal provisions, which may be adequate to protect the Councillors in times of normal business activity, are largely ineffective when trade is depressed and there is much unemployment. The policy adopted by the Courts before which appeals against dismissals are brought is also very important. As a whole they have undoubtedly endeavoured to avoid social injustice and to protect the Works Councillors where the latter have been able to make out a clear case. But it has been found extremely difficult to go behind the plea of economic necessity, usually put forward by the employers and it is often impossible for a Works Councillor to prove that he has been victimised.

THE QUARTERLY REPORT AND OTHER INFORMATION

By Section 71 of the Act, the Works Council of any undertaking which serves economic purposes is entitled to require the employer to grant it, or, in large concerns, the Works Committee, access to information respecting all operations of the business which affect the contract of employment or the activities of the employees, subject to the proviso that no business secrets are thereby endangered or legal provisions contravened. The employer must also lay before the Council, or its Committee, the wages books of the undertaking and must supply any other information necessary for carrying out existing Collective Agreements. It is expressly stated that the Works Council may only demand the above information for the purpose of fulfilling its official duties in accordance with the Act. The employer is further required to make a Quarterly Report to the Council on the position and progress of the undertaking and of the industry generally and, in particular, on the output of the undertaking and on the anticipated demand for labour. The members of the Works Committee or the Works Council must observe secrecy in regard to all confidential information supplied to them by the employer.

The right to secure the information specified in Section 71 is confined to "undertakings which serve economic purposes", for the reason that the information is intended to assist the Works Council in carrying out its duties under Section 66, Clauses (1) and (2).[1] In the case of undertakings whose fundamental *raison d'être* is non-economic, such as propaganda bodies, newspapers, religious, scientific or artistic organisations, etc., the employees as such are not permitted to express any views as to the general policy of the management or the way in which the aims of the undertaking are carried out. In all other undertakings, the Councils are given the duty of "supporting the management with advice" and, for this purpose, in order that their advice may be based on inside knowledge, they are allowed access to information which previously had been the property of the management alone.

If an undertaking has a number of separate establishments, in each of which there is a Works Council, the individual Councils may each demand information under Section 71 in regard to its own establishment; while if there is a Central Works Council for the whole undertaking, as in the case of Krupps at Essen, or the Allgemeine Elektrizitätsgesellschaft in Berlin, the Central Works Council can demand information on similar lines for the undertaking as a unit.

[1] Section 66. "It shall be the duty of the Works Council:
  (1) in establishments which serve economic purposes, to support the management with advice and thus to co-operate in securing the highest possible standard of production and the maximum degree of working efficiency;
  (2) in establishments which serve economic purposes, to co-operate and assist in the introduction of new labour methods."

As the Act merely empowers the Council to have access "to information respecting all operations of the business which affect the contract of employment and the activities of employees", without specifying more closely the nature of the data which come under this description, it is natural that many disputes have arisen over the interpretation of this paragraph. It can be urged that nothing which happens in the business is without its bearing, in the long or short run, on the activities of the employees[1] and, in practice, the Councils have often made very far-reaching demands on the employer.

But the history of Section 71 shows that the legislature intended the words referred to above to have a relatively restricted application, for the original wording of the Bill spoke of "all operations of the business affecting labour conditions", while this was altered during the discussion of the Bill to "all operations of the business which affect the contract of employment or the activities of the employees". Thus the employer can be regarded as having fulfilled his duty if he gives information regarding all operations which have a *direct* bearing on the contract of employment. Such information would have regard, for example, to the operation of piece-work rates in the establishment; contract work; the distribution of overtime; the shifting of workers from one department of the undertaking to another; the introduction of new labour methods; the carrying out of emergency work; the regulation of working shifts, etc. Matters of a more general character, which arise out of the conduct of the business as a whole and which involve questions of policy, are supposed to be dealt with by the employer in his Quarterly Report. It should be noted that the Council has no right to stay the hand of the management or even, in most cases, to require to be consulted before decisions are actually taken, but it can demand information as to the nature of these decisions and it is entitled to make such representations as it considers to be in the interests of the employees, the undertaking in general and the community.

The fact that the employer is empowered to refuse to give any information, through which business secrets might be endangered,

[1] Cf. Nörpel, *Aus der Betriebsräte Praxis*, vol. i, p. 88.

represents an important practical limitation to the scope of this Section. This is, however, less serious than might at first sight appear, because the Works Council can always, if it dares, appeal to the appropriate authority and obtain a ruling on the point at issue. The view generally adopted on appeal, is that the Works Council is required to observe secrecy in regard to all information declared by the employer to be confidential and heavy penalties are provided for the infringement of this rule; it is only under exceptional circumstances that the employer is legally entitled to refuse to give information under the plea of secrecy.

The wages books referred to in this Section include the detailed books showing how much each individual wage-earner receives. As the Act refers to wages books and not to salary books, it has been ruled that the management are not required to give this detailed information in regard to the earnings of salaried employees. It need only give a statement of the salaries paid to the employees falling within each salary group. It has also been ruled that the Works Council cannot demand access to the personal files relating to individual workers. In general, the Works Council has the right to obtain all data necessary for it to form a judgement as to whether the Collective Agreements are in fact being carried out, such as, for example, the amount of overtime worked, the numbers of different grades of workers employed, methods of calculating wage rates, the allocation of holidays, etc. This was the kind of task which, before the passing of the Works Councils Act, fell to the lot of the Trade Union delegates in each undertaking. But these delegates could only obtain their information by asking the individual workers and had no recognised status vis-à-vis the employer.

The Quarterly Report is intended to give the Works Council an opportunity of ascertaining the productivity of the business in relation to its working capacity and to the demand of the market, and thus to get an insight into the general economic conditions governing the business and to be able to judge, inter alia, of the necessity for the engagement or dismissal of workers. The whole purpose and intention of the Quarterly Report are well set out in a ruling given on January 22, 1922, by the Bavarian Ministry of Social Welfare, in a dispute which arose over some very comprehensive demands for information put forward by the Works Council of a Nürnberg firm:

The purpose of this Report is not to provide a basis for action in a particular case—that is the purpose of para. 1 of Section 71—by means of para. 2 it is intended that the Works Council should be given a general survey of the economic position of the whole industry and of the particular undertaking, so that it can adopt the right attitude to the questions with which it has to deal.... The fulfilment of the duty [of making a Report] involves a special measure of tact on the part of both employer and employees. The Report should deal with everything which is of material importance in estimating the position of the undertaking and of the whole branch of industry: the supply of raw materials and fuel; the technique of the process of production; market conditions; inventions which influence production; changes in legislation affecting taxation or customs duties at home or abroad; and changes in the general economic situation which may influence the section of industry concerned. The factors which are of importance will, to a large extent, be entirely unknown to the employees, and their attention will be drawn to them for the first time by the employer. ... It depends also entirely on the particular circumstances to what extent the Report should go into details. In a sound business, with plenty of work and with good prospects, the information can be of a more general character than in one which is in difficulties or which belongs to a section of industry whose economic existence is threatened.

The ruling proceeded to discuss the individual points at issue in the dispute between the Works Council and the firm. It was decided that the Council had the right to demand information as to the total number of employees, showing separately the wage-earning and salaried employees; the output of the business in general terms, unless the firm could prove that business secrets were thereby endangered; the total of overhead costs; the market prices of raw materials and fuel; and the state of the market and of the trade in general. On the other hand, the average selling price of the goods ex works; the actual prices paid for raw materials and certain other data, were declared not to come within the proper scope of the Report.

The intention at the back of this provision of the Works Councils Act is clearly that the worker should be taken to a considerable extent into the confidence of the employer, and be given an opportunity of realising the part played by his particular undertaking in the industry as a whole and of understanding the influence of the general economic situation upon the welfare of his own firm and so of himself. It is part of the attempt, in the words of the official memorandum accompanying the Act, to transform the workers "from automatic links in the productive process, unaware of the purpose of this labour, into responsible and willing co-operators in the work of production".

As with other of the more ambitious sides of the Works Councils Act, all the indications hitherto go to show that, in the great majority of cases, the Quarterly Report, as actually presented, is very far from providing a comprehensive and clear picture of the economic position of the establishment in its relation to the rest of the industry. The following extracts from the minutes of a Works Council in a large textile factory employing 2400 workers, in which the relations between the Council and the management were exceptionally good, summarise two Quarterly Reports made in 1924:[1]

The Director reported that there were many signs of a coming crisis in the establishment. He regretted the public attacks that were being made against the textile industry. Insufficient account was taken of the fact that raw cotton was three times the pre-war price. For the next few months there were enough orders for the factory. These orders would have been better had it not been for the recent strike. He appealed to the representatives to leave nothing undone to secure clean work. He would do everything that he could to prevent a reduction in the volume of labour required.

There was no discussion on the Report.

The Director reported that the general business position had improved owing to the acceptance of the Dawes Report. It had been widely believed that a settlement of the Reparation question would mean a sudden increase of employment. He was glad to be able to state that this had not occurred, for a slow improvement was more favourable for industry. The accumulation of large stocks of cotton and semi-manufactured products from the previous crop constituted a serious difficulty. As there had been an extraordinary fall in the price of the new season's crop, the stocks from the previous crop must necessarily be sold at a loss. It was a good sign of better business conditions that the higher qualities of cotton were in greater demand. As a result of this improvement he was able to state that it would be possible until further notice to work a five-day week.

There was no discussion on the Report.

[1] *Aus dem Tagebuch eines Betriebsrats*, 1925, pp. 25, 40.

These two Reports are probably characteristic in that they are confined to wide generalisations as to the state of business as a whole in the industry, and refrain from going in any detail into the real problems of management and policy in regard to the factory in question.

It would be going too far to say that this type of information is worthless or that it has no educative value, but it clearly throws no light on those questions which are of real importance so far as the practical working and administration of an industrial firm are concerned, for example, price policy; the allocation of overhead costs between different departments, etc. Many years of listening to vague general statements would not go far towards realising the hopes of the Socialists, or helping to produce men who would have a genuine insight into the methods of conducting a business. As a whole, employers are very chary indeed of giving away any information to their Works Council which could not be equally well obtained from, say, the columns of a trade paper. On the other hand, when skilful use is made of the right to ask questions at the end of the Report, it is sometimes possible to extract additional data which may prove of considerable value, either for their own sake or for use in subsequent negotiations.[1]

In the nature of things it is impossible to discover in how many cases Quarterly Reports are in fact demanded by the Works Councils and presented by the employers. In many small businesses the employer would be hard put to it to give anything more than the barest facts, already probably well known by the Works Council. It may, indeed, be taken for granted that the Quarterly Report has no practical importance and is not asked for in the vast majority of small concerns. In other cases, e.g. a big bank, such a Report would be as a rule of neither value nor interest to the employees. In the larger industrial concerns, immediately after the passing of the Act, when its provisions were novel and interest was keen, Reports were regularly made in many cases. But from all the evidence the writer has been able to collect, it would appear that very many Works Councils

---

[1] Cf. *Protokoll der Konferenz...der Betriebsräte...der Metallindustrie*, December 1924, p. 35.

now do not trouble to ask the employer for a Report and, though the employer is supposed to present one without being explicitly asked for it, in practice, at any rate in smaller undertakings, the whole matter is likely in that case to fall into abeyance. Since the stabilisation of the mark and the accompanying depression of trade and unemployment, members of Works Councils have had strong reasons not to thrust themselves upon the notice of the employer unnecessarily and thus, for practical and personal reasons, legal rights have been apt to go by the board. Considerations of this latter order are, however, only of a temporary character. In general, it must be borne in mind that the right to demand a Quarterly Report exists, and that here, as in other directions, the Trade Unions continually exercise their influence upon the Works Councils to take full advantage of all their legal rights.

THE SUBMISSION OF A BALANCE SHEET AND PROFIT AND LOSS ACCOUNT

In the Works Councils Act there is a short section (Section 72) in which it is stated that in all establishments (with few exceptions) employing not less than 50 salaried employees or 300 wage-earners, the Works Council may require that a balance sheet for the establishment and a profit and loss account shall be presented annually for the past business year, with suitable explanations. The more precise provisions for putting this section into force were left to a subsequent Act which was passed in February 1921.[1]

The novelty of this section lies partly in the fact that the obligation contained in it applies, not merely to the ordinary joint stock company with its published balance sheets, but also to partnerships, private undertakings, etc. and, in general, to every form of industrial, commercial or financial undertaking of the required size. As can be seen from the text of the supplementary Act, the items which have to be given correspond to the normal requirements of German company law, save that, in the case of the private undertaking, the personal capital of

---

[1] A translation of the text of this Act is given in Appendix III.

the employer, not used in his business, must be excluded from the balance sheet, and the data given must refer to the individual establishment and not to the undertaking to which it may belong. But the Act goes beyond this in imposing upon the employer the duty of expounding the various items to the Works Council, or, in a larger business, to its committee. Thus the employer may be asked to estimate to what extent the actual value of buildings, plant, etc., in the balance sheet diverges from their book value; how far the debts due to the establishment are good; what is the extent and nature of the reserves; how the chief items on the assets side are made up; how far the undertaking is working with borrowed capital, and so on. In the case of the profit and loss account, the Works Council may require the profits from appreciation of values, interest on invested reserves, etc., to be separated from the profits resulting from actual production, and similarly in the case of items on the loss side. It remains, however, within the discretion of the employer to refuse to give information which in his view would endanger his business. In no case may the Works Council demand to see the actual data from which the balance sheet and profit and loss account have been compiled; they are entirely dependent upon the verbal explanations of the employer. The difficulties of the Works Council in the examination of balance sheets are, to some extent, lessened by rulings of the Courts that the employer must provide comparative figures for the preceding year.

In a commentary for use of the Works Councils, published by the German Federation of Socialist Trade Unions[1] (which in 1922 was in its 13th–15th thousand), it is declared that the chief aims of a criticism and appreciation of a balance sheet are: firstly, to ascertain how the different items have been valued and to set off initially against one another the entries of assets and liabilities; secondly, to show the relation between the gross and net profit, on the one hand, and the total capital resources used in the business, on the other hand, and thus to enable the economic working of the business to be tested; thirdly, to investigate the allocation of the profits and, in particular, the division as between reserves and dividends.

[1] Paul Koske, *Wie beurteilt man eine Bilanz?*, p. 14.

Another view, also from the labour side, is as follows:[1]

> The Works Councils have every reason to devote the greatest attention to the question of the estimation of profits. Chiefly, because it is their duty to supervise the undertaking for which they must regard themselves as jointly responsible, and to pay particular attention to the technical efficiency of the undertaking even if the employer is only concerned with making profits. It must also be their endeavour to keep themselves so closely informed of all operations of the business that they can see through any manœuvres of those at present responsible for the management. Further, the Works Council has duties to the community, since for it the business in which it is employed is only a part of the economic whole and it knows that the neglect of technical consideration, the senseless distribution of profits and the ruthless forcing up of prices...involve exploitation of the community.

Other writers have gone further and have regarded one of the chief uses to which Section 72 could be put, as being the opportunity afforded for ascertaining when demands for higher wages could with advantage be pressed, the information thus obtained to be passed on (in direct conflict with the provisions of the Act) to the headquarters of the Trade Unions.

When regard is had to the terms of Section 72, as expanded by the supplementary Act of February 5, 1921, and to the very drastic claims put forward by representatives of labour while its provisions were being discussed, it is not surprising that the employers as a body should have felt the keenest misgivings and fears as to the way in which these novel rights would be handled by the Works Councils. Events, however, have justified neither the fears of the employers nor the expectations of the labour leaders.

Owing to the almost continuous inflation and depreciation of the currency, during the whole period from the passing of the Act down to the end of 1923, it was virtually impossible for anybody to draw valid deductions from balance sheets. Merely by valuing stocks at their replacement value it was often possible to turn a paper profit of hundreds of millions of marks into a very heavy loss. The employers themselves for the most part did not

---

[1] Dr Robert Einstein in *Betriebsrätezeitschrift...der Metallindustrie*, March 31, 1922, p. 264.

THE WORKS COUNCILS AND

know where they stood; still less could this be expected from the average member of a Works Council. It is clear that, in any case, the wage-earning members of the Councils could not possibly have the technical knowledge necessary to criticise intelligently the balance sheet of an undertaking, but, from the employers' point of view, the danger lay more with those members who were salaried employees.[1] The bulk of the organised salaried employees in Germany are affiliated to the "Free" or socialist Trade Union movement, and for a time after the Revolution, many of the salaried employees, especially in Berlin, were more radically inclined than the majority of the wage-earners. In practice, however, the fact that the employer need not show the Works Council any of the data from which the balance sheet, etc., have been compiled and that he need only give verbal explanations of the figures, the accuracy of which it is generally impossible for the Works Council to test, has proved a very effective safeguard against the disclosure of any information which he would prefer not to reveal.

In the case of all companies which are already compelled to publish balance sheets, it is the normal practice to place the printed balance sheet before the Works Council. Anyone who has any experience of the published balance sheets of joint stock companies knows how much it is possible to conceal and how misleading an impression can be given by figures which yet conform to legal requirements.

All the experience, hitherto, shows that the Works Councils have been unable to make any effective use of the rights nominally given to them by Section 72 of the Works Councils Act. In part this may be attributed to the abnormal currency conditions prevailing during the greater part of the existence of the Councils. During the inflation, as has been pointed out, comparable statistics from year to year were impossible. When the currency was stabilised all undertakings had to convert their book-keeping on to a gold mark basis—a highly complicated and difficult operation, and it is really only since 1925 that a certain degree of stability in accounting has been obtained.

[1] See above, p. 133.

186

The Works Councils are handicapped in their efforts to obtain practical results from their right of access to the balance sheets and from their still more important right of demanding information as to the composition of the different items, by two great hindrances in their way—firstly, their own lack of knowledge and understanding of the theory and practice of accountancy and, secondly, by the determined opposition of the employers to revealing any of the financial secrets of their businesses. It is clear that the ordinary workman, even if he has attended a course of, say, a dozen lectures on the methods of construction and interpretation of a balance sheet, is not in a position to do much more than demonstrate his own ignorance if he attempts to criticise a balance sheet, nor is he likely to know what sort of questions to ask. While the salaried employee is certainly in a better position in this respect, even he is not likely to know very much about the way in which the figures have been drawn up, unless he happens to be employed in the accountancy department of the business. Even assuming this to be the case, he is very unlikely to damage his future chances of promotion and, perhaps, run the risk of dismissal by asking questions which force the hand of the employer.

Thus, even with a reasonable degree of goodwill on the side of the employer, it is unlikely that the average Works Councillor would derive much advantage from the right to inspect the balance sheet and profit and loss account. Far less is this the case under existing conditions, when the employer does his utmost to prevent any sort of valid deduction from being drawn from the figures he is forced to supply. By amalgamating large numbers of different items under a single head, by writing down his fixed capital and stock out of profits and in many other ways, he can present a financial picture which is entirely misleading.

Most employers have a rooted and, to some extent, irrational dread of any disclosure of the inside workings of their businesses. If they are doing well they are afraid of public opinion, of the tax collector, of the demands of their employees and of the competition of their rivals: if they are doing badly they are concerned as to their credit and their contracts. There are, moreover, reasons that are by no means negligible why they should wish to keep the Works Councils in the dark. For most of the members of the Councils are also members of the Trade Unions or of one of the political parties, and the Unions are always pestering the Councils to send them information as to the profits, etc., of the individual firms, which would serve them as propaganda or as a basis for fresh wage claims. The ordinary employer, therefore, in a competitive industry, is far more inclined to present his figures in as misleading a form as possible than to give his Works Council a real insight into the facts about his business.

In practice the Councils are and realise themselves to be impotent to make a practical use of their rights under the Works Councils Act. In some measure this spurs them on to deepen their knowledge of the very complicated and difficult material with which they are confronted, but more often it embitters them and enhances that feeling of mistrust, based on the feeling that they are being deliberately hoodwinked, which it was one of the intentions of the Works Councils Act to dispel.

THE ELECTION OF WORKS COUNCILLORS ON TO THE CONTROL BOARDS OF COMPANIES

The Works Councils Act contains a general provision (Section 70) empowering Works Councils to elect, in some cases one, but in most cases two members to sit on the Control Board of every company or other form of undertaking, which, either by legal enactment or its own statutes, possesses a Control Board. As in the case of Section 72, which provides for the submission of balance sheets and profit and loss accounts, it was left to an Act to be passed subsequently to lay down in a more concrete form the conditions governing the election of Works Council members to the Control Board. This Act was passed after a prolonged and bitter agitation against it on the part of the employers on February 15, 1922,[1] or more than two years after the Works Councils Act became law. It aroused indeed a keener controversy both in the Reichstag and in the Press than was caused by any other of the rights granted to the Works Councils.

Under German company law a public company is administered by three organs—the General Meeting of shareholders;

---

[1] A translation of the text of this Act is given in Appendix IV.

the Management (*Vorstand*), which is the executive body responsible to the General Meeting for the administration of the affairs of the company; and the Control Board (*Aufsichtsrat*), whose function it is to supervise the activities of the Management in the interests of the shareholders. Thus the Control Board of a German company has not the same legal functions as those of a Board of Directors of an English company and the word "control" must be taken in the French sense of *contrôle*, or the right of inspection and supervision, rather than as implying the exercise of directive functions. The legal functions of a Control Board are set out in Article 246 of the Commercial Code:

> The Control Board shall supervise the conduct of the company in all branches of its administration and shall keep itself informed of the progress of the affairs of the company. It may at any time demand a report on these affairs from the management and may, either itself or through members which it nominates, inspect the books and files of the company and can investigate the state of the company's balance and its holdings of securities and goods. It shall audit the annual accounts, the balance sheets and the proposed distribution of profits and report thereon to the General Meeting of the company. It shall convene a General Meeting when this is desirable in the interests of the company. Other functions may be assigned to the Board of Control by the Statutes of the company.

In addition to these general provisions, the Board of Control is required, by other Articles of the Code, to examine and verify the accuracy of all data given in the prospectus of a company in process of formation. Further, if a resolution has been passed at a General Meeting for the increase of the capital of the company, the signature of all the members of the Control Board, as well as of the Management, are required for purposes of registration. The same provision holds good in regard to the capital of a new company, but it has been ruled, in both cases, that individual signatures cannot be withheld except on the ground of illegality of the proceedings.

The Control Board is also normally entrusted with the work of appointing "Procurists", i.e. officials who are entrusted with extensive managerial functions, such as the right of appointment and dismissal of employees, the right to sign contracts, etc.

In recent years one of the most frequent functions of the Boards has been to enter into commercial and financial agreements with other concerns (so-called *Interessengemeinschaften*).

The members of a Control Board are exposed to serious penalties in the event of misuse or gross neglect in the exercise of their legal functions, for they are liable to be sued individually for damages and are also subject to criminal prosecution.

It is evident from the foregoing account that, on paper, the powers of the Control Board of a company are very considerable and that it is entitled to obtain information in regard to practically every aspect of the commercial and financial working of the company, so that it can carry out its duties as the trustee of the interests of the whole body of shareholders, to whom it reports at the General Meeting.

It has, however, for a long time past been very generally recognised in Germany that many of the Control Boards are largely a form and are far from carrying out the duties entrusted to them by law. This has been due, partly, to the growth in the size and complexity of businesses and, therefore, of their accounts, which has made any really effective supervision impossible in the time at the disposal of the Board. Moreover, the members of one Board commonly sit on a number of others as well and are almost bound to accept without too much scrutiny the figures that are put before them. Finally, the Management, as a rule, is very anxious not to take the Control Board too much into its confidence, in view of the variety of interests probably represented on the Board. It is not uncommon for a Management to refuse altogether to supply certain information asked for by the Board. The only practical remedy in that case is likely to be the threat of resignation, to be followed by an explanation at the General Meeting—a course which is only rarely adopted. Repeated proposals have been put forward in the commercial Press and elsewhere for a reform of the law, in such a way as to give larger effective powers to the Control Boards, but so far without avail. These are facts which it is important to bear in mind when considering the rôle of the Works Councils on the Control Boards.

It has already been observed that the employers as a whole

190

did their utmost to prevent the admission of Works Council members to the Control Boards. The most vehement opposition came from the banks. When they realised that the measure would nevertheless be adopted, they put forward the claim that they should come under Section 78 of the Works Councils Act, which exempts businesses whose main purpose is non-economic, such as newspapers, from the provisions of Section 70. The banks, however, were unable to substantiate their contention and were forced to comply with Section 70.

When the new Act came into force in 1922 the employers immediately took a series of measures designed to lessen the danger from their point of view. Many companies promptly altered their statutes and attempted to remove from the competence of the Control Board important functions which hitherto they had been fulfilling and which were now transferred, either to the Chairman of the Board, or to Committees from which the Works Council members were expressly excluded.

A number of such cases were taken to the Courts and for the most part were decided against the companies, on the ground that it is laid down in Section 3 of the Act of February 12, 1922, that: "In so far as it is not otherwise provided in the Works Councils Act, provisions which hold good for the other members of the Control Board are applicable to the Works Council members who are elected to the Board". The employees based their case on the wording of Section 70 of the Works Councils Act, which says that Works Councils have the right to elect members to the Control Boards "in order to represent the interests and claims of the employees and their wishes regarding the organisation of the undertaking". It is argued from this that the Works Council members are only entitled to discuss and vote on those matters coming before the Board, which are directly concerned with labour conditions in the undertaking. This dispute has been to some extent settled by an important decision given recently by the Reichsgericht (the highest Civil Court of Appeal in Germany). It is laid down in this decision that, in so far as the statutes of an undertaking give to the Control Board additional functions to those enumerated in the Civil Code, it is permissible for such functions to be entrusted to other bodies on which the Works Council is not represented. But so far as the strictly legal functions of the Control Board are concerned, the Works Council members must be placed on exactly the same footing as the other members who have been elected by the General Meeting.

The employers, finding that the alteration of company statutes was open to legal objections, quickly modified their tactics and proceeded to take advantage of the very loose way in which the actual conduct of the business of the Control Boards is regulated by law. The Civil Code nowhere lays down the number of meetings which must be held annually by the Board and, although the entire cessation of all meetings would clearly be contrary to the law, not more than one or two meetings need be held during the year. Even before the Works Councils came on the scene this was common in a large proportion of companies and inevitably meant the transaction of a large amount of business in a very perfunctory manner. This tendency has now been reinforced by the desire to avoid any detailed discussion of important matters in front of the Works Council members. As the representatives of the shareholders are always in a majority on the Board, it is easy for them—and it is now the common practice —to delegate to sub-committees of their members the consideration of any question which it is desired not to go into thoroughly at the full meeting. One consequence of this development, which is by no means negligible, is that the effectiveness of the Control Boards as supervisory bodies is seriously impaired, even in comparison with pre-war conditions. An illustration of this was afforded by a recent criminal prosecution of the managing director of a German combine, for breach of trust.[1] It was found that the majority of the members of the Control Board knew nothing of the gross irregularities which were proved to have taken place. During the proceedings a memorandum was supplied by the directors of three leading German banks, in which it was stated that, since the introduction of the Works Councils Act, it had become impossible to obtain precise information as to the drawings of managing directors of such concerns, because this information was only made known to a small circle of members

[1] Cf. *Wirtschafts-Informations-Dienst*, August 1926, pp. 85–90.

of the Control Board. It is also worth noting that a member of the Control Board of the above undertaking, who was prosecuted for complicity, but was acquitted, was shown to have deliberately made false statements at a meeting of the Board at which the Works Council members were present. It was pleaded in his defence that it was not always advisable that the Works Councillors, who represented the principle of publicity, should be told the whole truth.

Apart from the appointment of sub-committees of the Board, there is also nothing to prevent the ordinary members of the Board from meeting informally as often as they like. When the full meeting takes place, the members are confronted with a large number of resolutions, which are voted on with as little discussion as possible, and the transactions assume a purely formal character. It is naturally difficult for the Works Council members to challenge proposals, concerning the inner history of which they know nothing. Where, as has often been the case, the Control Board has been entrusted with functions which go beyond the legal minimum laid down in the Commercial Code, such as the nomination of "procurists", or members of the management, the statutes are usually altered and special committees are appointed to do this work.

Finally, the great tendency to combination which has characterised German industry since the War has led to the formation of many holding, or "roof" companies, as they are called in Germany, which commonly assume a form of organisation in which the constitution of a Control Board is not legally necessary. Thus, in these companies, where the major decisions are taken on questions of policy affecting great groups of industry, the Works Councils have no rights of representation.

When full account has been taken, however, not merely of the practical weakness of the Control Board *vis-à-vis* the Management, except where some of its members have great influence or force of character, but also of the very successful and well-thought-out measures that can be taken to defeat the inquisitiveness of the Works Council representatives on the Board, it still remains true that every individual member has very considerable powers of extracting information, and these powers belong as much to the Works Council members as to any of the others. For example, any member can demand a report from the management on the following matters:

1. The volume and duration of contracts placed with the firm.
2. The prices and sources of supply of raw materials.
3. Marketing conditions.
4. Labour conditions.
5. Mode of estimation and determination of costs of production.

In regard to the balance sheet and profit and loss account, the Works Council members have the right to demand much fuller and more detailed information than they are likely to obtain from the management at the annual meeting of the Works Council, at which the balance sheet is laid before the Council. They can thus check the accuracy of the information there supplied and, if the company has control over more than one establishment, can compare the financial results of their own establishment with that of the others comprised in the company. They can require a report on the methods of valuation of buildings, materials, stocks, etc., the amount of depreciation, the distribution of overhead charges and their relation to the net profit, the sources of profits, whether from production or speculation or participation in other concerns. Thus all the economic conditions affecting a company can be brought under review by the Control Board and each individual member can point to his legal responsibilities and liabilities in justification of his demand for exact and complete information.

When we come to enquire to what extent the Works Council members have in fact been able to utilise their new and unprecedented rights to serve on the Control Boards of companies, we find a universal consensus of opinion amongst all parties, employers, Trade Unions and Works Councillors themselves, that down to the present time these rights have proved sterile, and for the most part devoid of any practical importance. Already in 1922 in the first year of operation of the supplementary Act it was observed in the Report of the Baden Factory Inspectors that "Many members of Works Councils have become disillusioned owing to their having cherished false ideas as to the

194

functions of a Control Board, or because they have felt that the workers' representatives have not been given the same full insight into the affairs of the business which the other members of the Board have enjoyed ". The history of the past three years has done practically nothing to weaken the force of this ob servation.

It is noteworthy that the Works Councils themselves and the Trade Unions are by no means disposed to throw the whole of the responsibility for this state of affairs upon the obstructive tactics of the employers. There is very general agreement that lack of education and of knowledge of the practical working of economic forces affords a great part of the explanation. If the Works Council member of a Control Board knew sufficient to take an active part in the proceedings of the Board and had sufficient force of character to refuse to be ignored or intimi- dated, he could undoubtedly exercise a considerable influence on the operations of that body. But even though these members are elected by the Works Council from their own number and not by the body of employees and, therefore, there is some pre- sumption that the most capable men have been selected, it is very rare to find anyone capable of holding his own against the other members of the Board. The writer has often been told by German employers that there was no difficulty in dealing with the Works Councillors at Board Meetings; all that was necessary was to give them a fat cigar and they were quite content and took no interest in the proceedings. This is also borne out on the employees' side.[1] The frequent changes in personnel, owing to the annual elections, make it exceedingly difficult to secure continuity of representation and, therefore, the accumulation of the necessary knowledge and experience. Moreover, there is a natural tendency for the Works Council members, when they do take an active part at a meeting, to confine themselves to details concerning labour conditions in the undertaking, which are really matters for discussion with the management at an ordinary Works Council Meeting. In the discussion of the broad economic problems with which it is the proper function

[1] Cf. *Protokoll über die Konferenz der Arbeiteraufsichtsräte der Textil- industrie*, June 1925, p. 62.

13-2

of the Control Board to deal, they very seldom take any part.[1]
When a speaker at a Conference of Works Council members of
Control Boards declared that 80 per cent. of such members in all
branches of industry did not understand the material that was
put before them at the meetings nor the point of the discussion,
he was probably under- rather than over-stating the case.[2]

One piece of favourable evidence of an unbiased nature may
be cited from the Reports of the Factory Inspectors for Baden
for the year 1925:[3]

> The administration of the Closing-down of Works Order would have
> involved greater hardship for both employers and employees had it
> not been for many valuable suggestions, based on knowledge of the
> businesses, which were put forward by capable Works Councillors.
> We also observed that in joint stock companies the Works Councillors
> were well informed as to conditions in their undertakings, owing to the
> fact that they had been present at meetings of the Control Boards
> and were therefore in a position to make noteworthy suggestions.
> However, in this year also, employees complained that they were con-
> fronted by accomplished facts in the meetings of the Control Boards,
> while the actual discussion had taken place in preliminary meetings
> without their presence. There were also many complaints of deliberate
> concealment of information regarding business conditions.

Taking the situation as a whole, the Works Councils have been
grievously disappointed in their hopes, either of obtaining concrete advantages for their fellow-workers, or of securing a real
insight into the problems and policies of business management.
They have failed in this, partly, because of the successful opposition of the managing bodies of many companies to too great
inquisitiveness of the Control Boards as a whole; partly, because
the management has made common cause with the rest of the
Control Board to prevent the Works Council members from
finding out more than is considered good for them; and partly,
because of the incapacity of the Works Councillors themselves
to enforce or make use of their position on the Boards.

[1] Cf. *Protokoll über die Konferenz der Arbeiteraufsichtsräte der Textilindustrie*, June 1925, p. 74.
[2] *Ibid.* p. 32.
[3] Report of Factory Inspectors for Baden, 1925, p. 15.

INDUSTRIAL SELF-GOVERNMENT

WORKS COUNCILS IN THE GERMAN
FEDERAL RAILWAYS

The German Federal Railways which, in 1922, employed 452,000 wage-earners and 566,000 officials, constitute one of the largest undertakings under a single management in the world. It is therefore of special interest to see how the problem of incorporating the system of local representation of the workers into a State concern of such magnitude, extending over the German Reich, has been solved.

Under Section 61 of the Works Councils Act, State undertakings are placed in a separate category and the representation of the worker in them falls to be regulated by Administrative Order. Such an Order was issued for the State Railways by the Federal Minister of Transport on March 3, 1921.[1] The Order as a whole is based very closely on the provisions of the Works Councils Act; the main practical differences have to do with the structure and organisation of the Works Councils.

Three distinct classes of Works Councils are set up in the Federal Railways: firstly, there are the local Works Councils and Works Stewards; secondly, the District Works Councils; and, thirdly, the Central Works Council (*Hauptbetriebsrat*) for the whole railway system.

The local Works Councils and Works Stewards are elected in each local work place (*Dienststelle*) and the former vary in size according to the numbers employed, in precisely the same way as in the case of undertakings which come under the Works Councils Act, save that the Works Councils in the railways consist only of wage-earners.[2] The term "work place" is not defined in the Order, but includes all the various industrial undertakings

[1] The transformation of the German State Railways, under the Dawes Scheme, into a species of Public Company subject to international control, has not affected either the status or functions of the Works Councils in the railway system.

[2] The relatively few genuine salaried employees in the sense of the Act come under the Federal Collective Agreement as to wages, etc., and count therefore as wage-earners. All the other employees (including engine drivers) rank as officials for whom special and separate representation is provided.

197

(power stations, locomotive and waggon works, etc.) coming under the Railway Administration.

The District Works Councils are set up for each of the District Railway Directorates in Germany, of which there are 26. Where 3000 or fewer wage-earners are employed, the District Works Council numbers five and for each additional 1000 wage-earners the number of members is increased by one, up to a maximum of 15. The District Works Council is elected by all the wage-earners entitled to vote in the district, at the same election as for the local Works Council.

The Central Works Council of 25 members is elected by the whole body of wage-earners employed by the Federal Railway Administration. Both the District Councils and the Central Works Council are elected annually and hold office for one year.

The functions of the local Works Councils are closely analogous to the functions of Works Councils in other undertakings; they have the same duties to fulfil and the same rights, with the exception of the right of inspection of the balance sheet and profit and loss account.[1] All questions as to working conditions, disputes, dismissals, etc., which arise in the work places and undertakings of the railways, come within the scope and competence of the local Works Councils. When however similar questions arise, which concern more than one local unit, the competent body is the District Works Council. Finally, the Central Works Council represents the wishes of the whole body of wage-earners *vis-à-vis* the Central Railway Administration.

If a dispute, or any other matter requiring settlement, occurs in a work place, the local Works Council must first seek to reach an agreement with the local representations of the Railway Administration; failing an agreement it can appeal to its District Works Council, which will then take the matter up with the District Board of Management.

If the matter is one which lies outside the competence of the

---

[1] Under State ownership and management there was no Control Board for the railways, and therefore no possibility of the workers securing representation in this form. The Central Works Council has put forward a claim to be represented on the new international Administrative Board of the Railways on the ground that this constitutes a Control Board, but this claim has been rejected.

Conciliation Board the decision of the Directorate is final, even though no agreement is arrived at with the District Works Council. In other cases the District Works Council can appeal to the District Railway Conciliation Board and, except when the Board and the District Works Council are agreed that the matter lies outside the competence of the local Works Council, the latter can also appeal direct to the Conciliation Board.[1] The Central Works Council, besides dealing with all questions which affect the interests of the workers in the railway system as a whole, can deal with disputes which arise between the District Works Councils and the District Boards of Management and are referred to it either by the Minister of Transport or the District Councils themselves. Here again, in those matters which do not come within the competence of the Conciliation Board,[2] the decision of the Railway Authority, in this case the Minister of Transport, is final. In other cases, appeal can be made to the Central Conciliation Board for the Railways. The Conciliation Boards, whether local or central, can only give decisions binding on both parties in regard to disputes over those sections of the Works Councils Act, where this power is given them by the Act. Otherwise the decisions have only the force of an award which the Railway Administration could, if it thought fit, refuse to accept. In certain cases appeal can also be made to the Federal Economic Council.

From the above survey of the organisation of the Works Councils in the Federal Railways it can be seen that, though three types of Works Councils have been set up, appeals cannot be pushed through from the local Councils to the Central Council. The District Works Councils can take up disputes of the local Works Councils, but if their representations to the District Board of Management prove ineffectual, they are powerless to lay the matter before the Central Works Council, but must

[1] By the *Schlichtungsordnung* of October 30, 1923, disputes arising out of the engagement or dismissal of individual workers; the election and procedure of Works Councils; the dissolution of Works Councils; and certain other matters, are dealt with in the German railways by special expert Railway Boards.

[2] These are, broadly, matters of a purely administrative character and disputes arising out of the functions of the Works Councils, for which no appeal to a Conciliation Board is provided by the Works Councils Act.

abide by the decision of the Board. The District Councils can only submit, officially, to the Central Works Councils disputes, which relate to the workers in general in their district or which cover a wider area than a single local work place. In practice, a good many individual disputes are put up informally to the Central Works Council and are settled by it by personal interview with the heads of the different departments in the Ministry of Transport.

This organisation has by no means remained merely upon paper: the Works Councils have, on the contrary, played an active and important part in the life of the railways and have caused changes in the status of the workers of no inconsiderable order. One factor differentiating the railway workers from those in most other industries must not be overlooked. The wages of the whole body of workers in the railways have been governed, since the War, by a single Collective Agreement. Thus the possibility was completely excluded of a participation of the Works Councils in questions of general wage policy; they have retained a certain importance for the local adaptation of piecework rates, but have not otherwise been concerned with the regulation of wage conditions. Further, before the War the Trade Union organisation of workers in State undertakings was legally prohibited, and the removal of that prohibition after the Revolution brought with it an enormous accession of strength to the railwaymen's Trade Unions. Although a certain number of isolated strikes took place without the sanction of the Trade Union headquarters, on the whole discipline was preserved to a very remarkable extent and it is noteworthy that no general strike in the railways has occurred since the War.

The railway Unions have throughout kept in very close touch with the Works Councils and have been successful in their aim of incorporating them completely into their organisation and using them merely as local organs of the Unions for the purpose of carrying out the functions allotted to them by the Works Councils Act.

At first there was a certain amount of inevitable friction due, partly, to the unwillingness of the higher railway officials to recognise that the existence of the Works Councils involved a restriction in some directions of their previously unfettered right to determine labour conditions and, partly, because the Works Councils endeavoured to put the widest possible interpretation on the rights granted to them by the Act. At present the relations between the Central Works Council and the Railway Administration appear to be good, but those between the local Councils and the local railway officials still leave much to be desired on both sides.

The local Works Councils are concerned with the multifarious incidents arising out of the daily working life of the individual railwayman. To them come, for instance, complaints of unfair treatment or discrimination, especially as to the allocation of work and of shifts between the different men. They have to investigate dismissals and to ascertain whether the agreed principles, laid down for the selection of men to be dismissed when the staff is being reduced, have been carried out. They have, further, to supervise the execution of the Collective Wage Agreement and its application in detail to those employed in their work place. Of special importance in the case of the railways is the duty of the Works Councils to strive to prevent accidents to the railway personnel. Besides these and other tasks, it is continually being impressed upon them by the Trade Union officials and their comrades in the District Councils and the Central Council, that it is incumbent on them to work for the greater efficiency, both technical and financial, of the railways, for example, by encouraging and supervising the collection of scrap material, etc.

In order that they may have the necessary facilities for carrying out their duties, one member in each local Works Council above a certain size is allowed a certain amount of time off during working-hours. In Works Councils with seven members nine hours free time are allowed each week, in those with eight to nine members 24 hours are allowed, in those with 10 to 12 members 36 hours, and in Councils with more than 12 members, 48 hours free of work are allowed in each week. In the case of all other members of the Works Councils, leave of absence from work is only granted if special urgency and necessity can be proved.

It has been stated above that the District Works Councils, besides acting as supervisory and appeal bodies to the local Councils, have independent functions, in that they are competent to deal with matters which extend beyond the sphere of a single work place. In practice, the District Works Councils have been inundated, hitherto, to so great an extent by complaints sent up to them by the local Councils that they have hardly been able to pay much attention to their own separate functions. The District Works Council meets in full four times in the year, but its current business is conducted by two members who are entirely freed from their ordinary work. These two members are selected by the Council, and live at the headquarters of the District Administration.

The Central Works Council, which is in very close touch with the headquarters of the railwaymen's Union in Berlin, constitutes a sort of General Staff for the whole of the Works Councils. Four of its members are freed from railway work and live in Berlin, receiving their normal wages plus an allowance to cover extra cost of living. Each man has under his charge certain sections of the work and functions of the Councils.[1]

The Central Works Council holds a full meeting four times in the year lasting two days, to which the remaining 21 members come from all parts of Germany. One day is devoted to a discussion of the events of the last three months and to the agreement of general lines of policy. The whole of the second day is taken up with the Quarterly Report given by the Railway Administration in accordance with the provisions of the Works Councils Act. This Report is given in sections by the principal experts in the various departments of the Ministry of Transport. Thus the expert from the Traffic Department describes the general transport conditions during the past quarter and explains why, perhaps, there has been an abnormal movement of goods from east to west, due, it may be, to transit trade from Czecho-Slovakia. He thus naturally has something to say about the economic conditions governing such movements. The repre-

[1] A scheme for the allocation of duties between the four members of the Executive Committee of the Central Works Council for the German Railways, elected for the year 1924–1925, will be found in Appendix VII.

sentative of the Finance Department sets out the earnings of the railways and the various forces, favourable and unfavourable, which have been at work. The controller of personnel shows the changes in the numbers employed and expresses an opinion on employment prospects in the near future. The engineering expert deals with the state of equipment of the railways and with various technical matters. Another expert will describe the progress of the organisation for utilising scrap, at the same time taking the opportunity to impress on his listeners that the success of the organisation depends upon the care and interest of the individual worker and, therefore, comes largely under the influence of the local Works Councils. In all cases the members present have the right of putting questions and elucidating points which may not be clear or which do not conform to their own practical experience. An animated discussion sometimes takes place lasting for a considerable time. The value of such a survey of the economic and technical conditions governing the progress of a great undertaking, in broadening the outlook and stimulating the interests of those to whom it is given, need hardly be stressed.

The Central Works Council has the very important and responsible task of agreeing upon the works rules with the Federal Ministers of Railways. Once the *Arbeitsordnung* is approved it becomes a Works Agreement in the technical sense of the term, and is legally binding on both parties. In 1922 new working rules for the whole of the railway system were thus agreed, after protracted negotiations, and it was claimed in the introduction to an annotated edition of the rules issued by the German railwaymen's Union, that the final form of the rules was a great improvement, from the point of view of the men, on the first draft prepared by the Minister of Railways. Before the passing of the Works Councils Act the employees would have had no say whatever in the determination of these rules, which govern absolutely the conditions under which they carry out their work. The limitation of the old autocratic power of the management is, moreover, enhanced by the fact that, if no agreement is reached, appeal can be made to the Central Conciliation Board, whose decision is final and binding in regard to a dispute over works rules

Partly, because the railways have always been administered as a public corporation and, partly, because the service which they render to the community is so very obvious and direct, the Works Councils have in this industry laid special and, to a real extent, successful emphasis on the importance of reducing costs and increasing the efficiency of service. Here, more than elsewhere, the Works Councils have given attention to the economic functions of their office and have left to the Trade Unions the task of disputing over the allocation of the proceeds of the industry. The Dawes Scheme, involving as it does enormously heavy financial burdens on the German railways on Reparation account, has stimulated this constructive attitude of the Councils because they have realised that surpluses must be obtained. They are sufficiently far-sighted to appreciate that one of the most important elements of costs is the wages of labour and that the only hope of preventing an attack on wages is to produce economies in other directions and to increase working efficiency.

This activity on the part of the Works Councils has frequently received recognition and commendation in the Quarterly Reports of the management.[1] The complaint is, however, made on the workers' side that the functions of the Central Works Council are too narrowly circumscribed by the management, with the result that both the Central and the District Councils are unable to exercise sufficient control and influence over the operations of the individual Councils.

Lastly, a factor of great importance in the operation of the Works Council system in the railways is the comparative continuity in the personnel, especially of the District and Central Works Councils.[2] The same men tend to be elected year after year and, on the whole, technical and other qualifications play a more important rôle in their selection than demagogic oratory. Thus a good class of man tends to serve on these bodies and is able to take advantage of the experience gained in successive years of office.

It should be noted that the rights under the Works Councils

[1] Seidel in *Die sozialen Probleme des Betriebes*, p. 131.
[2] *Ibid.* p. 130.

Act only refer to the wage-earners, who number less than half the total number of employees of the railways. The officials, numbering more than half a million, are in a different category altogether. It is true that they are allowed to elect Officials' Councils, but the powers of these bodies are very limited; in particular, they are not entitled to appeal to any form of Conciliation Board in the event of a dispute with the management of the railways. This is a serious limitation of the rights of a very large class of employees, and one which in the long run will probably not be able to be maintained in its entirety.[1]

WORKS COUNCILS IN MUNICIPAL UNDERTAKINGS

During the years of revolutionary ferment and unrest after the War, there were no types of undertakings which suffered more from the unruliness of their employees than the municipal undertakings. With the passing of the Works Councils Act in February 1920, these employees found themselves able to take advantage of the existence of statutory representative bodies with special privileges and considerable powers. In very many cases they made use of their powers and privileges to reduce the undertakings, in which they were working, to a condition of financial ruin coupled with a completely disorganised and unsatisfactory service to the public.

Those who were in charge of these undertakings were in a specially weak position in dealing with this situation, because they consisted to a large extent of socialist Town Councillors, who were powerless to resist the pretensions of their employees. The weaker the administrative body, the more extreme were the demands of the workers, who resisted all attempts at imposing discipline upon them. They held out, often with success, for abnormally high wages; they refused to allow any reduction in personnel, however excessive might be the numbers employed; and they laid down their own conditions of work, with small regard for either the convenience of the public or the efficiency of the undertaking.

Realising the importance of such essential services as gas,

[1] Cf. Potthoff in *Arbeitsrecht*, January 1925.

electricity, water, tramways, etc., the Communists concentrated their attention on them for political motives, hoping by their control of these services to acquire a strangle-hold on the community. The practical consequences of their agitation were, however, to strengthen the syndicalist tendencies of the workers, who ignored all wider conceptions and merely sought to use their power to exploit the rest of the public as far as possible.

The radical Works Councils, who were the actual leaders of the employees in each municipal establishment, could never have acquired such a dominant influence had it not been for the weakness of the Trade Union movement, which before the War had been forbidden in State and municipal services. Although Unions had come into existence after the War, they had not had time to become strong and their members were still untrained in any spirit of Trade Union discipline and solidarity. The employees in many cases had their heads turned by the Revolution; they felt that they had acquired the real power and they intended to allow no one to restrict them in their exercise of it. When the Unions tried to curb their excesses, they replied that the Works Councils were now the controllers of production and that they recognised no responsibility to the Trade Unions.

Thus it was in socialised undertakings, run directly by the community, that the worst abuses of the Works Councils were manifested. That similar conditions did not prevail in the railways was due, partly, to the greater power of the Trade Unions; partly, to the fact that the railways, not being concentrated locally in the same degree, the opportunity for communist agitation was much less; and partly, to the powerful influence of the officials who stood out for order and discipline.

In the course of time the Socialists lost their seats on the Town Councils; many municipal services were transformed into "mixed" undertakings, the capital of which was owned by the municipality, while the management was in the hands of a company; the influence of the Communists waned; and the Trade Unions extended their control and restored order in their ranks. Thus the abuses were removed and the Works Councils were forced back into a subordinate instead of a dominating position.

The history of the movement in municipal undertakings is instructive, because it demonstrates the syndicalist danger inherent in the Works Council type of representation, when not controlled by an independent management, as well as held in check and subjected to a strong and efficient Trade Union organisation. It also shows that the mere fact of working for a public instead of a private employer is not necessarily sufficient to secure the loyal co-operation of the employees in working for the efficient conduct of an undertaking.

WORKS COUNCILS IN VERTICAL COMBINES

The Works Councils Act provides for the formation of a Central Works Council under certain strictly defined conditions; namely, where a number of establishments, under the same ownership and of a similar type or forming part of the same economic process, are located in the same commune or in neighbouring, economically inter-dependent, communes. Where these conditions hold good, e.g. in the case of Krupps at Essen, a Central Works Council may be constituted, which consists of members of the Works Councils of the individual units, elected, not by the whole body of employees, but by the Works Councillors in each establishment. In the case of communal undertakings, Central Works Councils may be formed even where the undertakings are distinct in character, such as gas and water works, labour exchanges, slaughter-houses, hospitals, etc. But in State and Federal undertakings this is not permitted unless they belong to the same branch of the public service. The functions of such Central Works Councils are to deal with the broader questions of policy affecting all the establishments alike, while the individual Councils are restricted to matters peculiar to their establishment. Any one of the individual Councils may decline to elect representatives to the Central Works Councils and thereby preserve the whole of its freedom of action. But, if it decides to come in, it must accept without discussion agreements negotiated by the Central Works Council, in so far as they are of general application. Considerable use has been made in practice of the right to form these bodies. In the case of a number of public or semi-public undertakings, such as the Post

Office, the State mines, the railways, etc., where the organisation of Works Councils is regulated by administrative order, provision is made for the formation of Central Works Councils which play an important and responsible rôle in the undertakings in question.

In all the above instances the Central Works Councils referred to are statutory bodies, having the same rights and duties in their respective spheres of action as ordinary Works Councils.

Of greater interest, however, for the evolution of the Works Council type of labour representation, are the Central Works Councils which have been formed in many of the great vertical combines, whose plants are dispersed in more than one part of Germany, and which represent one of the principal developments of large-scale industrial organisation in Germany since the War. This type of Central Works Council is sharply distinguished from the statutory bodies described above, owing to the fact that it represents an organisation on a purely voluntary basis, not contemplated in any way by the Works Councils Act. This has the consequence that these *Konzernbetriebsräte*, as they are called, have not the rights and duties of the ordinary Works Councils. Their members are not entitled to be compensated for any working-time lost in the exercise of functions *quâ* delegates to the Central Works Council; the management is not liable for any expenses incurred with this body; nor can urgency be claimed in justification of the holding of a meeting in working-hours. The management would also be within its legal rights in refusing to recognise the existence of such a body or to enter into negotiations with it. Where the management is unwilling to meet such a Central Works Council and where the organised strength of the workers is insufficient to compel him to do so, the existence of a Central Works Council of this type is precarious and its members can do little except come together from time to time to exchange information; its practical importance is therefore small and its overriding authority is not likely to be recognised by the individual Councils. The most it is probably able to do is, in times of unrest, to extend a strike movement from one branch of the undertaking to others.[1] On the other hand a Central

[1] Winschuh, *Betriebsrat oder Gewerkschaft*, 1922, p. 86.

Works Council, which is recognised by the management, may be a real force and exercise a considerable influence over the separate Works Councils. This is not always without its advantages for the management, which finds a responsible and often an able and moderate body to negotiate with; and it fits in well with the centralised organisation of the whole undertaking.

In practice the formation of *Konzernbetriebsräte* and their finance have inevitably fallen into the hands of the Trade Unions, which alone have the funds necessary to enable the former to function. Reference has been made elsewhere[1] to the anxiety of the Unions lest the evolution of the Works Councils might lead to the emergence of a rival organisation of labour interests, with the result that the power and influence of the former would be weakened. This danger would seem to be present, to a special degree, in the grouping of the Works Councils within a vertical combine and explains the distrustful and unhelpful attitude of the Unions in certain cases. But, as a rule, when the pressure of events has been too strong and the opposition of the Union has been overborne, it has endeavoured, generally with success, to avert possible danger by taking over the organisation and finance of the Central Works Council.

A further difficulty in the way of effective co-operation arises from the fact that most vertical combines include workers belonging to a considerable number of crafts and, therefore, to different Trade Unions. It is no easy matter to secure unity of policy and agreement as to financial contributions, etc., amongst the separate Unions.

The organisation of *Konzernbetriebsräte* has been specially successful in the metal and engineering industries, partly, because the Union there is organised on an Industrial not on a Craft basis; partly, because vertical combines are most frequent in these industries; and partly, owing to the initiative and driving power of the leaders of the Metal Workers' Union, who have throughout laid great stress on the value and importance of the work to be accomplished by the Councils. In December 1924 a Conference was held of representatives from the Metal Workers' Union and from seventeen vertical combines in the metal

[1] See above, pp. 41–2.

industries, at which problems such as the relations between manual workers and salaried employees, the position of Works Councillors on the Control Boards of companies, etc., were discussed and views and experiences interchanged. The minutes of this and similar Conferences; the annual reports of the Central Works Council of the Siemens Combine; and other evidence, show that there is at least a nucleus of men in these large works who take their duties as Works Councillors seriously and do not regard themselves merely as a channel for the transmission of complaints to the employer.

The chief driving force behind the grouping and association of Works Councils in vertical combines is the general desire of the best brains among the workers to extend their organisation *pari passu* with that of the employers and to gain, as far as possible, a general survey of the whole prospects and economic conditions of the great undertakings in which so many of their fellows are employed. It is felt, in particular, that those who are elected to sit on the Control Boards of these companies are not in a position to understand the business transacted before them or to criticise intelligently, unless they have been in touch with Works Councillors in the various works throughout the country. Further, for the ordinary business of the Works Councils, it is often found desirable to be able to compare notes and perhaps to use concessions granted in one works as a lever for their extension to the others, thus tending to level up conditions in the different branches of the undertaking. A Central Works Council is also sometimes in a position to bring pressure to bear on the central management of the whole concern to remedy grievances in the individual works, the existence of which would otherwise certainly not have come to its notice.

A report of a Conference of the Works Councils of the Buderus Combine in 1922 states that:

The representatives from the different works agreed unanimously that a way must be found to link together the various Works Councils. The necessity of this has become apparent, owing to the increasing evidence from the individual works of the combine that the whole undertaking is highly centralised and that the operations of the individual works are controlled and determined by a central office. The discussion amongst the representatives afforded a picture of the character of the whole undertaking and of its position in the industry. It then became possible for the different Works Councils to see clearly their special tasks in the individual Works, and those who took part in the Conference separated with the conviction that for the first time it has been possible through this discussion to obtain a true appreciation of their duties as Works Councillors.[1]

Of a similar Conference in the Siemens Combine it was stated that:

Thereby it was possible to obtain a clear view of the whole welfare institutions of the undertaking; to gain a proper understanding of the balance sheet and quarterly report; and to find the basis for a clear and sober appreciation of the economic problems to which a giant business of this type gives rise.[2]

Trade Union leaders have informed the writer that the convocation of delegates from the Works Councils of these big combines has brought to light men of first-class ability, who had not previously taken any distinctive part in the Trade Union movement, but who had a real understanding for and keen interest in the economic conditions of the undertaking in which they were employed. This interest the Unions have sought to foster by holding special advanced courses of instruction for members of the *Konzernbetriebsräte* and, in particular, for those with seats on the Control Boards of the constituent companies. By such means it is hoped to build up a nucleus of trained minds, who will have had at least some first-hand knowledge of industrial management and organisation and who will supply a need, the existence of which has only lately become fully apparent to the leaders of the labour movement in Germany.

---

[1] *Betriebsrätezeitschrift...der Metallindustrie*, April 15, 1922, pp. 297–8.
[2] *Ibid.* p. 298.

CHAPTER VI

Summary and Conclusions

THE ORIGINS OF THE WORKS COUNCILS

It is impossible to appreciate justly the history of the Works Councils during the last five years except in the light of the peculiar circumstances in which they came into being.

In structure and to a large extent in functions they evolved directly out of the old voluntary factory committees, which had a precarious and unimportant existence before the War, but which, during the War, were made compulsory in all munition and other war establishments, as part of the price paid by the Government for the acquiescence of organised labour in the passing of the Auxiliary Service Act of 1916. But both in scope and in the extent of their rights and, above all, in their practical working, they were vitally influenced by the revolutionary wind which blew over Europe from the East. The Councils system of Soviet Russia acquired a hold over the imagination of the masses, which was more formidable than that of any other idea since Karl Marx exploded "Bourgeois Economics" in *Das Kapital*, and popularised the doctrines of revolutionary socialism. Only a very few of the leaders of the left wing of the German labour movement understood the political uses to which the Councils system had been put in Russia, and they were so hopelessly divided, as to the methods of its application to German conditions, that there was lacking in Germany any such compact body of men, directed by a leader of genius, as had uprooted the old order of things in Russia and produced a Dictatorship of the Proletariat. To the German masses, however, the workers' councils stood for the democratisation of the industrial system and the attainment, in the economic sphere, of the same rights of self-government and self-determination as they thought they had achieved by the Revolution of 1918 in the political sphere. For a short time it appeared as though they had been successful in this, when the Councils system was "anchored" in the Constitution of Weimar by Article 165. But when it came to the practical working out of the basic and, to the individual workers, the most important part of the structure—the Works Councils, they found that the bulk of the political leaders of labour were in league with the employers to prevent any too wide extension of powers to these Councils. The outcome of the prolonged parliamentary struggle which resulted was that the Works Councils, both in composition and functions, mainly perpetuated the old factory committees; moreover, permanent organs of control were set over them in the guise of the Conciliation Boards, which likewise had been part of the machinery set up by the war-time Auxiliary Service Act. The greatest care was taken to prevent the Councils from encroaching on the sphere of operations of the Trade Unions; they were not allowed to have funds of their own and absolute priority was given to Collective Agreements, thus largely shutting out the Councils from the all-important field of wages and hours of work.

There are, however, also in the Works Councils Act the germs of certain constructive ideas deriving their origin from that new conception of economic democracy which has received so decisive an impulse from the great Russian experiment—an impulse which, in the next hundred years, may well have as vitalising an effect on the development of economic organisation in the western world, as the French Revolution had on the growth of political institutions in the nineteenth century.

THE WORKS COUNCILS AND THE
TRADE UNION MOVEMENT

When the German Works Council Act first made its appearance on the statute book, many of the German workers saw in it a more effective means of giving effect to their economic hopes and aspirations than the Trade Unions, the leaders of which had become discredited owing to the imputation of time-serving to which their co-operation with the Government during the War had laid them open.

The political Revolution of October 1918, paralleled as it was by the much more complete transformation of society in Russia, had resulted in the widespread expectation of a new economic status for labour through the dethronement of the individual capitalist from his position of uncontrolled autocracy.

The startlingly sudden abolition of the monarchy throughout Germany and its replacement by a democratic republican State, had given the masses an enormous self-confidence and belief in their own capacity to govern, and it is not surprising that this was carried over into the economic sphere. The Trade Unions, with their cautious policy, their centralised bureaucratic organisation and their attitude of holding the sole monopoly of leadership of the workers, appeared to many to be a part of the old machinery of social government, adapted to the State as it used to be, but requiring fundamental reconstruction under the new social conditions. The Works Councils, endowed with the glamour lent to them by their association in the popular mind with the success of the Russian workers, came on the scene just at the right moment to crystallise the impatience and discontent of a section of labour into a definite form.

The progress of inflation and the legal sanction given to Collective Agreements prevented any widespread secession from the Trade Unions, but the left wing of the socialist Unions, in conjunction with the Communists, made strenuous endeavours to develop the Works Councils into a separate organisation of labour, only co-operating with the Trade Unions when it was convenient to them and regarding themselves as the spearhead of the proletarian assault on capitalist supremacy. The struggle for the control of the Councils was decided in principle at the National Congress of Works Councils held in Berlin in October 1920, when the disciplined forces of the Trade Unions overcame the enthusiasm of their ardent but unorganised opponents, with the result that the Works Councils were declared to be subordinated to the Trade Unions. From then onwards the Unions secured a control over the Works Councils which, though never complete and sometimes gravely imperilled, has been the dominant factor in the development of the Councils. The enduring dissensions between the right and left wings of the labour movement in Germany have contributed more than anything else to weaken the effective power of the Trade Unions and to bring about the *débâcle* of 1924. Even in the absence of the

Works Councils, these dissensions would have remained, but there can be no doubt that the existence of the Councils provided the opposition to the official labour movement with what it stood most in need of—a form of organisation distinct from that of the Unions. On the one side, this has reacted on the Trade Unions by lessening their control over the forces of labour and giving rise to disharmony and mutual recrimination within their ranks. On the other side, the Councils have often lost through their own actions the backing of the Unions and have exposed themselves to the danger, which to a considerable extent materialised in 1924, of being devoured piecemeal by the employers. Further, the short-sighted exploitation by some of the Councils of their power, in the first two or three years, consolidated the opposition of the employers to their pretensions and helped to bring the whole institution into discredit. The danger to the Trade Unions was perhaps at its greatest in 1924, when in a few months their membership had declined by 40 per cent., and when the employers took advantage of the situation to substitute, as far as possible, agreements with the individual Councils for Collective Agreements between the Trade Unions and Employers' Associations. That the employers should have had comparatively little success, at a time when everything seemed to be in their favour, is a testimony to the reality of the control of the Unions over the Councils and to the effective propaganda carried on by means of newspapers, Trade Union schools and personal contact between the Works Councillors and Trade Union officials.

The decisive factor in the victory of the Unions, apart from the discipline of the majority of Trade Unionists and their natural reaction to the bitter attacks of the extremists, has been the failure of their opponents to create anything in the nature of a widespread regional organisation of Works Councils. The wisdom of the provision of the Works Councils Act, refusing to the Councils the right to raise funds on their own account, has become apparent, for it is lack of money which has been chiefly responsible for the breakdown of repeated attempts to build up an independent system of Works Councils linked together by some permanent centralised machinery. The Trade Unions have been supported in this matter by the employers and by the Conciliation Boards, both of which have opposed the development of an extra-legal organisation of Works Councils.

Although the extremists have found the Works Councils a useful tool in their struggle either to capture or destroy the Trade Unions, the latter have in turn been able to make use of the Councils in many cases as valuable *points d'appui* against the employers. The Councils have acted in a large measure as the agents and representatives of the Unions: they have supervised the execution of Collective Agreements, conducted propaganda amongst the employees on behalf of their Unions and, in general, supported their policy within the works. As a result of the institution of Works Assemblies, the officials of the Unions have been brought into closer and more direct touch with the body of workers and have been enabled to explain their policies and defend their actions against attacks. It is undeniable that, especially in the early stages, there was a certain measure of jealousy and rivalry between the Works Councils and the socialist Trade Unions, which resulted in a lack of co-operation that was detrimental to both organisations, but this has been much less marked in recent years.

In general, the history of the last six years has shown that there is no place in labour organisation for a system of Works Councils acting independently of and as an alternative to Trade Unions. In the absence of a strong and compact Trade Union organisation, the Works Councils would either be reduced to complete impotence or would fall victims to syndicalism in one or other of its forms.

The recognition of the necessary subordination of the Works Councils to the Trade Unions does not preclude the possibility that the former may react on the latter to an important extent. There is evidence that the Councils are influencing the Trade Union movement in three main directions: (1) the structure of the Unions; (2) the policy of the Unions; (3) the leadership of the labour movement.

(1) The Works Councils are essentially an inter-Union type of organisation, embracing not merely wage-earning but also salaried employees, and comprising every kind of Union,

216

whether of Socialist, "Christian", "Hirsch-Duncker", Syndicalist or other persuasions.

On the one hand, this has strengthened the prevailing tendency, which is specially strong among the socialist Unions, in
favour of the industrial as opposed to the craft Union; while on the
other hand, the Councils have brought into close contact with one
another men with very varied industrial status and experience
and, in particular, have provided a common meeting ground for
members of the different groups of Unions. Co-operation between different sections of labour has been hindered in the past
by the excessive preoccupation with political considerations and
by mutual rivalry and suspicion. At present any substantial
unity within the ranks of German labour is not within sight,
but the Works Councils (which are essentially industrial bodies,
much though they were involved in politics during their early
years for special historical reasons) are accomplishing something
in the direction of greater unity and solidarity, through their
practical work in a field where there is much less scope for
divergent opinions than in the wider sphere of labour
politics.

(2) The whole outlook and policy of the Trade Unions have
been based on the continuous and never ending struggle with the
employers over the division of the product of industry and over
the conditions of employment. Their organisation is a fighting
organisation and the mentality of their leaders has been con-
ditioned by this fact. The Works Councils represent in part a
different principle, for they are representatives of the interests,
not merely of the workers *quâ* employees, but also of one of the
great factors of production. The Works Councils have already
contributed much to the Trade Unions in the way of a new outlook on the position and functions of labour in the economic life
of the community. Trade Union Congresses since the War have
given evidence of a more constructive spirit than formerly and
of a much greater attention to fundamental economic problems.
It would be absurd to attribute this wholly to the Works Councils, but there can be no doubt that their experiences, and the
relations which have been formed between Union officials and
Works Councillors, have directed the attention of the Unions

towards problems of production, which previously they had neglected in their exclusive preoccupation with distribution.

(8) The problem of leadership is a dual one, for it involves the capacity to be led as well as the capacity to lead. Since the passing of the Works Councils Act a very large number of employees have served for a period on the Councils and have been brought into touch with industrial relations. They may be expected to bring a greater comprehension to Trade Union problems than hitherto and, at the same time, by their influence in the individual establishments, to permeate the mass of the workers with Trade Union sentiments and ideals. This is a slow process, however, and by no means a uniform one, for a section of Works Councillors is hostile to the existing Unions and to those in control of them. Of more immediate importance is the effect of the Councils in evolving a new class of labour leader of a type distinct from the Trade Union official.

The ever increasing centralisation of the Unions has developed a class of bureaucratic officials, which is out of touch and, to some extent, out of sympathy, with the rank and file. The Works Councillor is much better placed so far as contact with his fellows is concerned and can more readily appreciate their point of view and requirements. There is room in the labour movement for both types of representation and the Councils, working in harmony with the Unions, can supply a direct personal relationship with the workers, in which the Unions are deficient. The Works Councils Act has given a considerable stimulus to working-class education of a kind that previously had not been attempted. Works Councils schools and newspapers have enlarged the vision of those who have attended them, while even the Works Councillor who has not taken advantage of the educational facilities provided, has yet acquired, during his term of office, a considerable amount of practical experience of negotiation with the employer—experience which hitherto has been the monopoly of the Trade Union official. Moreover, the Works Councillor gains an insight, however faulty and imperfect it may be, into questions of management, such as costings, marketing, etc., which lie outside the view of the Trade Union official as such.

The development of this new class of leader cannot leave the Trade Unions unaffected. Men can now come to the fore who would not have been attracted by the career of a Union official, but who find scope in the Works Councils for abilities which otherwise would not have been discovered. These men, in time, tend to demand also a voice in Trade Union policies and to seek to be associated with the Unions in important negotiations with the employers. Hitherto, the Unions have resisted such pretensions as far as possible, but it is probable that in the future they will increasingly realise both the necessity and the desirability of a closer co-operation with the Councils. It is not impossible that, ultimately, the Works Councils may help to provide a remedy for one of the chief economic defects of Trade Union policy—the excessive rigidity of Collective Agreements—and may make possible a greater elasticity and differentiation in the application of general standards to particular cases.

THE WORKS COUNCILS AND INDUSTRIAL RELATIONS

The history of the relations between the Works Councils and the employers since 1920 is a chequered one.

In 1920 the passing of the Works Councils Act coincided with a period of great social unrest in Germany. The tide of revolutionary unrest was, it is true, already on the wane, but it still had a good deal of strength. In Berlin and in the Ruhr district, in particular, revolutionary organisations of the Works Councils were set up which defied the Trade Unions and, disregarding their advice, conducted a campaign against the employers in which they went far beyond any legal authority they possessed. Although, taking Germany as a whole, these revolutionary Works Councils were, even in 1920, in the minority, they were mainly concentrated in a few areas where their subversive activities attracted a disproportionate amount of attention. Hence, at the outset, the Works Councils as a whole seemed to be heavily tarred with the revolutionary brush and the attitude of the employers towards the institution in general was profoundly influenced by this circumstance.

The employers, finding themselves on the defensive, banded together to resist encroachments on their authority which were not sanctioned by the Act, but they often went further and sought to restrict unduly the legal rights of the Councils by an excessively narrow interpretation of its legal provisions. This gave rise to much friction and to embittered disputes. Moreover, at first there was a great deal of legitimate ground for conflicts of opinion in regard to the precise meaning of the Act. The tribunals responsible for settling disputes—the Conciliation Boards —were themselves new to the work; they were not well adapted to the task of giving decisions on purely legal issues; and they were flooded with an enormous number of appeals. As there was no central court responsible for giving definite rulings, divergent awards were the rule rather than the exception and, for a time, confusion reigned supreme. As neither side knew beforehand what the verdict on a particular case would be, it was generally worth while to appeal rather than to come to an accommodation. Thus the initial result of the coming into force of the Works Councils Act seemed to have been that occasions for dispute were greatly multiplied and that the Councils were supplying an added irritant to industrial relations.

There is, however, another side to the picture: the times were turbulent for many reasons which had nothing to do with the Works Councils as such, although, being ready to the hand of the extremists, they came to play an important part in the disorders. But over a large area of the country and, to a considerable extent, even in the most disturbed districts, many of the Councils were in the hands of experienced Trade Unionists, moderate men, who used their influence to restrain the wilder spirits. Against the vast amount of working-time lost in excited talk and discussion, must be set the value of the Councils as safety-valves for blowing off emotions which often would have been far more dangerous if bottled up. The Works Councils had at least the advantage of a definite procedure and certain assigned duties. This would not have been the case with the *ad hoc* bodies, which would certainly have been set up in the absence of the Councils and which would have had much less sense of responsibility. Finally, in spite of the difficulties under which the Conciliation Boards laboured, they undoubtedly did valuable work in their rôle as guardians of the interests of the community. They refused to countenance gross abuses on the part of the Works Councils, and the employer who was able to prove such abuses could always secure (but often only after considerable delay) the dissolution of the offending Council.

During the two following years, 1921 and 1922, the Works Councils were settling down to the exercise of their functions under more favourable conditions than in 1920. The worst of the revolutionary danger was over; the German workman had had his fill of disturbances and only asked to be left alone to get on with his work. The new elections in the spring of 1921 saw the disappearance of many of the agitators and extremists from the Councils and their replacement by the older and more responsible employees. The Works Councils, aided by the advice of the Trade Union officials and of the Factory Inspectors, were becoming more familiar with their duties and, in every area, rulings had been given by the Conciliation Boards, which threw light on the many controversial issues raised by the Act. Above all, a greater sense of responsibility was growing up amongst the Works Councillors, many of whom did their utmost to assist the employers in maintaining order and discipline in the works.

This evolution was naturally accompanied by an improvement in the relations between the Councils and the employers as a whole, which were further affected by the very active state of trade. Up to a point the Works Councils fell into the same category as welfare schemes, which always flourish in times of booming trade, when the employer is relatively indifferent to overhead costs and when he is anxious to keep his men contented and prevent them from being enticed away by his competitors. Thus employers often found it wiser to adopt a conciliatory attitude over such matters as the expenses of the Councils, release of their members from productive work, etc., which diminished the opportunities for friction.

The reaction of the employers towards the activities of the Councils varied widely in different parts of Germany and in different types of undertaking during this period. In general, the Councils were most disliked and most firmly opposed in

221

the east of Germany, where industry has long been highly individualistic, and in Berlin, where communism was specially strong. In the west of Germany employers were accustomed to negotiating with Trade Unions and were more willing to co-operate with the Works Councils, in so far as the latter were not controlled by extremists, out for war at any price. Further, relations tended to be better in the very large undertakings and also in those in which the quantity of capital per head of employees was very large.

During this period, in which the Works Councils were relatively active and powerful, the employers may be divided into three categories so far as their practical policy in relation to the Councils was concerned. Firstly, there were employers who, either on principle or in order to avoid trouble, willingly recognised the Councils as the statutory representatives of their employees. They invited the co-operation of the Councils in many matters both large and small; they made considerable concessions wherever these could be granted without interfering with the efficiency of management; and they endeavoured to strengthen the prestige of the Councils in order to use them as a mediating influence in the works. A second section of employers resented bitterly the existence of the Works Councils and lived in a state of continuous conflict with them. A third section made a show of accepting the Councils, but did their utmost to paralyse their activities; sometimes by various forms of inducements ranging from open bribery to the granting of special privileges and hints of favour to come; sometimes by overloading them with duties, especially in the nature of welfare work, which left them no time for other activities; and sometimes by deliberately undermining their influence among the employees.

There can be no doubt that, during this period, Works Councils were a troublesome thorn in the side of many employers. Disputes arose continually over the most trivial issues. Works Assemblies would then be convened, where inflammatory speeches were made and the whole of the employees brought to a state of excitement and anger with the employer. Even where this did not actually lead to a strike, it created an atmosphere of unrest, which was very detrimental to the efficiency of working and the Works Councils were at times able to organise a sort of passive resistance to decisions of the employer that was very difficult to overcome. Where employers were most hardly hit, however, was through the amount of their time taken up, both by discussion with the Councils and by their enforced attendance at meetings of the Conciliation Boards, to which the Councils appealed on every possible occasion. One result of this, particularly in the larger works, was that it was found necessary to set up special labour departments, whose whole business it was to control and supervise the labour policy of the undertaking and to represent the management in all questions to do with the Works Councils. These departments were greatly resented by the Councils, partly, because they diminished their opportunities of putting personal pressure on the actual heads of the undertakings and partly, because, being staffed for the most part by legal experts, they were able to outmanœuvre the Councils on many occasions and to defeat their appeals to the Conciliation Boards.

The year 1923 was a decided turning point in the development of the Works Councils. For the first time an appreciable halt was called to the apparent prosperity of industry and commerce, which had ruled since the War. The occupation of the Ruhr occasioned serious difficulties in regard to coal supplies and many establishments had temporarily to close down or go on short time. But the chief factor was the amazing rapidity with which the currency descended into the abyss of inflation. The Works Councils, in common with all other social institutions, were drawn into the vortex. Their gradual evolution, away from the chaotic struggles which characterised the first year or two of their existence, towards a more practical and constructive rôle in industry, received a big set-back. All over the country, Works Councils Schools had to be closed down and almost every side of their activities was paralysed. The one great exception was wage negotiations, the need for which arose out of the incessant modifications in wage rates, owing to the fantastically rapid depreciation in the value of money. The Councils were not, it is true, concerned with changes in basic rates, but with the practical application of coefficients of increase to meet the rising cost of living. Questions as to the time and mode of payment also became of great importance. It is widely admitted by German employers that the Councils fulfilled a valuable and, in some cases, an indispensable function, by acting as a medium through which the employer could explain the nature and necessity of the changes that were being made and with which he could discuss the best method of meeting the ever greater difficulties that arose in regard to wage payments. The Councils were also able to be of considerable service in mitigating the hardships of unemployment, which was setting in increasingly as inflation progressed. Employers frequently left to them the task of selecting those employees whom it was impossible for economic reasons to retain, and they appear to have performed this duty well and conscientiously. Apart from wages and dismissals, most of the Councils had neither the time nor the inclination, under the prevailing conditions, to concern themselves with their other functions. On the whole, then, the relations between the Works Councils and the employers, during this very abnormal period, were characterised by less friction than at any other time since the Councils had come into operation.

In November 1923 the devaluation of the mark was successfully accomplished; a new currency was introduced and thenceforward Germany was in possession of a relatively stable standard of value based on gold. For the next two years, however, throughout 1924 and 1925, the country suffered greatly from the after-effects of the prolonged inflationist debauch. Circulating capital was exceedingly scarce and the rate of interest on short term loans correspondingly high. Bankruptcies were numerous and most employers were forced, for a time at least, to restrict the scale of their operations. The consequence, of course, was unemployment affecting millions of workers. A severe reaction set in against all forms of collective bargaining as soon as the employers, for the first time since the War, found themselves in a position of almost undisputed supremacy. The Trade Unions suffered a great loss of membership, as the main portion of those who had joined the movement since the War seceded, either remaining unorganised or becoming associated with communist or Fatherland ("yellow") organisations. A wave of deep discouragement swept over labour, which saw itself threatened with the loss of almost all the achievements of the Revolution, including the eight-hour day, without being able to make any resistance.

The Works Councils, deprived of the active support of the Trade Unions and weakened by dissensions amongst their members and in the ranks of the employees, were left alone to face the employers. They were not long in discovering the practical consequences for them of bad trade and unemployment. It was easy for an employer to get rid of any employee who was unwelcome to him, and not even the special protection to the Works Councillors themselves was adequate to safeguard them from dismissal under the plea of economic necessity. It is true that most employers did not take advantage of their regained supremacy to make a deliberate onslaught on the Works Councils as such. But they were in a position, of which they made full use, to eliminate individual Works Councillors who had shown what they considered to be an undue or misdirected vigour in the exercise of their duties. By no means all of these were of the agitator type; not a few were efficient and conscientious men, who had fallen into disfavour because of their refusal to disregard the policy of the Trade Unions, or because they insisted on their rights in regard to the disclosure of information.[1] A sufficient number of examples was made to intimidate the bulk of the Councils and to reduce them to a state of inglorious quiescence. Thus, for the time being, the whole institution appeared to suffer eclipse and employers ceased to regard the Councils as any longer of importance, except in so far as they could make use of them for their own ends. While it would be easy to bring forward individual instances, for which the description just given would not be valid, this state of inertia was broadly true

[1] One of the chief reforms desired by the workers, as a result of their experience of the operation of the Act, is the strengthening of the protection accorded to Works Councillors against dismissal. It has been proposed recently that more adequate protection be given to the Councillors themselves and that the same protection be extended to the Election Committee and also to all those nominated on the list of candidates, and to Works Councillors for six months after they have ceased to hold office. Only in this way, it is contended, will victimisation be avoided and the workers feel really safe in exercising their rights under the Act. The present writer is strongly of opinion that the complaints of the workers are justified in this respect and that further safeguards against unfair discrimination on the part of employers are called for.

of the mass of Works Councils, except in a few districts where, for special reasons, the Trade Unions remained powerful. The one important class of Councils, which formed an exception to the general rule, was the Central Works Councils in the great vertical combines. These often had more influence on the conditions of employment than the Trade Unions themselves. They owed their exceptional authority, partly, to the great size of these undertakings, employing as they did many thousands of men, which both made the existence of the Councils advantageous to the employers and also rendered the Works Councillors relatively independent of the employees; and partly, to the process of selection, which caused the Councillors often to be men of unusual ability and force of character.

During the latter part of 1925 and the first half of 1926, there were signs that the worst of the industrial depression was over, although unemployment continued on a great scale. The membership of the Trade Unions increased somewhat; they were considerably more powerful than they had been in 1924, and they had largely regained control over the labour situation. These altered conditions did not fail to have their effects on the Works Councils. The available evidence points to an appreciable quickening of interest in the Councils on the part of the workers. At the Works Councils elections held in the spring of 1926, the proportion of employees voting at the election of Councils was considerably greater than in the two preceding years and in other directions also the activity of the Councils was increasing. The Trade Unions were now in a position to give more effective support and encouragement to the Councils, on whose behalf they had been conducting a vigorous propaganda amongst their members. It is too early yet for results, but if success attends the efforts of the Trade Unions and if trade revival brings about a reduction of unemployment, the Works Councils will assuredly become once again a factor to be reckoned with in the relations between labour and capital.

In surveying the course which the relations between the employers and the Works Councils in Germany have taken during the last six years, the following considerations stand out as of chief importance:

(1) The whole evolution of the Works Councils has been warped and diverted owing to their initial association with the revolutionary movement in Germany, which derives its inspiration from Soviet Russia and its force from the chaos which followed the collapse of the War. Most of the undeniable abuses and excesses, of which the Works Councils were guilty in their early period, were due to these causes and it is not likely that they would be repeated, even if labour were again to assume a very strong bargaining position in relation to employers.

(2) Virtually the whole of the short period, during which the Works Councils have hitherto been in operation, has been characterised by abnormal economic and political conditions. There has thus been little opportunity for a continuous orderly development of the Councils on normal lines. In their effects on the attitude and preoccupations of the workers, the political, especially the external conditions, have been almost as important as the economic.

These two factors alone make it not merely difficult, but dangerous, to be dogmatic about any phase of the activities of the Councils during their short period of existence. What was true in 1920 was no longer true in 1922, while still greater changes were to be observed in 1924. But these transformations were themselves not the result of an organic evolution, but rather of a series of violent and discontinuous changes in the economic environment. Equilibrium has not yet been reached and there is no stable basis from which to draw final deductions.

(3) The practical experience of the Councils, down to the present day, shows the enormous importance of the relative bargaining strength of employers and employees for the operation of any form of representative machinery. Despite the fact that the duties and powers of the Works Councils are regulated by statute with extreme detail, the actual extent of these powers, the degree to which they can be enforced in practice and the use made of the facilities provided, are chiefly dependent upon those general economic forces which decide, when it comes to a trial of strength, whether the employing class as a whole or the employees as a whole have got the upper hand in industrial relations.

(4) The Trade Unions provide an indispensable support and backing for the Works Councils, without which the latter would for the most part be helpless. Any change in the bargaining strength of the Unions is almost immediately reflected in a corresponding change in the strength of the Councils.

(5) The employers, as a class, have already become accustomed to the existence of the Works Councils as statutory bodies and are not actively hostile to a large part of the provisions of the Act. Although parts of the Act are unpopular, there is no general agitation or desire for its repeal as a whole. In fact, there is a wide consensus of opinion among the more enlightened employers in large undertakings, that they stand to gain more than to lose from the existence of representative bodies with legally defined functions, with which they can negotiate. Through the medium of the Councils they are enabled to ascertain the feelings and wishes of their employees, to correct abuses which otherwise would not have been brought to their notice and, in turn, to use the Councils to clear up misunderstandings or doubts as to the intentions and policy of the management.

(6) The extent to which there is co-operation, in fact, between the employers and the Works Councils is mainly a question of the personalities on either side. A Works Council is merely a piece of social machinery; how it functions depends on the character and tact of the members of the Council and of the employer with whom they come in contact.

Hence any broad statements as to the working of the Councils must be understood to be limited by the impossibility of accurate generalisation about an institution, which varies in every instance in response to the mutual reactions of the persons concerned and which is never the same in any two cases.

(7) A system of statutory Works Councils, with functions prescribed and defined by legal provisions, presupposes some method of appeal in the case of disputes. The German Conciliation Boards and Labour Courts have acted, on the whole, with much success as the guardians of the interests of the community and as upholders of equity. They have supplied a vital safety valve for the whole system, without which industrial relations would either have become intolerable, or it would have been necessary

drastically to curtail the functions and powers of the Works Councils.

THE WORKS COUNCILS AND INDUSTRIAL DEMOCRACY

Before the War, German labour legislation, apart from the social insurance laws of Bismarck, was chiefly confined to the protection of the individual employee in regard to certain aspects of the labour contract, agreed upon between himself and his employer. The legal system embodied the view that the labour contract was fundamentally analogous to other contracts made between individuals for their mutual profit and advantage. Such contracts were, therefore, subject to private law, in the same way as other enforceable contracts freely entered into by both parties. The exceptions to this general rule, such as the restrictions on the employment of women and children, the establishment of uniform conditions for the prevention of accident and disease, and so on, were confined to the minimum which experience had shown to be essential under modern industrial conditions. Such exceptions were, moreover, attributable to the concern of the State to secure the physical well-being of its citizens, rather than to a recognition of any fundamental peculiarities of the labour contract requiring the application of special legal principles. On the other hand, the conception of the labour contract as an individual contract between the employer and his employee was so strongly felt, that the State looked askance at labour combinations and restricted to an important extent the freedom of association of the workers.

The transformation of this whole system and the construction, in the few years which have elapsed since the War, of a great body of labour legislation giving expression to new and far-reaching principles, is an astonishing achievement, the magnitude and merits of which have not been sufficiently appreciated in other countries. In contrast to the old principle of individual contract, subject only to a certain minimum of protective regulation by the State, a great part of the new labour legislation is based on the principle of the collective contract, by which the individual employee ceases to have any direct immediate influence on the conditions of his employment, but is bound by the collective bargain to which he is a party. He may be a party to the bargain through his membership of the Trade Union by which it was concluded with the employer, or merely through working in conjunction with other employees for whom a Collective Agreement has been established, or, finally, through an autonomous decision of part of the administrative machinery of the State (a Conciliation Officer, or the Minister of Labour of the Reich). The last-mentioned possibility illustrates another of the outstanding characteristics of the new system—the intervention of the State, by statutory provisions and by the organs it has created, in the regulation of labour conditions. This action is no longer only protective and preventive; it is an active and controlling intervention in many aspects of the labour contract and of the issues arising from it. But although in many directions, e.g. the conclusion of Collective Agreements, the extension of hours of work, etc., the State has assumed compulsory powers, it is an essential condition that these should be used rarely and only in cases of real necessity and that, so far as possible, the action of the State should be confined to mediating between the great self-governing bodies of employers and employees. A third ruling principle is the introduction, at present under a very restricted form, of the constitutional in place of the absolutist system in the unit of industry—the individual works or establishment.

The Works Councils Act is a most significant reflection of the new trend in labour legislation, for it gives to a large proportion of all employees in industry and commerce the statutory right to elect representative bodies. Such bodies have the dual function of upholding the rights of the workers against the employer and of co-operating with the employer in increasing the efficiency of production. While, on the one hand, the Works Councils constitute an additional piece of machinery designed to promote the class interests of a particular social group; on the other, they may be regarded as the leaders, in every establishment, of one of the great and indispensable partners in the process of production, whose interests, *quâ* producers, are identified with those of all the partners, in the volume and continuous disposal of the collective product. With the distribution of the product, the Works Council, as such, is not in principle concerned; for that is a matter for bargaining between the Trade Unions and the employers, and this remains true whether the employers are private individuals or some authority appointed by the State.

The Works Councils, in their capacity as representatives of the interests of the workers in each establishment, are entrusted with duties which are of varying practical importance. In the first place, they are called upon to supervise, on behalf of the Trade Unions and the State, the executions of all provisions affecting the contract of labour which have legal force; such provisions are those contained in all ruling Collective Agreements and in the whole body of labour legislation. They are, however, given no independent power of enforcement in regard to these provisions, but are required to report any infringement they may observe to the Trade Unions or to the Factory Inspector. For this purpose, their members can move freely throughout the works, any working-time lost in the performance of their duties being paid for by the employer. There is a general consensus of opinion amongst Trade Union officials that the effectiveness of Trade Union policy has, on the whole, been enhanced by the Works Councils, even when allowance has been made for instances of revolt and refusal to accept the advice and instructions of the Unions. When the employers' attack on the Unions and on the principle of Collective Agreements was at its height in 1924, the majority of the Councils remained loyal and declined to give their sanction to proposals that conflicted with the policy of the Unions. Many of them, in consequence, suffered the loss of their employment, others were overborne, but the net result was a considerable support to the Unions at a time when the latter most needed it. When we come to the supervision of labour legislation, we find a different picture. The available evidence serves to show that, despite praiseworthy exceptions, the Councils have relatively little to their credit in this sphere. This is true also of the very important field of the prevention of accidents and occupational diseases, in which the Councils are not limited to the task of supervision, but have the positive function of putting forward suggestions for improvement. The explanation is to be found, partly, in the volume and complexity of the

231

legislation in force and the lack of expert knowledge on the part of most Works Councillors; partly, in the constant changes in membership of the Councils; partly, in the disturbed economic conditions prevailing since 1920; and partly, in the lack of understanding and frequent opposition manifested by the employees towards any endeavours by the Councils to modify conditions of work to which they had become accustomed. The wiser employers have willingly co-operated with the Works Councils in such matters and have sought their assistance wherever possible, but an appreciable proportion has resented the interference of the Councils, both on grounds of principle and from the fear that they would be involved in additional expense.

It is still much too soon to say whether the Works Councils will, in time, come to make a more important contribution to the welfare of their fellow-workers in such matters as accidents and health. On the one hand, the instability of membership of the Councils in the larger works appears to be diminishing and, consequently, there is a real accumulation of knowledge and experience: moreover the Trade Unions are doing their best to encourage and stimulate the interest of the Councils in this side of their work, by technical courses, propaganda, etc. But on the other hand, the inherent difficulties remain very great and experience has shown how hard it is to find men, who are willing to devote much time and energy to a task which has little immediate bearing on the economic welfare of themselves and their fellows and where spectacular results are scarcely to be looked for.

In the second place, the Works Council is interposed as a sort of buffer between the employer and the employees. It is responsible for keeping the peace between the employees themselves and also between them and the employer.

In all disputes over the levying of fines, the individual application of piece-work rates, the granting of holidays, the transfer of workers from one machine to another or to a different department, etc., the Works Council is the standing body to which the worker can carry his grievances and ask for redress. It can thus exercise a very important mediating influence within the works. This is a side of its work which comes least into the public eye, but which is none the less of great practical importance. Everything depends here on the tact and strength of character of the members of the Council, on the one side, and on the nature of its relations with the employer, on the other. A good Council can smooth over many difficulties in the works, provided that it enjoys the confidence and support of the employees and that the employer is reasonably conciliatory, but where the Council is in the hands of extremists, or the employer is hostile to any intervention on its part, the result is likely to be much disturbance and unrest.

In the event of a dispute between employer and Works Council, in which neither party is willing to give way, the deadlock can be resolved by appeal to the Labour Court, against whose decision there is no further appeal. It can be seen that the statutory rights of the Works Council to uphold the interests of the employees and, if need be, to appeal to a Labour Court for a ruling, constitute a considerable advance towards industrial democracy in comparison with pre-War conditions.

Thirdly, the Works Council is competent to conclude a Works Agreement with the employer on all matters which are not already regulated by a Collective Agreement. Although wages are generally so regulated, it not infrequently occurs that there is an interval between the termination of one Collective Agreement and the conclusion of a new one. In this interval, the responsibility for coming to an interim agreement with the employer rests with the Works Council, which is required, however, to act in conjunction with the Trade Union. On the other hand, hours of work can only be legally modified by a Collective Agreement.

Under normal conditions the chief form of Works Agreement is the *Arbeitsordnung*, which lays down disciplinary regulations, the time and methods of wage payments, penalties for breaches of discipline, rest pauses, and the hours for beginning and ending work, etc. Works rules are required by law in all save very small industrial establishments and the counter-signature of the Works Council is necessary for their validity when first issued, as well as for any subsequent modifications. In the event of disagreement between employer and

233

Works Council, appeal can be made to the Conciliation Board for a final ruling. On paper, this would appear to represent a most fundamental change in the status of labour and to make a big breach in the long-established autocratic control of the employer. In practice, this right of the Works Council is less important than appears at first sight, because the custom has grown up since the War of regulating works rules in most industries by Collective Agreement. The works rules of each establishment must, none the less, be countersigned by the Works Council, but it is constrained to accept what has previously been approved by the Trade Unions. The improvement in the status of labour remains, but it is associated more with the Unions than with the Councils. Nevertheless, the powers of the Councils remain in principle and can be used effectively when the employer endeavours to modify the provisions of the *Arbeitsordnung* to the detriment of the workers.

Fourthly, unquestionably the most important of all the practical rights of the Works Council is its power of intervention in regard to the dismissal of employees. The right of the Council to defend a worker, who declares that he has been unjustly dismissed, either because he contests the grounds of dismissal or because he can claim special hardship, constitutes a real safeguard to the employees against arbitrary dismissal. It is, in practice, the most valued of all the statutory powers of the Council. Although the necessities of economic life make it impossible that the Council should have the last word and this is left to the Labour Court, the employee knows that his case, if taken up by the Council, will be defended by his own representatives, who are probably more competent to do so than he would be; while the ultimate decision is in the hands of an impartial tribunal. It is true that, if the verdict goes in his favour, he cannot claim re-employment as a right, but the alternative of a monetary compensation, which may be very substantial, is a considerable alleviation of his lot. It is this privilege, more than anything else, which has maintained the interest of many of the workers in the institution of Works Councils, because the appeal to the individual is direct and cogent.

To sum up the achievements of the Works Councils Act in

this sphere: The employees have now a share in the determination of the conditions under which their working life is carried on, which is more direct and more intimate than that afforded by the Trade Unions. This share is given to the employees as a statutory right and not as a concession wrung from individual employers by force, or granted, like so many welfare schemes, in order to keep the men quiet. The German Works Councils, with their legal charter and prescribed functions, have a theoretical as well as a practical importance; for the recognition that the propertyless employee has rights as well as duties is at least a step forward towards a new conception of the status of labour in the State.[1] It is true that the Works Councils do not and, indeed, cannot alter the fundamental relationship of subordination and authority, which is bound up with the contract of employment in the modern wage system. But they undoubtedly help to reduce the mass of avoidable hardship and injustice hitherto associated with that system and they give to the individual worker the feeling that he is under a constitutional and not a despotic rule.

Nevertheless, it is important not to attribute too much to the Works Councils by themselves, for, besides their right to represent the employees and to argue their case with the employer, they are empowered to appeal in case of dispute to an independent tribunal—the Labour Court or the Conciliation Board—whose decision, in the great majority of cases in practice, is final and binding on both parties.

These tribunals are the most positive and effective contribution of the post-War labour legislation of any country towards the extension of industrial democracy. It is in fact they, rather than the Works Councils themselves, which constitute the real limitation on the autonomous power of the employers within their own establishments; for it is they who have the ultimate decision in cases of disputes. In practice, the majority of

---

[1] Maine, in his *Ancient Law*, drew attention to the immense advance involved in the transformation of society from the feudal basis of status to the new basis of contract. The pendulum has swung back, though over a very different course, and the need now is for a partial return to status in a form which will give labour a sense of security, dignity, and organic relationship within the productive mechanism of the modern State.

disputes are settled "out of court", because neither party is anxious to expose itself to the loss of prestige consequent on an adverse judgement; with the result that the existence of courts of appeal increases very materially the bargaining power of the Councils, so long as they keep within their legal functions.

At the time that the famous Article 165[1] of the new Constitution was drafted, there were many people in Germany who entertained a naïve belief in an innate constructive ability of labour, by virtue of which it could throw off the shackles of the system of private enterprise and enter into immediate possession of its birthright, through the direct control of production in the factories. There is scarcely any one left, even amongst the communists, who now believes this to be possible. The experience of the last five years has sufficed to disillusion those who cherished such hopes, and the advocates of an ambitious Councils system based upon the Works Councils have practically disappeared. It is significant that none of the schemes, propounded by the leaders of German labour for the future democratisation of industry, proposes to extend materially the existing functions of the Works Councils. It has come to be realised that the broad lines of economic policy for industrial groups and the inter-relations among these groups, must be determined by some central authority on uniform lines. Any other alternative would involve all the evils of syndicalism. Modern factory industry requires discipline, with its corollary, the subordination of the many to the few and it is clear that, whatever else the democratic control of industry means, it does not and cannot mean the freedom of the individual employee, or body of employees, to determine their own conditions of work irrespective of the general plan. So far as the Works Councils are concerned, therefore, narrow limits are necessarily set to their functions, whatever may be the future basis of the economic system. In practice, however, their rôle in a democratically organised system would be of even greater importance than under the present individualist regime; for the more democratic the basis

[1] See above, pp. 9–11.

of industry, the more would its success or failure depend upon the willingness of the masses of labour to accept and follow the leadership of those whom they had elected (even though indirectly) to control the economic organisation of the State.

Under the Works Councils Act, the Councils are mainly required to act as advisory bodies, so far as the wider sphere of industrial democracy—the co-operation of employees in problems of management and policy—is concerned. They have, however, certain positive duties. They are required, in the interests of production, to keep the peace within the establishment and to exercise their influence both over their fellow-workers and over the employer to prevent demands from being put forward, or acts committed, which would be detrimental, not merely to the productive interests of their establishment, but also to the welfare of the community. They must, further, co-operate with the employer in the introduction of new and more satisfactory labour methods and must assist him, by advice, in order to secure the maximum technical and productive efficiency of the undertaking. All these duties are clearly based on an entirely different conception of the functions of the Works Council from that of a representative body, confronting the employer in defence of the separate and often diverging interests of the employees. Here the emphasis is on the fundamental partnership of labour and of management in command of capital, in the productive process.

The Works Council has no power to interfere with the employer in the conduct of his business; it can only give him advice and support. It has long been a contention of labour, in all industrial countries, that the employees, out of their practical experience, could make valuable suggestions to the employer, but are hampered by the absence of any recognised channel through which to make suggestions and by the fear that they would merely be told to mind their own business. The Works Council provides a solution of this difficulty. But, over and above the possibility that minor technical improvements might result, it was held by the framers of the Works Councils Act that there was a manifest need for a more constructive attitude towards the operation of the economic system than had been hitherto shown by labour. For the Trade Unions are combative organisations,

237

the whole of whose strength and energies are absorbed by struggles with the employers. Might it not be possible to initiate the employees to some extent into the difficulties and problems of management and, thereby, to awake in them a sense of responsibility and a realisation of the common interests of all the producers in the success of the undertaking from which they draw their livelihood? It was in this hope that the Works Councils were given a voice, even if only an advisory voice, in the broader questions of economic policy and were not restricted merely to matters arising directly out of the contract of employment. But, if the Works Council is to give advice which is to be of any value at all, it must have cognisance of information which previously had been shared by the employer with no one, except to a limited extent with his banker and the tax collector. It is on these arguments that are founded—and this is perhaps the most novel and constructive side of the Works Councils Act—the right of the Councils to receive quarterly reports on the activities and economic situation of the businesses in which they are employed and to put questions to the employer; the right to inspect balance sheets and profit and loss accounts in all save small businesses; and the right to sit on the Control Boards of Companies.

That the Works Councils, taken as a whole, have signally failed to show either the capacity, or, for the most part, the desire to co-operate with the employer in increasing the efficiency and productivity of industry, is universally admitted and not least by their own spokesmen. The period since the War has been one of far-reaching change in labour methods and of the introduction, on a large scale, of a modified form of scientific management—the so-called *Rationalisierungsprozess*. This has taken place in the face of the opposition and obstruction of organised labour and, so far as they dared, of the Works Councils.[1] In general, the Works Councils have shown but little under-

[1] In fairness to the Works Councils, it should be pointed out that they have legitimate reason in many cases to complain of the unwillingness of the employers to co-operate with them. If new labour methods are to be brought in, it is rare for the Works Council to be consulted beforehand, or for any of its members to be appointed to the committee engaged in working out the new scheme. The Works Council is only asked its opinion

standing of the requirements of industry under post-War conditions, and have been justly reproached by the employers with the stubborn, unreasoning adoption of the traditional Trade Union policy of opposition to any and every change in conditions of work. One of the intentions of the institution of Works Councils was to restore a more organic relationship between the employee and his work, which has suffered from the ever-increasing division of labour and the impersonal organisation of production in modern large-scale industry. Apart from a few isolated exceptions, there is no evidence that the Works Councils have played any part in reconciling the employee to his normal functions in the industrial system, or in bringing about an appreciation of the underlying economic conditions which govern industry.

The employers must bear a considerable share of the responsibility for this unsatisfactory result. From the outset they have been more strongly opposed to the rights of the Works Councils to gain an insight into the financial and other conditions of private enterprises, than to any other part of the Act. When their parliamentary resistance was broken down, they proceeded, with a great measure of success, to render nugatory the statutory rights of the Councils which were chiefly obnoxious to them. As a whole, they have thwarted the intention of the legislature—by meagre and unsatisfactory statements in their Quarterly Reports; by compiling balance sheets from which no proper deductions could be drawn; and by rendering the position of the Works Councils on the Control Boards of companies virtually a farce. While complaining bitterly of lack of co-operation on the part of the Councils, they have themselves failed to implement those sections of the Works Councils Act on which it was intended that such co-operation should be based. At the same time, it cannot be denied that the employers have had certain grounds for their action.

Even apart from the revolutionary menace, with which the

when the proposals have already taken shape and are about to be introduced. Suggestions for modification at this stage are difficult to make and easily give rise to the accusation of mere obstructiveness. Employers are too often reluctant to allow the Works Councils an opportunity to give advice at a stage when this could be both practical and helpful.

Works Councils were so closely associated during the first two years of their existence and which rendered them suspect to the employers, the latter have been fearful lest they should be prejudiced by the leakage of confidential information. The Works Council is, it is true, pledged to secrecy, but the employer is not unnaturally inclined to take the view that what is every man's secret is no man's secret and, therefore, to tell the Works Council as little as possible that it does not already know. Moreover, it is widely known that the Trade Unions look to the Councils for information which would be of assistance to them in their wage negotiations or their propaganda. Of all the statutory powers of the Works Council it is these rights to information which are the most obnoxious to the employers, and the Works Councillor who ventures to put awkward questions, even when he is within his legal rights, is likely to find himself marked down as a dangerous man to be got rid of at the earliest opportunity.

Since the trade depression and unemployment of 1924, the employers have very widely given it to be understood that inconvenient curiosity will be dangerous, not only to hopes of promotion, but also to the maintenance of employment. In this way, they have largely shut the mouths of the salaried members of the Councils, whose better education and knowledge of figures might make them dangerous, and have driven the wage-earning members to other and less controversial activities. The result is that the workers are exacerbated by the knowledge that they are being prevented from exercising rights which are legally theirs. They see just enough to realise that anything that they are told, or allowed to see, in regard to the financial results of the business, is not the whole truth and they are not any more inclined to believe the employer when he puts forward figures showing that expenses must be reduced, say, by dismissing staff or working short time. Partly as a result of recent American statistics, which have been widely circulated in Germany, there is a very prevalent belief amongst employees that inefficiencies and undue costs of management are responsible for a great deal of waste and consequent lack of success in the competitive market. The wage-earner has every interest in the elimination of this source of loss before the burden of lowering costs is trans-

240

ferred to his shoulders. In practice, however, he finds himself unable to penetrate behind the barriers which the employer raises against all attempts to secure information on these matters.

Taking a long view, it seems very doubtful whether the employers have been well advised in their own interests in circumscribing so narrowly the activities of the Works Councils. For in their anxiety to repel even the smallest encroachment on their domain as controllers of industry, they have lost an opportunity of attracting some of the best brains and finest characters amongst the workers to co-operate with them in the organisation of production. The alternative course would have involved greater immediate risks, but with a big prospect of ultimate gain. The history of representative institutions proves that it is responsibility which breeds moderation and which also attracts the best men to assume arduous duties.

But the employer is not by any means solely responsible for the scanty success of the Works Councils in their rôle as partners in industry. There are many factors on the workers' side which must be taken into account.

Firstly, the shortness of time which has elapsed (the Works Councils Act was passed in 1920 and the supplementary Acts dealing with the right of inspection of balance sheets and of electing members to Control Boards, in 1921 and 1922 respectively) since the Councils have been in operation and have been able to exercise their powers, is such that it would be absurd to expect any considerable achievements already. This part of the Works Councils Act is a new and constructive experiment, calling not merely for knowledge and experience, which the great majority of employees do not yet possess, but also for a fundamentally different conception of the position of labour in the productive process. Most of those who are now members of Works Councils have grown up in the old school of Trade Union policy and it may be necessary to wait till a new generation of workers arises who bring with them a fresh outlook on industry.

Secondly, a large proportion of German labour, comprising nearly all the members of the socialist Unions, is strongly Marxist in sympathy and certainly shares his views on the exploitation of labour under the present industrial system. There exists, therefore, a conflict between their loyalty to the *Klassenkampf* or Class War, and their position under the Works Councils Act as partners in the concern in which they are employed. Indeed, they find this antinomy in the terms of the Act itself, which directs them to do nothing that would be harmful to the interests of the community as a whole. How, they ask, is this provision to be reconciled with the private ownership of capital and with the profit system? The psychological bases for a whole-hearted co-operation between the Works Councils and the employers, in the interests of the maximum efficiency of production, are thus in a large measure absent.

Thirdly, most members of Works Councils lack the intelligence, the education, the experience and the time necessary to understand the complicated structure and problems of modern business. The ordinary primary education is not much of a background from which to build up protagonists capable of holding their own with German business men with their expert staffs of University trained officials. Moreover, there is the difficulty, which is a very real one, of obtaining even a minimum of experience in the face of the obstacles so generally placed in the path of the Councils by the employers. This difficulty is enhanced by the fact that the office of Works Councillor is only held on an annual tenure, and changes in membership are frequent. Also, most Works Councillors are men engaged on heavy productive work for eight or nine hours a day; their duties are multifarious and they have rarely got the physical or mental vigour to do much more than the ordinary routine tasks that come their way.

Fourthly, the Works Council is a democratic institution and its members are dependent for their election each year upon the votes of their fellow-workers. To be successful in co-operating with the employer the Council must be able to rely on the support of its electors. But it is notorious that the employees are generally much less willing to adopt new methods than the Council itself, and narrow limits are therefore imposed on its actions even where it is willing to use its influence in favour of co-operation.

The fact that the experience of the last five years has proved that the Works Councils have been weakest and least effective

SUMMARY AND CONCLUSIONS

in that part of their functions which is concerned with the productivity of industry, does not imply that this side of the Act has been a complete failure. The writer, in making enquiries in different parts of Germany, has come across instances, admittedly exceptional, in which the Councils have done valuable service by putting forward constructive and helpful proposals in regard to the organisation of the works, or to marketing, or even to general questions of financial policy. But much more important than the small amount of actual achievement, hitherto, has been the stimulus which these functions have given to the education, both practical and theoretical, of the workers. However imperfect the administration of the Act may be in practice, it remains true that tens of thousands of employees by serving on the Works Councils are being brought each year into touch with the wider aspects of industry and are given the opportunity of realising something of the work of management. They commonly start their duties full of the valour of ignorance and convinced that the employer is merely a man who is in a position to exploit their necessities in order to acquire a large income for himself, out of which he can live luxuriously. In time they learn to appreciate some of the difficulties of management and, above all, the limitations, that are largely outside the employer's control, which hedge him in on every side—limitations in regard to capital, credit, raw materials, labour supply, etc. They may ultimately come to see how closely their employment and their wages are bound up with the prosperity of the business as a whole. In addition to this practical experience, the institution of the Councils has done a great deal to encourage adult education in such subjects as economic theory, industrial organisation, the finance of industry, book-keeping, etc. Some, at least, of those who have sat on the Control Boards of companies and have listened to discussions which they have not been able to understand or to follow, have been impelled to go to school again and to spend laborious hours after work in puzzling at problems of whose very existence they were previously unaware. It is not pretended that these men form a considerable proportion of the whole, but in the long run they may prove to be a very important leaven in the lump of German labour.

248

16-2

Finally, attention must be drawn to a significant phenomenon —namely, what may be termed the drift from the Works Councils. Beginning already as early as 1922 and acquiring ever greater proportions each year, there has manifested itself an unwillingness to take advantage of the machinery set up under the Works Councils Act. Although the Works Councils are universal and compulsory, in the sense that a Council should be elected in every establishment above a certain size, there is no penalty attached to the failure of the employees to elect a Works Council, other than the loss of any privileges that they would have enjoyed under the Act. In view of the importance of the protection afforded to employees against arbitrary dismissal, which is only available where a statutory Works Council has been formed, it is surprising that there should be such widespread evidence throughout the country of the absence of Councils where they should exist. It still remains true that they are almost universally to be found in large undertakings, where the employees are numbered by the thousand. But in establishments with less than 1000 employees, it is becoming increasingly common to find no Works Council, and the pages of the Factory Inspectors' Reports are full of observations of such cases. Sometimes there is no Works Council because the employees take so little interest in the institution that they cannot be prevailed upon to go to the trouble of holding an election. But it is more common to find no one willing to assume the office of Works Councillor, all the previous holders having resigned and refused to stand for re-election. One of the chief causes seems to be the very evident drawbacks attendant on an honorary and unpaid office, the holders of which are exposed, on the one side, to the hostility of the employer, and on the other, to continuous abuse and recriminations from their fellow-employees. So long as the Councils had the charm of novelty, while there was little risk of unemployment, and Councillors were largely released from productive work, the office was not without its attractions, but all these conditions have now disappeared, and the kicks are far more in evidence than the ha'pence. Another factor is the disillusionment of the employees as a whole and of the Works Councillors themselves with the practical operation of the Act. They had hoped for far more real power and believed for a time that they actually had got it, only to be undeceived by the rulings of the Conciliation Boards and Labour Courts and by the successful obstruction of the employers. Since unemployment became rife, the power of the Councils to protect the employees and even their own members against dismissal or victimisation has greatly diminished, which is an important additional cause of discouragement.

The early enthusiasm has given way to a wide measure of indifference on the part of employees and, even where Councils are elected, they often cease to meet or to exercise any functions. An extreme instance of this is provided by a case noted in the Factory Inspectors' Reports for 1924, where the employees did not know the names of their representatives on the Council and a Works Councillor was himself ignorant of the identity of his own colleagues.

In estimating the importance of this trend for the future of the Works Councils a sharp distinction must be drawn between different types and sizes of establishments. In commercial undertakings of all kinds the Works Councils have dwindled into insignificance, except in some of the great banks and similar very large establishments. But even in these they are often more of a fiction than a reality. To some extent, this may be attributed to the altogether exceptional period of unemployment in the commercial world which followed the stabilisation of the mark at the end of 1923, but the real cause is deeper than this. There is, in the nature of things, not much scope for the Works Council in commerce, where conditions of work are governed by a well-established routine, where the average number of employees is small as compared with industry and where the individual employee is accustomed to have direct personal access to his employer. In normal times there is a high degree of continuity of employment in commerce and, above all, the future of every employee is bound up with his chances of promotion, which he is not anxious to imperil by assuming an office in which he may be called upon to oppose the wishes of his employer.

In industry the same factors also tend to weaken the co-operation of the salaried employees on the Works Councils and to deprive the wage-earners, in many cases, of their advice and

245

support. So far as the wage-earners themselves are concerned, it seems probable that the tendency to refrain from participation in the election and operation of Works Councils will continue in the smaller works, despite all the efforts of the Factory Inspectors and Trade Unions to the contrary. For these works the election procedure is too complicated, while the necessity for specially elected Councils is far less than in the big works. There can be little doubt that in the latter the Works Councils have come to stay, for there they correspond to a real need which the Trade Unions cannot fill. During the prolonged period of depression beginning at the end of 1923, the Works Councils have lost very greatly in prestige and influence, with the result that many people in Germany regard them already as an effete institution and one which need be reckoned with no longer. But this is to ignore altogether their real significance. In modern large-scale enterprise they have an enduring value, as a piece of representative machinery, which in any case would ensure them a permanent place in industrial organisation. But of greater importance than this is their relation to the ideology of German labour. The nineteenth century saw the struggle for the recognition of Trade Unions and the principle of collective bargaining. This struggle has been won and the great, slow-moving, but in the long run immensely powerful forces of labour are now pushing onwards towards the extension of industrial democracy in other directions. The Works Councils constitute a new thrusting forward of the line of assault on the strongholds of capitalism. The gain is modest, but it has been seized hold of tenaciously by the Trade Unions, which have converted the Councils into their own outposts.

No one who has followed the proceedings of the Trade Union Congresses since the War, and especially of the last Congress held in Breslau in 1925,[1] can doubt that the leaders of the German labour movement are both sincere and determined in their endeavour to secure for labour a greater voice in the control of industry, with the ultimate hope of attaining to a socialist State. While it is not contemplated that the Works Councils should

[1] Cf. the resolution on the democratic control of industry, a translation of which will be found in Appendix VIII.

play the leading rôle in this development, it is recognised that no system of socialised industry, whatever form it might take, could function successfully without the whole-hearted co-operation of the individual workers, based on an understanding of the economic laws which govern the productive process. The course of events in Russia has been closely followed by the German Trade Unionists, who have learned a great deal about the difficulties which a Socialist State would experience in managing its industries with efficiency, while according to the employees even as much freedom as they now possess under the capitalist system. Without thousands of working-class experts and an educated and disciplined body of employees, there could be no hope of success. Moreover, the carry-over, into a Socialist State, of an unmodified Trade Union psychology amongst the mass of workers would inevitably lead to the old hostility to the private employer being transferred to the new managing bodies set up on behalf of the State.

It is for these reasons that the ablest leaders of the Trade Unions, who are looking a long way ahead, realise that the Works Councils have an indispensable rôle to play in their schemes for the future reorganisation of industry on a collectivist basis. They are not prepared to see the Councils sink into oblivion, as a result either of the intimidation of the employers or the lack of interest of the employees. Additional legal powers for the Works Councils have an important part in their programme and, in the meantime, they are engaged, by propaganda and practical support, in doing their utmost to stimulate the interest of the employees in the exercise of the rights which the legislature has given them.

The future of the Works Councils depends, almost more than on anything else, upon the way in which their relations with their fellow-employees develop. It has been very apparent since 1920, that the greatest difficulties and discouragements with which the Works Councils have been faced have come, not from the employers, but from their own fellow-workers. The German people are noted for their willingness to submit to authority imposed on them from above, but they have had little experience hitherto of democratic forms of government. Unlike the mass of

English workers, they are full of ideas and difficult to lead by persuasion. The Trade Union movement in Germany has always been split up into numerous rival factions and this disunity has been accentuated latterly by the growth of a powerful communist and syndicalist agitation. Even within the Trade Unions, discipline was gravely impaired after the War and matters were much worse in the case of the Works Councils, which were a new form of organisation with no traditions behind them. Hence the Works Councils have suffered severely from lack of loyalty on the part of the employees towards their own elected representatives, who were thus deprived of the support they needed in their negotiations with the employers.

Like every other democratic innovation in its early stages, the Works Councils were premature, in the sense that the men who had to administer them and those for whose benefit they were established were not ripe for the new duties and responsibilities imposed upon them as the counterpart of their privileges. To make this admission is not necessarily to condemn the innovation, for time and experience and, above all, education, are necessary to make any democratic institution function properly.

A considerable part of the present difficulties with which the Works Councils in Germany are confronted is due to economic causes, which are temporary and of which the greatest is unquestionably the prevalence of unemployment and the consequent liability to victimisation. In the long run, the more serious, because the more fundamental danger, comes from within, in the shape of the disunity and dissensions which ravage the ranks of the employees and it is this danger which, more than any other, imperils the future progress of the Works Councils. Time alone will show whether it will be possible to achieve conditions of loyalty and discipline amongst the employees, such as will attract men of character and ability to the Works Councils, or whether the German workers will ultimately prove themselves unfit for even the relatively restricted rights of self-government extended to them by the Works Councils Act.

Act to establish Works Councils. *February* 4, 1920

I. GENERAL PROVISIONS

§ 1. In order to safeguard the common economic interests of employees (salaried and wage-earning) as against the employer, and to support the employer in the efficient conduct of his business, Works Councils shall be constituted in all establishments normally employing not less than 20 persons.

§ 2. In establishments where less than 20 persons, but not less than five persons entitled to vote, are normally employed, of whom not less than three are eligible for election in accordance with §§ 20 and 21, a Works Steward shall be elected.

Where such establishments employ not less than five wage-earning and five salaried employees entitled to vote, a common Works Steward may be elected. If an agreement cannot be arrived at by the majority of each group, the wage-earning and salaried employees shall each elect a Works Steward.

§ 3. In establishments which employ not less than 20 out-workers (Section 119 *b* of the Industrial Code), who usually work for the same firm and do not themselves employ others, a special Works Council shall be constituted for the out-workers. Detailed regulations shall be drawn up by the Federal Minister of Labour, subject to the approval of a Committee of the Reichstag consisting of 28 members.

§ 4. Sections 1 and 2 shall apply to establishments in agriculture and forestry and subsidiary undertakings, provided that only permanent employees are taken into account in reckoning the number of persons employed. In such establishments a Works Steward shall not be elected unless at least 10 persons are regularly employed, of whom not less than three are eligible for election under §§ 20 and 21.

§ 5. The formation of bodies representative of persons employed by ocean and inland navigation undertakings shall be dealt with in a special Act.

§ 6. In order to safeguard the special economic interests of wage-earning and salaried employees as against the employer, Councils of wage-earning and of salaried employees shall be constituted in every establishment where both wage-earning and salaried employees are represented on the Works Council.

§ 7. In establishments where two Works Stewards are elected, each of them shall represent the special interests of the group by which he is elected.

In establishments where only one Works Steward is elected, he shall represent the common interests of both, and also the special interests of each group.

§ 8. The right of the economic associations of wage-earning and salaried employees to represent the interests of their members shall not be affected by the provisions of this Act.

§ 9. For the purposes of this Act, the term establishments shall include all public and private establishments, businesses, and administrative establishments.

Subsidiary establishments or departments of an undertaking, which are linked together either by management or industrial process, shall not be deemed to be separate establishments, provided that they are situated within the same commune or in adjacent and economically interdependent communes.

§ 10. For the purposes of this Act, the term employees shall include wage-earning and salaried persons other than members of the employer's family.

The following shall not be deemed to be employees:

(1) Public officials, and persons awaiting permanent appointment as officials.

(2) Persons who have not taken up an occupation primarily for the sake of remuneration, but mainly for the sake of physical health, vocational training, moral improvement or education, or who are actuated by motives of a charitable, religious, scientific or artistic nature.

§ 11. For the purposes of this Act, the term wage-earning employees shall include all persons who work for remuneration in the services of others or who are employed as apprentices, but shall exclude salaried persons.

The term wage-earning employees shall further include out-workers (§ 3), resident in the same commune as the establishment or in an adjacent economically interdependent commune, who work mainly for the same firm and do not themselves employ others.

If a special Works Council is constituted for out-workers under § 3, these shall be excluded from calculations of the number of employees in the works.

§ 12. For the purposes of this Act, the term salaried employees shall include all persons who work for remuneration in any of the occupations specified in § 1, paragraph 1, of the Salaried Employees' Insurance Act, even if they are not compulsorily insured. Further, the term salaried employees shall include apprentices who are going through a regular training for one of these occupations, and persons employed in offices on work of a subordinate or purely mechanical nature.

For the purposes of this Act, the term salaried employees shall not include directors and legal representatives of public and private corporations and associations, nor managers and executive officers of businesses, in so far as they have independent power to appoint or dismiss the other employees in the establishment or its branches, or in so far as they hold a power of attorney or general authority to take action.

§ 13. The Federal Government may decide, by Order, for public authorities and enterprises of the Reich as well as for the public bodies which come under Federal supervision in respect of the conditions of employment of their officials, that certain classes of permanent officials and persons awaiting permanent appointment as officials shall be considered as wage-earning or salaried employees for the purposes of this Act.

For the public authorities and enterprises of the individual States, communes and federated communes, as well as for the public bodies which come under the supervision of the individual States in respect of the conditions of employment of their officials, the necessary regulations may be made by the Governments of the said States.

Where this is done, § 78, paragraphs 8 and 9, §§ 81 to 90 and 96 to 98 shall not apply.

In the same way it may be determined that certain groups of employees, who have a prospect of being raised to the grade of officials or who are employed by public authorities on the same or similar work to that performed by permanent officials and persons awaiting permanent appointment as officials, shall not be regarded as employees for the purposes of this Act, provided always that they enjoy the same rights as officials in the constitution of the officials' representative bodies (Officials' Councils and Committees).

§ 14. In cases where the employer is not a single individual, the rights and duties of employers under this Act shall be assigned

    (1) In the case of private corporations and associations, to the legal representatives thereof.

    (2) In the case of the Federal Government, the States, communal unions, communes and other public bodies, to the chiefs of each department, subject to the provisions to be laid down by the supreme Federal authority for the undertakings of the Reich, and for public bodies which come under its supervision in respect of the conditions of employment of their officials, and by the central State authority for all other bodies.

An employer may be represented by any person empowered to act on his behalf.

II. CONSTITUTION OF WORKS REPRESENTATIVE BODIES

A. Works Councils (Councils of Wage-earning and of Salaried Employees)

1. *Composition and Election*

§ 15. A Works Council shall consist:

In establishments with not less than 20 and not more than 49 employees, of three members.

In establishments with not less than 50 and not more than 99 employees, of five members.

In establishments with not less than 100 and not more than 199 employees, of six members.

The number of members shall be increased:

In establishments with not less than 200 and not more than 999 employees, by one for every further 200.

In establishments with not less than 1000 and not more than 5999 employees, by one for every further 500.

In establishments with not less than 6000 employees, by one for every further 1000.

The total number of members shall in no case exceed 30.

The Councils of wage-earning and of salaried employees shall consist of the wage-earning and salaried members of the Works Council respectively. Even if there are in either case only one or two members, such members shall have the rights and duties of a Council for wage-earning or salaried employees. If the number of wage-earning or of salaried employees is so great that either can claim more representatives on its Council, on the basis of calculation specified in paragraphs 1 to 3 above, than it has on the Works Council, a corresponding number of supplementary members shall be added.

If an establishment for which a Works Council has to be set up has fewer employees who are eligible for election than the number of Works Council members required under paragraphs 1 to 3 above, the Works Council shall consist of three members; provided that if less than three employees are eligible, Works Stewards shall be elected.

§ 16. If both wage-earning and salaried persons are included among the employees, each group shall be represented on the Works Council in proportion to its relative numbers at the time of fixing the date of the election.

Each group shall have at least one representative.

Minority groups shall be represented as follows:

For a group of not less than 50 and not more than 299 employees, at least two members.

For a group of not less than 300 and not more than 599 employees, at least three members.

For a group of not less than 600 and not more than 999 employees, at least four members.

For a group of not less than 1000 and not more than 2999 employees, at least five members.

For a group of not less than 3000 and not more than 5999 employees, at least six members.

For a group of 6000 or more employees, at least eight members.

The numerical proportions shall be determined by the Election Committee, in accordance with the regulations for the management of elections, on the proportional representation system (§ 25).

A minority group shall not be represented if it does not include more than five persons, unless they constitute more than one-twentieth of the employees of the establishment.

§ 17. Members may be allotted to groups otherwise than as provided in § 16, if a majority in each group voting separately by secret ballot so decides.

If a group includes fewer eligible persons than the number specified in § 16, it may elect members of the other group as its representatives.

§ 18. Those members and supplementary members (§ 15, paragraph 4) of a Works Council who are wage-earners shall all be chosen at the same election by the wage-earning employees of the establishment from among their own ranks by direct ballot vote on the system of proportional representation, and shall hold office for one year, and the members and supplementary members who are salaried employees shall be similarly elected by the salaried employees. Members shall be eligible for re-election.

If the number of persons employed is temporarily increased by more than 100 per cent., but in any case by not less than fifteen, including three who are entitled to vote, the persons temporarily employed shall ballot for a representative, who shall be a member of the representative body for the establishment where such exists. In default of a representative body, the said representative shall have the status of a Works Steward.

If the number of temporary employees exceeds 100, a new Works Council may be constituted on a resolution to that effect adopted by a majority of the employees entitled to vote. In agriculture, forestry and subsidiary establishments, under the same conditions, the temporary employees shall ballot for two representatives, who shall be members of the representative body for the establishment.

§ 19. The representatives of wage-earning and of salaried employees shall be chosen at a single election for all employees, if the wage-earning and salaried employees who are entitled to vote so decide before each election by a two-thirds majority in each group voting separately by ballot.

The constitution of Councils of wage-earning and salaried employees under § 6, and the provisions of §§ 15 and 16, shall not be affected by the above provision.

§ 20. All male and female employees who have attained the age of 18 years and who are in possession of civic rights shall be entitled to vote.

Persons who are entitled to vote shall be eligible for election if they have attained the age of 24 years and are German citizens, have completed their vocational training and have, on the day of the election, been employed for not less than six months in the establishment or undertaking and for not less than three years in the branch of industry or occupation in which they are engaged on the said day.

An employee shall not be eligible for election in respect of more than one establishment.

§ 21. If an establishment or an undertaking has been in existence less than six months, the requirement as to duration of employment therein shall be deemed to be satisfied by any person who has been employed in the said establishment or undertaking since its foundation.

The requirement as to six months' employment in the establishment shall not apply in the case of temporary employees in any establishment in which it is the rule to employ some or all of the employees during part of the year only.

If in any establishment there is not a sufficient number of employees who are eligible for election under § 20, paragraph 2, the requirements as to six months' employment in the establishment and (if necessary) also as to three years' employment in the industry or occupation may be waived in respect of the said establishment.

Disabled persons, as defined in the Order dated 9 January, 1919 (R.G. Bl. p. 28), who owing to their disablement are obliged to adopt a new occupation, shall be exempt from the requirement as to three years' employment in the same branch of industry or occupation.

§ 22. In the composition of a Works Council regard shall be had so far as possible to the various occupational groups of male and female employees in the establishment.

§ 23. A Works Council shall, not later than four weeks before the expiry of its term of office, appoint by a simple majority vote an Election Committee consisting of three persons entitled to vote, and appoint one of these three to be chairman.

If the Works Council fails to fulfil the above obligation, the employer shall nominate an Election Committee consisting of the three senior employees who are entitled to vote, on which both wage-earning and salaried employees shall be represented if both are employed in the establishment. The Election Committee shall in this case appoint its own chairman.

The same rule shall apply in the case of a newly-established undertaking, or one in which the prescribed minimum number of employees for the constitution of a Works Council is attained for the first time.

The Election Committee shall, immediately upon its appointment, make preparations for the election, which shall take place within six weeks of its appointment.

§ 24. Wages or salaries shall not be reduced on account of loss of time due to the exercise of electoral rights or to activities as members of an Election Committee. Clauses in agreements which are contrary to this provision shall be void.

§ 25. Detailed regulations as to election procedure shall be issued by the Federal Minister of Labour, subject to the approval of a Committee of the Reichstag consisting of 28 members.

2. Procedure

§ 26. If a Works Council consists of fewer than nine members, it shall appoint a chairman and vice-chairman from among its members by a simple majority vote. If the Works Council includes both wage-earning and salaried employees, the chairman and vice-chairman may not belong to the same group.

§ 27. If a Works Council consists of not less than nine members, it shall elect a Works Committee from among its own members according to the principle of proportional representation. If the Works Council includes both wage-earning and salaried employees, the members of the Works Committee shall not all belong to the same group. The Works Committee shall appoint a chairman and vice-chairman from among its members in accordance with the provisions of § 26, *mutatis mutandis*.

§ 28. The chairman or his deputy shall represent the Works Council in negotiations with the employer and before the Conciliation Board.

§ 29. The Election Committee shall convene the Works Council, not later than one week after its election, to make the appointments specified in §§ 26 and 27. The chairman shall convene all subsequent meetings, and shall draw up the agenda and conduct the proceedings. On the demand of not less than one-fourth of the members of the Works Council, the chairman shall call a meeting and shall place on the agenda the subject brought forward by them for consideration. The same procedure shall apply if a meeting is demanded by the employer.

The employer shall only be present at meetings to which he is invited and at meetings called at his request. He may take the chair at such meetings.

An appeal shall not be made to the Conciliation Board until the matter in dispute has been discussed with the employer at a meeting to which he has been duly invited and of the agenda for which he has been notified, or unless he or his representative has failed to attend the said meeting though duly invited.

§ 30. A Works Council shall meet outside working-hours as a rule and whenever possible. The meetings shall be private.

When it is necessary to hold a meeting during working-hours, the employer shall be given adequate notice.

§ 31. At the request of one-fourth of the members of a Works Council, one official of each of the economic associations of employees represented thereon shall be invited to attend meetings in an advisory capacity.

The employer may require that one official of each of the economic associations to which he belongs shall be invited to attend in an advisory capacity meetings at which he is entitled to be present.

§ 32. A resolution of the Works Council shall not be valid unless all the members have been summoned to the meeting and notified of the agenda, and unless at least half the members of the Council are present. Members may be represented by their substitutes in accordance with § 40.

Resolutions shall be passed by a simple majority vote of the

255

members and substitutes present. In the case of an equality of votes the resolution shall be deemed to be defeated.

§ 33. Minutes shall be kept of every meeting of the Works Council, stating at least the text of resolutions and the majority by which they are passed, and shall be signed by the Chairman and one other member.

If the employer has made a statement in the course of a debate, the minutes thereof shall be submitted to him for signature. He shall be furnished with a copy of the minutes of any proceedings in which he is entitled to take part.

If those wage-earning or salaried members of the Works Council, who find themselves in the minority as a group, regard a resolution passed by the Works Council on a matter affecting both wage-earning and salaried employees as gravely injurious to important interests of the employees whom they represent, the said members shall be entitled to express their views in a special resolution and to present the same to the employer.

§ 34. Other provisions respecting procedure may be embodied in standing orders drawn up by each Works Council for itself.

§ 35. Members and substitute members of Works Councils shall fulfil their duties without remuneration, as honorary functions. Unavoidable loss of working-time shall not be made a ground for reduction of wages or salary. Any agreement to the contrary shall be void.

§ 36. The necessary expenses arising out of the proceedings of the Council, including allowances for personal expenses where necessary, shall be borne by the employer, unless other provision is made for them under a Collective Agreement. He shall place rooms and other office requisites at the disposal of the Works Council for its meetings, interviews and current business, regard being had to the scope and nature of the establishment and the duties imposed by law upon the Council.

§ 37. It shall not be lawful for contributions to be collected from the employees and used for any of the purposes of Works Councils.

§ 38. Sections 29–37 shall apply correspondingly to the procedure of Works Committees, and § 26 (first sentence) and §§ 28–37 to the procedure of the separate Councils of wage-earning and salaried employees.

3. *Termination of Membership*

§ 39. Membership of a Works Council shall be terminated by resignation therefrom, by the expiry of the contract of employment, or by loss of eligibility.

At the request of the employer, or of not less than one-fourth of the employees entitled to vote, the Regional Economic Council, or, where none exists, the Conciliation Board, may resolve that the membership of a representative be terminated on account of gross misfeasance of duty.

Termination of membership of a Works Council shall entail

termination of membership of the separate Councils of wage-earning and salaried employees.

§ 40. If a member retires, a substitute (as provided for in the Election Regulations) shall take his place. Similarly substitutes may attend in place of members who are temporarily detained.

Substitutes shall be chosen in rotation from among the eligible but not elected persons belonging to the same list of nominations as the members replaced.

§ 41. At the request of the employer, or of not less than one-fourth of the employees entitled to vote, the Regional Economic Council, or, where none exists, the Conciliation Board, may resolve that the Works Council be dissolved on account of gross misfeasance of duty.

§ 42. If the total number of members and substitutes of a Works Council falls below the number of members of the Works Council required under §§ 15–16, steps shall at once be taken to hold a new election.

The same rule shall apply in the case mentioned in § 41, and also on the retirement of the whole Works Council. In the cases referred to in this paragraph substitute members shall not be called on to serve.

§ 43. If a new election of the whole Works Council is necessary, the members of the existing Council shall remain in office until the new Council is constituted.

In the case specified in § 41 the Regional Economic Council, or, where none exists, the Conciliation Board, may convene a temporary Works Council.

§ 44. Sections 39–41 shall apply correspondingly to termination of membership of a Council of wage-earning or salaried employees.

Termination of membership of a Council of wage-earning or salaried employees shall entail termination of membership of the Works Council.

A new election shall not be necessary if the number of supplementary and substitute members of a Council of wage-earning or salaried employees falls below the number required under § 15, paragraph 4.

If a Council of wage-earning or salaried employees is dissolved or retires, a new election shall be held to appoint members of the said Council who are also members of the Works Council, and as many supplementary members as before, for the remainder of the term of office of the Works Council. Section 43 shall apply correspondingly.

4. Works Assemblies

§ 45. A Works Assembly shall consist of the employees of one establishment.

If on account of the nature or magnitude of an establishment it is impossible to hold a meeting of all the employees together, the Works Assembly shall be held in sections.

§ 46. The chairman of the Works Council shall be entitled to call a

Works Assembly, and shall do so on the demand of the employer or of not less than one-fourth of the employees entitled to vote.

The employer shall be notified of any meeting held at his demand. He shall be entitled to appear at the said meeting, or to send a representative, and to take part in the proceedings either in person or through his representative, but not to vote.

A Works Assembly shall, as a general rule, take place outside working-hours; the consent of the employer shall be required if, in urgent cases, it is necessary to depart from this rule.

§ 47. One official from each of the economic associations of employees represented in the establishment shall be entitled to take part, in an advisory capacity, in a Works Assembly.

§ 48. A Works Assembly may forward requests and proposals to the Works Council. The meeting shall deal only with matters within its competence.

§ 49. Sections 45–48 shall apply correspondingly to separate Works Assemblies of wage-earning and salaried employees.

B. Central Works Councils

§ 50. If several establishments of a similar nature or forming part of the same economic process and belonging to the same proprietor are situated in the same commune or in neighbouring and economically interdependent communes, a Central Works Council may be constituted in addition to the Councils for individual establishments, if resolutions to that effect are adopted by the separate Councils.

§ 51. Under the aforesaid conditions a Common Works Council may be constituted instead of a Central Works Council, to take the place of the Councils for individual establishments.

The employees in any one of the associated establishments, who are entitled to vote, may withdraw from the arrangement on passing a resolution by a simple majority vote not later than six weeks before the expiry of the term of office of the Common Works Council.

A Common Works Council shall be constituted under the conditions specified in paragraph 1, in the case of establishments for which a representative body under §§ 1, 2 and 62 could not otherwise be formed.

§ 52. A Council for an individual establishment, or the employer, may propose the substitution of one or more Common Works Councils for the Central Works Council, in any case in which material simplification of business procedure would result therefrom without injury to the interest of employees. If the individual Works Councils do not all pass resolutions agreeing thereto, the Regional Economic Council, or, where none exists, the Conciliation Board, shall decide as to the proposal.

The employees entitled to vote in any one of the associated establishments may propose the dissolution of the Common Works Council on passing a resolution by a simple majority vote not later than six weeks before the expiry of the term of office of the Council. If resolutions agreeing thereto are not passed in all the works concerned, the Regional Economic Council, or, where none exists, the Conciliation Board, shall decide as to the proposal.

§ 53. Sections 50–52 shall apply to establishments carried on by communes and federated communes, even if they do not form part of the same economic process, but they shall apply to establishments carried on by other public bodies only in so far as they belong to the same branch of industry.

§ 54. For the purpose of electing a Central Works Council two electoral bodies shall be formed, one consisting of all the wage-earning members and the other of all the salaried members of the individual Works Councils. Each of these electoral bodies, under the direction of the three senior chairmen of the individual Works Councils, shall elect by ballot from among its own members its allotted number of members of the Central Works Council, on the principle of proportional representation. The number of members of the Central Works Council, and the constitution of the same, shall be determined in accordance with §§ 15 and 16.

Separate Councils of wage-earning and of salaried employees shall not be formed within a Central Works Council.

§ 55. Sections 26–37 shall apply correspondingly to the procedure of a Central Works Council.

§ 56. A Central Works Council shall be elected for one year.

Sections 39 and 41–43 shall apply correspondingly to the termination of membership of a Central Works Council.

The withdrawal of a member from a Central Works Council shall entail his withdrawal from the individual Works Council. The converse shall also apply.

In both cases the member who has withdrawn shall be replaced by his substitute on the individual Works Council.

§ 57. In undertakings in which Central Works Councils exist, the Works Assemblies of individual establishments shall be substituted for the Works Assembly of the undertaking.

C. Works Stewards

§ 58. A Works Steward (§ 2) shall be elected for one year by the employees entitled to vote, on a simple majority of votes by ballot. He shall be eligible for re-election.

Sections 20–21 and 23–25 shall apply correspondingly to the election of a Works Steward, with the following modifications of § 23, namely, that an election officer shall be substituted for the Election Committee and that the period of four weeks provided for in § 23, paragraph 1, shall be reduced to one week.

§ 59. Sections 28 and 35–37 shall apply correspondingly in respect of a Works Steward.

§ 60. Section 39, paragraphs 1 and 2, and § 43 shall apply correspondingly to the termination of service as a Works Steward.

D. Special Representative Bodies

§ 61. In undertakings and administrative departments carried on by the Federal Government, States, and federated communes, which extend over a considerable part of the Reich or of a State or into several communal areas, the constitution of individual and Central Works Councils and the determination of their respective powers and duties in relation to the form of the undertaking or administrative department shall be regulated by Order.

The said Order shall be issued by the Federal or State Government concerned, after consultation with the economic associations of the employees in question.

The said Order may also determine which parts of an undertaking or administrative department shall be deemed to be separate establishments in the sense of § 9, paragraph 2.

§ 62. A Works Council shall not be constituted, or, if already existent, shall be dissolved, if special difficulties are encountered in respect of its constitution or activities on account of the nature of the establishment, and if some other body representative of the employees of the establishment already exists or may be constituted on the basis of a Collective Agreement declared to be binding on all concerned. The said representative body shall have the powers and duties of a Works Council under this Act.

If such a Collective Agreement lapses, the representative body set up in accordance with paragraph 1 of this Section shall remain in office until a new Collective Agreement has been concluded and declared to be universally binding, or until a Statutory Works Council has been elected.

§ 63. If it is proposed that a Collective Agreement be declared to be binding on all concerned, the Federal Ministry of Labour may, on a proposal from persons entitled to put forward the same (§ 3 of the Order of 23 December, 1918, R.G. Bl. p. 1456), order the postponement of the election of Works Councils for establishments within the scope of the said Agreement, pending a decision as to its binding nature.

§ 64. If the said Agreement does not cover all the employees of an establishment, a representative body shall be constituted in accordance with the provisions of this Act for the workers to whom the Agreement does not apply, in order to safeguard their interests.

§ 65. If in an undertaking for which a Works Council is constituted there exists an officials' representative body (Officials' Council or Committee) for the public officials belonging thereto, the Works Council and the officials' representative body may meet for the joint consideration of matters of common interest which are within the competence of both bodies.

The chairman of the Works Council and of the officials' representative body shall preside in turn at alternate joint meetings. The sending out of notices of meetings and the drawing up of the agenda shall be carried out jointly by the two chairmen.

The Federal Government may issue more detailed regulations for the public authorities and undertakings of the Federal State and public bodies, which come under federal supervision in respect of the conditions of employment of their officials, and the Governments of the individual States may likewise issue regulations for the public authorities and undertakings of States, communes, federated communes and public bodies, which come under the supervision of the said Governments in respect of the conditions of employment of their officials.

III. POWERS AND DUTIES OF WORKERS' REPRESENTATIVE BODIES

A. Works Councils

§ 66. It shall be the duty of the Works Council—

(1) In establishments which serve economic purposes, to support the managing body with advice, and thus to co-operate in securing the highest possible standard of production and the maximum degree of working efficiency.

(2) In establishments which serve economic purposes, to co-operate and assist in the introduction of new labour methods.

(3) To guard the establishment against disturbances, and especially—without prejudice to the rights of economic associations of wage-earning and salaried employees (§ 8)—to appeal, in case of disputes between the Works Council, the whole body of employees or any group or part thereof, and the employer, to the Conciliation Board, or some other organ of conciliation or arbitration selected by agreement, in any case in which a settlement cannot be arrived at by negotiation.

(4) To supervise the execution of awards affecting the establishment as a whole which have been accepted by both parties, and which have been promulgated by a Conciliation Board or some other organ of conciliation or arbitration selected by agreement.

(5) To come to an agreement with the employer as regards works rules applicable to all employees and amendments thereof, subject to the terms of existing Collective Agreements, in accordance with § 75.

(6) To promote a good understanding among the employees themselves and between them and the employer, and to intervene to safeguard the employees' right of association.

(7) To receive complaints from the Councils of wage-earning and salaried employees and to endeavour to secure the removal of the grievances in question by negotiation with the employer.

(8) To take measures to prevent accidents and injury to health in the establishment, and to support the factory inspectors and other officials in the task of combating these dangers by means of suggestions, advice and information, and to co-operate in the execution of the provisions respecting the regulation of industrial conditions and the prevention of accidents.

(9) To participate in the administration of pension funds and housing or other welfare schemes attached to the establishment; in the last case, however, subject to the proviso that existing statutes of administration or existing testamentary dispositions do not prevent such participation or provide for the representation of the employees in some other manner.

§ 67. Section 66 (1) and (2) shall not apply to establishments which serve political, trade union, military, denominational, scientific, artistic or other similar purposes, in so far as the application of these paragraphs would conflict with the essential aims of those establishments.

§ 68. The Works Council shall endeavour in carrying out its duties to prevent either party from making demands and taking measures which are contrary to the interests of the community.

§ 69. The management of the establishment shall put into force any decisions arrived at in agreement with it. The Works Council shall not have the right to interfere with the management of the establishment by issuing orders on its own initiative.

§ 70. In an undertaking where a Control Board (*Aufsichtsrat*) exists, and where provision has not been made under any other Act for similar representation of the employees thereon, one or two members of the Works Council shall be appointed delegates to the Control Board in accordance with the provisions of a special Act to be issued hereafter on this matter, in order to represent the interests and claims of the workers and to put forward their opinions and desires in respect of the organisation of the undertaking. The said representatives shall have the right to attend and to vote at all meetings of the Control Board, but shall receive no remuneration other than repayment of out-of-pocket expenses. They shall be bound to preserve secrecy in respect of confidential matters communicated to them.

§ 71. A Works Council in an establishment which serves an economic purpose shall, for the purpose of fulfilling its duties, be entitled to require the employer to grant to the Works Committee, or, where none exists, to the Works Council, access to all transactions of the establishment which affect the contract of employment or the activities of the employees, and to the wages books and information required in connection with the carrying out of existing agreements, in so far as business or trade secrets are not endangered thereby and legal provisions do not forbid the same.

The employer shall further make a quarterly report on the position and progress of the establishment and of the industry generally and, in particular, on the output of the establishment and on anticipated requirements in respect of labour.

The members of the Works Committee or Works Council shall be bound to preserve secrecy in respect of confidential matters communicated to them by the employer.

§ 72. In an establishment in respect of which the owner is bound to keep accounts, and in which there are normally not less than 300 employees in all or 50 salaried employees, the Works Council may require that, every year from 1 January, 1921, onwards, a balance sheet for the establishment and a profit and loss statement for the past business year shall be presented for the inspection of the Works Committee, or, where none exists, the Works Council, and explained to the same, not later than six months after the end of the said business year, in accordance with a special Act dealing with this subject.

The members of the Works Committee or Works Council shall be bound to preserve secrecy in respect of confidential matters communicated to them by the employer.

§ 73. Sections 70 and 72 shall not apply to the establishments specified in § 67, if they would conflict with the essential aims of the establishment.

Undertakings or establishments may, on application, be exempted by the Federal Government from the obligations imposed under §§ 70 and 72, if important national interests necessitate such exemption.

In the cases specified in paragraphs (1) and (2), the Works Committee, or, where none exists, the Works Council, in any establishment for which a Control Board exists, shall be entitled to bring before the said Control Board proposals and recommendations in respect of the conditions of employment and the organisation of the establishment, and to make representations thereon to the Board through one or two delegates. The chairman of the Control Board shall, at the earliest possible moment, call a meeting and place the subjects thus raised on the agenda. The representatives of the Works Council shall have the right to speak and to vote at the said meeting.

§ 74. If, in consequence of the extension, reduction, or suspension of the establishment, or of the introduction of new technical processes, or new methods of organising or performing work, it becomes necessary to engage or dismiss a large number of employees, the employer shall communicate with the Works Council (or the Works Committee, where such exists, if any confidential communication is involved), as far as possible in advance, as regards the nature and scope of the necessary engagements and dismissals, and of the means for avoiding hardship in the latter case. The Works Council or Works Committee may require that the said information be communicated to the Central Employment Bureau or to an employment exchange designated by the latter.

§ 75. If general works rules are agreed upon under § 66 (5), the employer shall submit to the Works Council the draft of all provisions thereof not based upon existing agreements. If an agreement cannot be arrived at as to the said draft, either party may appeal to the Conciliation Board, whose decision shall be binding. The decision shall, however, not be binding in respect of the duration of working-hours.

The same procedure shall apply in respect of amendments of the rules of employment.

§ 76. In an establishment where more than 100 persons are employed, the Works Council may arrange for regular hours for interviews on one or more days in each week, when employees can make requests and complaints. If the hours for interviews fall within working-hours, the arrangement must be made by agreement with the employer.

§ 77. One of the members of the Works Council shall be invited to attend any enquiry into an accident which is undertaken at the works by the employer, the factory inspector or any other official concerned.

B. Councils of Wage-earning and of Salaried Employees

§ 78. It shall be the duty of the separate Councils of wage-earning and of salaried employees, or, where none exist, of the Works Council—

(1) To see that legal provisions for the benefit of employees, Collective Agreements, and also decisions, accepted by the parties, of a Conciliation Board or of any other organ of conciliation or arbitration agreed upon, are carried out in the establishment.

(2) To take part, in conjunction with the economic associations of the employees, in the fixing of wages and other working-conditions, in so far as these are not already regulated under Collective Agreements, in particular as regards—

the fixing of contract and piece-rates of wages or the bases for fixing such rates;

the introduction of new methods of remuneration;

the fixing of working-hours, with special regard to extensions and reductions of normal hours;

the regulation of holidays; and

the removal of grievances relating to the training and treatment of apprentices in the establishment.

(3) To come to an agreement with the employer respecting works rules or regulations of service affecting a group of employees, within the terms of existing Collective Agreements, and in accordance with § 80.

(4) To investigate grievances and to endeavour to secure their removal by negotiation with the employer.

(5) To appeal in case of disputes to the Conciliation Board, or to any other organ of conciliation or arbitration agreed upon, if the Works Council refuses to appeal.

(6) To take measures to prevent accidents and injury to health of

members of their group in the establishment, and, in connection with the said action, to assist industrial inspectors and other officials concerned, by means of suggestions, advice and information, and to co-operate in the carrying out of the provisions respecting the regulation of industrial conditions and the prevention of accidents.

(7) To do their utmost, by means of advice, suggestions and intervention, to influence the employer and their fellow-workers in the defence and on the behalf of persons disabled in the war or by accidents, so as to ensure for such persons employment on work suitable to their strength and capacities.

(8) To come to an agreement with the employer as to the general principles for the engagement of employees in each group in the establishment, in accordance with §§ 81–83, in so far as this matter is not regulated by existing Collective Agreements.

(9) To intervene in cases of dismissal of employees in each group, in accordance with §§ 84–90.

§ 79. Sections 68–69 shall apply correspondingly to separate Councils of wage-earning and salaried employees.

§ 80. Section 75 shall apply correspondingly to works rules or other regulations of service agreed upon for a group of employees under § 78 (3).

The determination of penalties provided for in § 134 b (4) of the Industrial Code shall be carried out by the employer jointly with the Council of wage-earning or of salaried employees. In case of dispute the Conciliation Board shall decide.

If the works rules in force were issued before 1 January, 1919, new rules shall be issued within three months after the date on which this Act comes into operation.

§ 81. The general principles agreed upon under § 78 (8) shall include a proviso that the engagement of an employee shall not be dependent upon his political, military, religious or trade union activities, or on his membership or non-membership of any political, religious or trade society, or any military organisation. They shall not include any proviso whereby engagement is made to depend upon a person's sex.

The provisions of paragraph 1 shall not apply to the establishments specified in § 67, in so far as the application of this paragraph would conflict with the essential aims of these establishments.

If an engagement is based upon obligations imposed by law, by a Collective Agreement, or by the decision of a Conciliation Board, or of any other organ of conciliation or arbitration agreed upon, the said obligations shall in every case have precedence over the general principles.

The employer shall decide independently, in accordance with the guiding principles, without either the co-operation or the supervision of the Council of wage-earning or of salaried employees, as to the engagement of individual employees.

§ 82. In case of an infringement of the principles agreed upon, the Council of wage-earning or of salaried employees may protest against the same within five days after receiving information thereof, but in no case later than fourteen days after the person concerned has taken up his employment.

The reasons for the protest and the evidence in support thereof shall be adduced by the Council of wage-earning or salaried employees in the course of the negotiations with the employer.

If a settlement is not arrived at by the said negotiations, the Council of wage-earning or of salaried employees may, within three days after the ending of the same, appeal to the competent Conciliation Board or to any organ of arbitration agreed upon.

A protest against an engagement and an appeal to the Conciliation Board or organ of arbitration shall not have suspensory or annulling effect.

§ 83. The decision in proceedings before the Conciliation Board as regards a protest shall be final. The person whose engagement is challenged shall be heard before the decision, so far as circumstances permit. If it is decided that a contravention of the principles agreed upon has been committed, it may at the same time be provided that the person engaged be deemed to be given notice of dismissal from his employment as from the date on which the decision becomes enforceable, the legal term of notice being duly observed. The decision shall have the force of law in respect of the employer and employee concerned.

§ 84. An employee who is given notice by his employer may, within five days after the date of the notice of dismissal, protest against the same and appeal to the Council of wage-earning or salaried employees—

(1) if there is ground for suspecting that notice was given on account of the sex of the person concerned, on account of his political, military, religious or trade union activities, or on account of his membership or non-membership of any political, religious or trade society, or any military organisation;

(2) if the notice was given without any reasons being stated;

(3) if the notice was given as a consequence of the employee's refusal to undertake regularly some work other than that agreed upon at the date of his engagement;

(4) if the dismissal appears to be unjust and involves hardship which neither the conduct of the employee nor the circumstances of the undertaking can justify.

If an employee is dismissed without notice for any reason which legally justifies termination of employment without observance of the period of notice, a protest may be based upon the alleged absence of any such reason.

§ 85. The right to protest under § 84 (1) shall not apply to the establishments specified in § 67, in so far as the application of this paragraph would conflict with the essential aims of these establishments.

The right to protest shall not apply—

(1) in cases of dismissal based upon obligations imposed by law, by Collective Agreement, or by the decision of a Conciliation Board, or other organ of conciliation or arbitration agreed upon;

(2) in cases of dismissal necessitated by total or partial suspension of the work of the undertaking.

§ 86. In connection with an appeal, the reasons for the protest shall be stated, and evidence adduced in support thereof. If the Council of wage-earning or salaried employees considers that the appeal is justified, it shall endeavour to bring about an understanding with the employer by negotiation. If an understanding is not arrived at within a week, the Council of wage-earning or salaried employees or the employee concerned may appeal to the Conciliation Board within the next five days.

In the case specified in § 84, paragraph 2, the Conciliation Board shall stay proceedings if judicial proceedings are pending in respect of the dismissal or if either of the parties claims a stay of proceedings in order to procure a judicial decision. Proceedings shall take their course if the withdrawal of the complaint is not notified within four weeks of the making of the claim for a stay of proceedings, or if an enforceable judicial decision is pronounced to the effect that dismissal without notice was not justified.

A protest against dismissal and an appeal thereon to the Conciliation Board shall not have suspensory effect.

§ 87. The decision in legal conciliation proceedings as regards a protest (§ 84) shall be final.

If the decision is to the effect that the protest against dismissal is justified, the employer shall at the same time be ordered to pay compensation in the event of his refusal to re-employ the person concerned. Compensation shall be proportionate to the total number of years during which the said person has been employed in the undertaking, and shall be reckoned at the rate of not more than one-twelfth of the last year's earnings for each year, but shall in no case exceed six-twelfths in all. In reckoning compensation, due regard shall be had to the economic situation of the employee and the financial capacity of the employer. The decision shall have the force of law in respect of the employer and employee concerned.

The employer shall, within three days after receiving information that the decision on the conciliation proceedings has become enforceable, notify the employee, either verbally or by post, whether he elects to re-employ him or to pay compensation. In default of the said notification he shall be deemed to have refused to re-employ him.

§ 88. If employment is resumed, the employer shall be bound to pay the employee wages or salary for the interval between his dismissal and his re-employment, in any case in which dismissal has in the meantime actually taken place. Section 615, sentence 2, of the Civil Code shall apply correspondingly. The employer may further take into account statutory payments, which the employee has received during the interval out of the unemployment or poor relief funds, and shall in such case refund the amounts to the authorities by whom the payments were made.

§ 89. An employee shall be entitled to refuse re-employment with his former employer if he has in the meantime entered into a contract of service with another. He shall notify the employer of his refusal, either verbally or by post, immediately upon receipt of the notification from the employer provided for in § 87, paragraph 3, but in no case later than one week after receiving information that the decision on the conciliation proceedings has become enforceable. In default of notification the right of refusal shall lapse. If he avails himself of the right of refusal, and if dismissal has actually taken place, he shall be paid wages or salary for the interval between his dismissal and the date on which the decision in the conciliation proceedings became enforceable. Section 88, sentences 2 and 3, shall be correspondingly applicable.

§ 90. If in any case specified in §§ 81–89 the observance of the time limits is prevented by natural occurrences or other inevitable accidents, the *status quo ante* shall be restored in accordance with the detailed provisions laid down in the administrative regulations.

C. Central Works Councils

§ 91. If a Central Works Council exists in addition to the Councils for individual establishments, the latter shall have the powers and duties of Works Councils only in respect of the individual establishments which they represent.

The Central Works Council shall deal with matters common to several separate establishments and matters concerning the whole of the establishments or undertakings.

D. Works Stewards

§ 92. A Works Steward shall have the powers and duties assigned to Works Councils (Councils of wage-earning and salaried employees) under §§ 66, 78 (1) to (7), 71 and 77.

Sections 67–69 shall apply correspondingly.

IV. SETTLEMENT OF DISPUTES

§ 93. The Regional Economic Council shall decide in case of disputes concerning—

(1) the necessity for constituting workers' representative bodies under this Act, the appointment and composition thereof;

(2) the right of any employee to vote or to become a candidate for election;

(3) the establishment, competence and procedure of workers' representative bodies and Works Assemblies;

(4) the necessity for expenditure in connection with the proceedings of workers' representative bodies;

(5) all disputes arising out of elections provided for in this Act.

§ 94. If an undertaking or an administrative organisation extends beyond the area of a single Regional Economic Council, or comes under the supervision of a State Government in respect of the conditions of employment in connection with it, the State Government shall declare it to be within the competence either of the State Economic Council or of a Regional Economic Council. If an undertaking or an administrative organisation extends beyond the area of a single State, or comes under the supervision of the Federal Government in respect of the conditions of employment in connection with it, the Federal Economic Council shall decide.

V. PROTECTIVE AND PENAL PROVISIONS

§ 95. An employer or his representative shall not hinder employees in the exercise of their right to vote in elections of the workers' representative bodies, or in the acceptance and exercise of their legal functions as workers' representatives, or place them at any disadvantage on that account.

§ 96. An employer shall not give a member of a workers' representative body notice of dismissal or transfer him to another works without the consent of the said workers' representative body.

The said consent shall not be necessary—

(1) in case of a dismissal based on obligations imposed by law or Collective Agreement or by a decision of a Conciliation Board or of any other organ of conciliation or arbitration agreed upon;

(2) in case of dismissal necessitated by the closing of the works;

(3) in case of dismissal without notice for any reason which legally justifies termination of employment without observance of the period of notice.

In the case specified in paragraph 2 (3), a protest may be made in accordance with § 84, paragraph 2, and § 86, paragraph 2.

If the dismissal of an employee without notice (paragraph 2 (3)) is pronounced by an enforceable judicial decision, or a decision of the Conciliation Board, to be unjustifiable, the dismissal shall be deemed to have been cancelled by the employer. Section 89 shall apply correspondingly.

§ 97. If a workers' representative body refuses its consent in any case in which the same is required, the employer may appeal to the Conciliation Board, whose decision shall take the place of the consent refused by the workers' representative body. It shall not take the place of the said consent in any case in which the Board determines that dismissal is a breach of the obligations imposed by § 95. The employer shall continue to employ the worker concerned until the Conciliation Board gives its decision.

§ 98. Sections 95–97 shall apply correspondingly to the representative bodies specified in §§ 62 and 63.

They shall apply to Works Stewards, subject to the proviso that a majority of the employees entitled to vote shall be substituted for the workers' representative body.

§ 99. An employer or his representative, who wilfully contravenes the provisions of § 95 itself or as applied under § 98, shall be punished by a fine not exceeding 2000 marks, or by detention.

A like penalty shall be imposed on an employer or his representative who wilfully contravenes the provisions of § 23, paragraphs 2 and 3.

An employer or his representative shall be liable to similar penalties if he wilfully refuses to grant the Works Council access to matters provided for in §§ 71–72, to furnish reports, to submit or explain wages books, information required in connection with the carrying out of existing Collective Agreements, and balance sheets or profit and loss statements, or if he wilfully neglects to fulfil these obligations in due time.

Any person who intentionally makes false statements or suppresses facts in the accounts, reports and surveys of the position of an undertaking furnished in discharge of his obligations under §§ 71 and 72, in order to deceive employees and with intent to injure them, shall be liable to imprisonment for not more than one year and to a fine not exceeding 10,000 marks, or to one of these penalties.

Criminal prosecutions shall be instituted only on demand of a workers' representative body. The suit may be withdrawn.

§ 100. Any person who, without authority, discloses confidential information or secrets of an undertaking or a trade which have become known to him through his membership of a workers' representative body, and of the confidential nature of which he has been notified, shall be liable to a fine of not more than 1500 marks or to detention.

Any person who commits the aforesaid offence for the purpose of obtaining pecuniary benefit for himself or another, or of injuring an employer, shall be liable to imprisonment for a period not exceeding one year. A fine not exceeding 3000 marks may be imposed in addition to imprisonment. If extenuating circumstances can be proved, the fine alone shall be imposed. In addition to the fine, the sum gained by means of the criminal action may be confiscated.

Prosecution shall take place only on demand of an employer. The suit may be withdrawn.

VI. ADMINISTRATIVE AND TEMPORARY PROVISIONS

§ 101. The Federal Minister of Labour shall be empowered to issue administrative regulations under this Act, subject to the consent of the Federal Council and of a Committee of the Reichstag consisting of 28 members.

§ 102. The Workers' Committee shall discharge the duties assigned to the Works Council under § 23, paragraph 1, in respect of the first election, which shall take place not later than six weeks after this Act comes into operation; it shall appoint the Election Committee at a meeting convened by its chairman and held jointly with the salaried employees' Committee where such exists. Where no Workers' Committee exists, the salaried employees' Committee shall act in its place.

If the Committee of workers or of employees fails to fulfil its obligations, or in any case where the said Committees do not exist, the procedure specified in § 23, paragraph 2, shall be adopted.

The employer shall nominate the three senior employees entitled to vote to act as election officers for the first election of a Works Steward (§ 58, paragraph 2).

§ 103. The central authority for the State shall appoint another body to act as substitute for the Regional Economic Councils under § 93, pending the constitution of the said Councils. Pending the constitution of State Economic Councils and the Federal Economic Council, the State Government shall appoint another independent body to deal with cases under § 94, first sentence, and the Federal Government shall make similar provision for all other cases.

§ 104. The following amendments shall come into operation simultaneously with this Act:

(1) Sections 7–14 of the Order respecting Collective Agreements, workers' and employees' Committees and the settlement of industrial disputes, dated 23 December, 1918 (R.G. Bl. p. 1456) are hereby repealed.

(2) Section 19 of the above-mentioned Order shall be amended to read as follows: "Special Conciliation Boards may be constituted for State and Federal undertakings and administrations. The Federal Government shall issue an order respecting the constitution of the said Boards for Federal administrations and the State Governments shall likewise issue orders for State administrations".

(3) Sections 20 *et seq.* of the above-mentioned Order shall be amended by the substitution throughout for the workers' and employees' Committees in establishments specified in § 1 of this Act, of the Works Council, or of the Councils of wage-earning and salaried employees under §§ 6 and 78; and in establishments specified in § 2 of this Act, of Works Stewards; and the representative bodies constituted under §§ 62 and 63 of this Act

shall be substituted in the aforesaid sections for those constituted under § 12 of the Order.

(4) Section 134 *a*, paragraph 2, and § 134 *b*, paragraph 3, of the Industrial Code shall be amended so as to assign to the employer jointly with the Works Council the responsibility for issuing the works rules and supplements to the same. The signature of the chairman of the Works Council shall be deemed to be the signature of the Council.

(5) Sections 134 *d* and 134 *h* of the Industrial Code are hereby repealed.

(6) Section 134 *e*, paragraph 1, of the Industrial Code shall be amended to read as follows: "The works rules and every supplement to the same, shall be transmitted in duplicate to the lower administrative authority within three days of their issue".

(7) Section 13, first sentence, of the Order relating to a provisional Agricultural Labour Act, dated 24 January, 1919 (R.G. Bl. p. 111), shall be amended to read as follows: "In those undertakings in which there exists a Works Council, works rules shall be issued and posted up in a conspicuous place".

(8) In references in other Acts and Orders and in Collective Agreements to workers' and employees' Committees, Works Councils or Councils of wage-earning or salaried employees under §§ 6 and 78 shall be substituted for the said Committees in the case of undertakings specified in § 1 of this Act, and Works Stewards shall be similarly substituted in the case of establishments specified in § 2 of this Act, and the representative bodies provided for in §§ 62 and 63 shall be substituted in the case of undertakings there specified.

§ 105. If the Act referred to in § 72 respecting the balance sheets of undertakings has not come into operation before 31 December, 1920, a balance sheet and profit and loss statement in accordance with the provisions of the Commercial Code shall be submitted to the Works Council.

§ 106. This Act shall come into operation on the day of its promulgation. The Acts of individual States respecting Works Councils shall be repealed on the same date.

Existing Works Councils, Councils of wage-earning employees established for special undertakings, and workers' and employees' Committees, shall be dissolved immediately upon the completion of the first election which takes place after this Act comes into operation.

Regulations governing Elections under the Works Councils Act

I. ELECTION OF WORKS COUNCILS AND OF COUNCILS OF WAGE-EARNING AND SALARIED EMPLOYEES
(§§ 15–25 of the Act)

A. General Provisions

§ 1. *Management of elections. Calculation of time limits.* In the election of the Works Council the wage-earning and salaried employees shall elect separately their own representatives on the Works Council.

In the formation of the wage-earners' and salaried employees' Councils supplementary members shall be added to the wage-earning and salaried employee members of the Works Council. The number of members of the individual wage-earners' and salaried employees' Councils shall be determined in accordance with the same principles as those governing the members of the Works Council itself (§§ 15, 16 of the Act).

The management of the election shall be in the hands of the Election Committee (§§ 23, 102 of the Act).

The provisions of the Civil Code regarding the calculation of time limits shall apply correspondingly.

B. Preparation for Election

§ 2. *Register of elections.* It shall be the duty of the Election Committee to draw up a register of those entitled to vote, showing separately the wage-earning and salaried employees. Existing lists (sickness insurance lists, wages lists) may be used.

§ 3. *Writ of election.* The Election Committee shall issue a writ of election, not later than 20 days before the last day for voting (§ 10, para. 1). The writ of election shall state the number of Works Councillors and supplementary members to be elected from each group of the employees (wage-earners and salaried employees), and where the election register can be inspected; it shall state that objections on the ground of exclusion from the register are to be brought to the chairman of the Election Committee within three days after the register has first been posted up (para. 3) and, in order that lists of candidates shall be presented for each group of Works Council members, it shall state that only such lists of candidates will be accepted as have been handed in to the Election Committee not later than a week after the lists were first posted up, and that voting is confined to the accepted lists of candidates. It shall further be stated where the lists of candidates can be inspected by the electors after their acceptance (§ 6); where the electors can obtain the voting envelope, and also when and where (§ 10, para. 1) they can give up the voting envelope with their voting card. Finally the election writ shall state where the Election Regulations may be inspected. The election writ shall give the address of the chairman.

A copy or off-print of the election writ shall be posted up and kept in a legible condition, in one or more places accessible to all electors, to be designated by the Election Committee, until the last day for voting (§ 10, para. 1) or until the day on which it is announced that no voting will take place (§ 8, para. 2).

§ 4. *Decisions on objections to the register of electors.* The Election Committee shall decide as quickly as possible as to any objections against the register of electors. If the objection is held to be justified the register shall be altered accordingly. The objector shall be notified of the decision before the commencement of the time limit allowed for voting (§ 10, para. 1); the decision may only be contested if the validity of the whole election is contested.

§ 5. *Lists of candidates. Proposers.* Each list of candidates shall contain the names of at least twice as many eligible candidates as the number of Works Councillors and supplementary members to be elected by the group in question (wage-earners, salaried employees). In drawing up the lists regard shall be had as far as possible to the different categories of male and female employees in the establishment. The individual candidates shall be ranked under consecutive numbers or in some other recognisable order and designated by their family and Christian names, occupations and dwellings. Their agreement in writing to the appearance of their names on the list shall be appended.

The lists of candidates must be signed by at least three persons eligible to vote. If one of the signatories is not expressly designated as proposer of the list of candidates, each signatory may be regarded as proposer of the list. The proposer of the list shall be entitled and required to give to the chairman of the Election Committee any information necessary to avoid objections. If an elector signs more than one election list his name shall only be counted on the first list handed in and must be deleted from the other lists. If several lists of candidates are handed in at the same time, which are signed by the same elector, the signature shall be valid for that list which is designated by the signatory within a period of grace allowed him of not more than two days. If the signatory fails to do this the issue shall be decided by casting lots. If a list of candidates does not contain the requisite number of signatures, owing to deletion, the proposer of the list shall be given a time limit within which to procure the missing signatures. If all the signatures are deleted the list is invalid (§ 7, para. 1).

An amalgamation of lists of candidates is invalid.

§ 6. *Notification and approval of lists of candidates.* The Election Committee shall give numbers and names to the list of candidates handed in, according to the order in which they were received and, so far as the lists are not invalid (§ 7, para. 1, sentence 1), shall forthwith inform the proposers of the list of any objections (§ 7, para. 1, sentences 2 and 3). A time limit shall be allowed for dealing with objections. Not later than three days before the beginning of the time limit fixed for voting, the approved lists of candidates shall be posted up or deposited, in a suitable manner, for the inspection of those taking part in the election. Until this takes place a list of candidates can be withdrawn by a declaration signed by all the signatories of the list.

If, in spite of an objection raised by the Election Committee, a declaration is not forthcoming or is not made in time, the name of the candidate concerned shall be deleted from the list.

§ 7. *Invalid lists of candidates.* Lists of candidates shall be invalidated if they are handed in too late, or if they do not carry the requisite number of signatures. Those lists shall also be invalid on which the candidates are not shown in a recognisable order of sequence (§ 5, para. 1, sentence 3), if this defect is not corrected in time (§ 6, sentence 2).

If a proposed candidate is not designated in the manner required by § 5, para. 1, sentence 3, and if the proposer of the list does not carry out in time the instruction of the Election Committee to complete the list (§ 6, sentence 2), the name of the person whose designation is incomplete may be deleted.

§ 8. *Case in which no lists are valid. Election without polling.* If no valid list of candidates is handed in for the election of members of the wage-earners or of the salaried employees, this must be notified by the Election Committee (§ 3, para. 3) and an additional period of grace of one day, as from the date of notification, must be allowed for the handing in of lists. If a valid list of candidates is still not forthcoming, the Election Committee shall announce, in the same manner as is prescribed for the election writ, that no voting can take place (§ 3, para. 3).

If only one list of candidates is approved for the election of wage-earners or salaried employees, those candidates on it whose designation is valid shall be deemed to be elected, in the order in which their names appear on the list. Para. 1, sentence 2 shall apply correspondingly.

C. Voting

§ 9. *Voting cards and envelopes.* The elector may give his vote only for one of the approved lists of candidates (§ 6). The voting card must contain the ordinal number of the approved list. In place of, or in addition to the ordinal number, one or more names of the candidates on the list may be cited. Voting papers which are signed, which contain names from more than one list of candidates or which are ambiguous or which contain a protest or objection against all the candidates or which have an identification mark, are invalid.

The elector must give up his voting paper in a voting envelope. The envelopes, on which are written or printed the words, "Election for the Works Council of (name of establishment)", are to be obtained from the employer.

The voting envelopes shall be supplied to those entitled to vote, in accordance with arrangements made by the Election Committee.

If several voting papers are found in one envelope, they will only count as one vote if they are the same in all particulars, otherwise they shall all be deemed to be invalid.

§ 10. *Handing in of voting cards.* The elector shall, on the day appointed for voting, hand in his voting card in the open or closed voting envelope at the place appointed by the Election Committee, giving his name.

The person entrusted with the receipt of the voting envelope and the voting papers shall, in the presence of the voter, put the envelope into the box prepared for the purpose, and shall mark off the vote on the register of electors.

The box for voting papers must be locked by the Election Committee and so constructed that the envelope with the voting papers, placed inside the box, cannot be removed from it without the box being opened.

If members of the wage-earners and of the salaried employees are to be elected, the voting papers shall be given up separately for each group of employees.

D. Ascertainment of Election Results

§ 11. *General.* The result of the election shall be announced not later than the third day after the termination of voting.

§ 12. *Reckoning of votes cast for each list.* After the box or boxes containing the envelopes have been opened by the Election Committee, the voting papers shall be taken out of the envelopes and the votes cast for each list aggregated. At the same time the validity of the voting papers shall be investigated.

§ 13. *Distribution of vacancies between lists.* The votes given for the separate lists shall be placed in a row, side by side, and shall all be divided by 1, 2, 3, 4, and so on. The quotients resulting shall be placed in order of magnitude under the numbers of the first row. The division shall be continued until it can be assumed that no maximum numbers will appear, which are higher than those in the earlier rows which come into question for the allocation of seats.

From the numbers thus found, as many maximum numbers shall be extracted and placed in order of magnitude as there are members and supplementary members of the Works Council to be elected.

Each list of candidates will receive as many seats as the quantity of maximum numbers which it contains.[1] If one maximum number is to be found in several lists, lots shall be cast to decide to which list the next seat falls.

If one list contains fewer candidates then the quantity of maximum numbers credited to it, the surplus votes shall be transferred to the maximum numbers of the other lists.

§ 14. *Order of candidates in each list.* The order of the candidates in each list is determined by the order of nomination on the list. If a person should be elected several times over, owing to his nomination on more than one list, he shall be deemed to be elected on the list for which his maximum number is the greatest. Where the maximum numbers are equal, the issue shall be decided by casting lots. On the other lists, the next candidate in order of nomination will take the place of the candidate already deemed to be elected.

§ 15. *Substitute members.* The candidates next in order after the elected members on each list are their substitute members, subject to the proviso, that the supplementary members belonging to the same list are at the same time the first substitute members for the Works Council.

§ 16. *Records of the Election Committee.* In so far as voting has taken place in accordance with §§ 9 and 10, the Election Committee shall record in writing the total number of the valid votes cast by each group of employees, the votes cast for each list, the resulting maximum numbers, their distribution amongst the lists, the number of votes declared to be invalid, and the names of the Works Councillors and supplementary members elected by each group of employees.

Similar procedure is to be adopted if the election has taken place without voting, in accordance with § 8, para. 2, sentence 1.

The records are to be signed by the Election Committee.

§ 17. *Notification to persons elected.* The Election Committee shall notify in writing the elected Works Councillors and supplementary members of the fact that they have been elected. If the person elected does not declare within a week that he declines election, he is deemed to have accepted.

In the event of refusal to accept election, the next person on the

---

[1] [If, for example, there were six vacancies and three lists for which a total of 260 votes were cast, of which 120 were for List I, 90 for List II, and 50 for List III, the result of the election would be as follows:

List I		List II		List III	
Candidate 1	**120**	Candidate 1	**90**	Candidate 1	**50**
„ 2	**60**	„ 2	**45**	„ 2	25
„ 3	**40**	„ 3	30	„ 3	$16\frac{2}{3}$
„ 4	30	„ 4	$22\frac{1}{2}$	„ 4	$12\frac{1}{2}$

In this case candidates 1, 2, 3 on List I, candidates 1, 2 on List II, and candidate 1 on List III would have been declared elected.]

same list of candidates, who has not yet been elected, is deemed to be elected.

§ 18. *Publication of result of election.* As soon as the names of those elected are finally settled, the Election Committee shall announce them by displaying them for two weeks in the same place where the writ of election was posted up.

E. Disputed and Invalid Elections

§ 19. *General.* The validity of the elections may be disputed during the period for which the names are displayed (§ 18). Objections must be brought before the authorities mentioned in §§ 93, 94, 103 of the Act.

Decisions of the Election Committee may only be disputed by disputing the election as a whole.

If the whole election is invalid, the procedure for a new election must forthwith be set in motion.

§ 20. *Invalid elections.* The election is invalid if there has been any infringement of the essential provisions governing election procedure, and if a subsequent adjustment is not possible, and if it cannot be proved that the result of the election could not have been affected by the infringement.

§ 21. *Invalid elections of individuals.* The election of an individual is invalid, if he was ineligible at the time of the election and has not become eligible in the meantime.

The election of an individual is also invalid if he, or others on his behalf, have illegally (compare especially §§ 107 to 109, 240, 339 of the Criminal Code). or by giving or promising bribes, influenced his election, unless such action could not have affected the result of the election.

Section 17, para. 2 applies correspondingly.

F. Final Provisions

§ 22. *Preservation of documents. Expenses.* The election documents shall be kept by the Works Council until the termination of its period of office.

The material expenses (provision of the Election Order, the voting envelopes, the necessary boxes for voting papers, etc.) shall be borne by the employer.

G. Special Provisions for Election of the Works Council
by all Employees voting together (§ 19 of the Act)

§ 23. *General.* Sections 1–22 apply correspondingly, except in so far as the following sections provide otherwise.

§ 24. *Constitution of the Works Council.* The Works Council is elected by a single election for all the employees of the Works Councillors and substitute members.

§ 25. *Writ of election.* In the writ of election (§ 3) the Works Councillors and supplementary members to be elected shall be enumerated separately as wage-earners and as salaried employees.

§ 26. *Lists of candidates.* In drawing up the lists of candidates (§ 5), it is to be noted that each group of employees must be represented on the Works Council in accordance with §§ 15, 16 of the Act.

§ 27. *Distribution of vacancies.* In the lists of candidates the wage-earners' seats, together with their supplementary members, are, in the first instance, distributed and then, by a separate count, the salaried employees' seats with their supplementary members. To each list of candidates as many seats are allotted from each group of employees as correspond to the maximum number falling to it on the separate count.

§ 28. *Order of candidates in each list.* In allocating the wage-earners' seats only those candidates belonging to the wage-earners' group, and in allocating the salaried employees' seats only those candidates belonging to the salaried employees' group, come in question.

II. THE ELECTION OF THE CENTRAL WORKS COUNCIL
(§ 54 of the Act)

§ 29. *Management of the election, calculation of time limits.* The Central Works Council is elected by the vote of all wage-earning and all salaried employee members of the individual Works Councils, each group forming a separate electoral body for the election of its representatives on the Central Works Council.

The management of the election in each electoral body is in the hands of the Election Committee (§ 54 of the Act).

Section 1, para. 4 of the Election Order applies correspondingly.

§ 30. *Writ of election.* Time and place of the election shall be notified in writing, about 20 days before the election, to all those entitled to vote in each electoral body. The notification must state the number of the members to be elected and must point out, with reference to the handing in of lists of candidates, that only such lists can be considered as are handed in to the chairman of the Election Committee by a stated date, about a week after the issue of the writ of election, and that voting is confined to this list of candidates. The writ of election must give the name and address of the chairman of the Election Committee.

§ 31. *Lists of candidates.* Sections 5 to 8 of the Election Order apply correspondingly, but § 5, with the proviso, that only the actual number of members of the Central Works Council is to be nominated, and that two signatures to the writ of election are sufficient, § 6, with the proviso, that the written communication of the election lists to those entitled to vote takes the place of the posting up of the lists. This communication is to be enclosed with the voting envelope.

APPENDIX II

§ 32. *Carrying out of the election.* The provisions of §§ 9 to 14, 16 to 22, apply correspondingly. A definite period of time shall be fixed for the election. All electors are entitled to vote who put in an appearance before the termination of voting. Substitute members (§ 15 of the Election Regulations) are not elected.

During the period of time allotted for voting any list of candidates may be withdrawn by those who have signed it provided that none of the electors who have appeared during the voting period objects, and new lists may be presented and withdrawn. Voting may also take place on the newly presented lists.

III. THE ELECTION OF THE WORKS COMMITTEE
(§ 27 of the Act)

§ 33. The election of the Works Committee shall take place in the Works Council meeting convened for this purpose (§ 29 of the Act) under the management of the oldest Works Councillor. It is incumbent on him to ask for lists of candidates to be handed in and to point out that voting is confined to the lists. Two signatures to the list of candidates are sufficient. Lists handed in may be withdrawn by the signatories.

The election is open.

The distribution of the elected amongst the lists of candidates shall take place in accordance with §§ 13, 14 of the Election Regulations.

Sections 19, 20, 21, paras. 1 and 2, apply correspondingly: the time limit for objections runs from the date of the election.

IV. THE ELECTION OF THE WORKS STEWARD
(§ 58 of the Act)

§ 34. The Works Steward is elected by ballot on a simple majority at an election conducted by the oldest employee in the establishment. In the event of equality of votes lots must be cast.

Sections 19, 20, 21, paras. 1 and 2, apply correspondingly. The period of grace for objections runs from the date of the election.

If two Works Stewards are to be elected the person who conducts the election in each group of employees is the oldest employee in that group.

Act regulating the Construction of Balance Sheets and Profit and Loss Accounts of Establishments. February 5, 1921

§ 1. The establishment balance sheet which is to be submitted in accordance with § 72 of the Works Councils Act of February 4, 1920, shall set out, in accordance with the legal provisions governing the preparation of the balance sheet of the undertaking in question, the separate items of the assets and the liabilities of the undertaking in such a way that the financial position of the establishment can be ascertained, without investigation of any other data. The statement of accounts shall not comprise any property belonging to the employer but not devoted to the purposes of the undertaking.

§ 2. For the purpose of explaining the balance sheet, information shall be given regarding the significance and inter-relation of the individual items. The information must be based on the data from which the balance sheet has been drawn up, such as the inventory, trial balance, cash account, overhead charges of production and marketing. The submission of the actual data from which the balance sheet has been drawn up is not obligatory. Reference must be made to any important changes which have taken place during the business year. If in the course of the business year any assets or liabilities have been transferred from funds devoted to the establishment to funds not devoted to the establishment, or *vice versa*, these shall be shown separately when the balance sheet of the establishment is submitted.

If an undertaking consists of more than one establishment the business position of the individual establishments shall be explained, when the balance sheet is submitted, in so far as the special conditions of the undertaking and of the separate establishments make this possible.

§ 3. The right to require the submission and explanation of the establishment balance sheet (§§ 1, 2) shall belong to the Central Works Council as well as to the individual Works Councils.

§ 4. The provisions of §§ 1 to 3 shall apply correspondingly to the establishment profit and loss accounts to be submitted in accordance with § 72 of the Works Councils Act.

§ 5. The submission and explanation of an establishment balance sheet as also of an establishment profit and loss account shall be required for the first time for the last business year preceding January 1 1921.

§ 6. This Act shall come into force as from February 1, 1921.

Act regulating the Election of Members of Works Councils to Control Boards. February 15, 1921

§ 1. A Control Board, in the sense of Article 70 of the Works Councils Act of February 4, 1920, shall be taken to comprise any organ of a joint stock company, of a partnership based on shares, of a company with restricted liability, of a registered co-operative society, of a mutual insurance society and of a mining undertaking, which is described as the Control Board in the laws governing these undertakings, irrespective of the designation of such organ under the articles of association of the undertaking in question.

§ 2. If one or more Works Councils or Central Works Councils exist for the employees in one of the corporate bodies named in § 1, the election of Works Council members to the Control Board shall be regulated in accordance with the following provisions.

§ 3. Unless it is otherwise provided in the Works Councils Act or in what follows, the legal provisions which apply to the other members of the Control Board shall also apply to the Works Council members elected to the Board.

§ 4. Two Works Council members shall be elected, if in accordance with the articles of association of the undertaking in force at the time of the election, more than three Control Board members may be elected, or if both sections of employees (wage-earners and salaried employees) are represented on the Works Council. In all other cases one only shall be elected.

For each member to be elected two substitute members shall be elected to replace those whose membership of the Control Board may lapse.

§ 5. In corporate bodies which have a single Works Council or a Central Works Council this Council shall form the electoral body for the election of Works Council members to the Control Board, but where there are several Works Councils the sum of these shall constitute the electoral body, irrespective of whether they are partly combined into a Central Works Council.

All members of the electoral body shall be eligible for election who at the time of the election have been employed for one year in the undertaking and have not within the preceding two years been compulsorily retired by an award under § 39 of the Works Councils Act. The condition that members shall have been employed for one year shall be waived if the number of eligible persons is fewer than four times the number of members to be elected.

In the case of registered co-operative societies, § 9, para. 2 of the

Act concerning co-operative societies shall only apply to the Works Council members to be elected to the Control Board if membership is open to them and can legitimately be attributed to them.

§ 6. The election shall take place by secret ballot and by a single majority vote of all those belonging to the electoral body. If two members are to be elected, the minority group of the employees (§ 16 of the Works Councils Act) may resolve by an equal or majority vote that a representative of their group shall be elected, provided that not less than two members of the electoral body belong to the group: in this event there shall be a divided election by each of the two groups of employees.

Re-election shall be permissible.

The Federal Labour Minister shall draw up detailed regulations for the electoral procedure.

§ 7. Membership of the Control Board shall lapse only through loss of membership of the Works Council to which the member belongs.

§ 8. If a Works Council member withdraws from the Control Board, a substitute member shall take his place in accordance with the provisions of the Election Order. If there is no substitute member available a new election shall be held.

§ 9. If a corporate body, which has been founded but has not yet been registered, has already a Control Board, Articles 1 to 8 shall apply correspondingly.

§ 10. This Act shall also apply to the workers' representative bodies described in § 62 of the Works Councils Act, if the representative bodies are constituted for the establishments of one corporate body only, and if they are composed of employees of this corporate body.

§ 11. The Act shall come into force on February 1, 1922. The first elections shall be held within three months of the coming into force of the Act.

APPENDIX V

The Questionnaire[1] of the "Bergwerks-Zeitung"[2]

Question 1. In what proportion in the year 1922 did the unproductive costs occasioned by the Works Councils stand to the total wages and salaries paid?

Answer. The question as to the unproductive costs to which the Works Councils give rise is answered differently by various works. In many cases, especially in the smaller and medium-sized works, there were no costs at all or else they were so slight as to be insignificant. Other works observe that, owing to the lack of data, they cannot give an exact return. According to some of the larger works, the costs consist chiefly of the earnings of the Chairman when released from productive work and, further, of the loss of working-time during meetings and interviews. To these should be added the costs arising from the action of the wage-earners' Council in keeping workers from their work, as has often occurred. In any case the costs occasioned by the activities of the Works Council are not inconsiderable.

Q. 2. What has been the nature of the co-operation with the Works Council?

A. The co-operation with the Works Council has been very varied. In the medium and smaller works there are fewer complaints than in the larger works. In individual cases, a relatively good co-operation is reported, which is chiefly attributed to the fact that older and experienced workers were elected to the Works Council. In larger works, especially in Dortmund, Gelsenkirchen, Bochum, Düsseldorf and Duisburg, the contrary was the case. Co-operation with the Works Council was confronted then by many difficulties, which were greater or less according to the political convictions of the members of the Works Council. The chief obstacles in the way of co-operation have arisen because the Works Council has been double-faced, and has said one thing to the management of the works and something quite different to the body of workers. It has also occurred that co-operation with individual members of the Works Council was better than with the whole Council. To sum up, it may be stated that the nature of the co-operation was dependent on the personal and political attitude of the members of the Works Council, and on their experience and age.

Q. 3. What was the composition of the Works Council? Were chiefly the older, more experienced workers, represented on it?

A. The composition of the Works Council was better in the medium and smaller works than in the larger ones. In the more rural districts also, where patriarchal relations still remain in some measure, it was mostly the older and experienced workers who were given mandates to the Works Council. The larger works have, for the most part, had an unfavourable experience of the Works Councils, since, frequently, it was not the best and most experienced workers, but the political agitators and demagogues, who were elected to the Councils. The electoral lists were almost entirely drawn up in accordance with political or Trade Union membership.

Q. 4. Has the Works Council been able to assist the works from the economic standpoint? Or has it damaged the works, and, if so, in what manner?

A. To this it can be replied that, only in very rare instances, can the

---

[1] See above, p. 115.

[2] *Deutsche Bergwerks-Zeitung,* November 18, 1924, and December 17, 1924.

Works Council be said to have been of positive value. Such value has consisted, chiefly, in the fact that reasonable Works Councils have been able, especially in small works, to prevent threatened strikes from occurring. Some works have had the experience that the co-operation of the Works Council in the fixing of piece-rates and in other negotiations, and also in preventing unrest, is of value, inasmuch as permanent representatives of the workers are less inclined to put forward extravagant demands than spokesmen who have been elected *ad hoc* in times of excitement. In general, however, the Works Councils have done more harm than good, chiefly because they have either stimulated strikes in certain cases, or else, on the outbreak of a strike, have kept themselves in the background in a cowardly fashion and have not opposed the radical elements among the workers with sufficient determination. On such critical occasions they frequently left the leadership entirely to the extremists. From the economic standpoint they have caused loss mainly through much waste of time by unnecessary meetings and discussions.

Q. 5. Has the Works Council accomplished anything of importance in labour matters, especially in the protection of labour against sickness and accident?

A. It was only reported in one case that the Works Council had achieved anything in the sphere of labour protection. For the rest, it is declared almost unanimously that its activities in this field have been entirely negative. In other labour matters also, no achievement can be recorded, since any suggestions made were based purely on political motives. Quite frequently proposals and demands have been put forward without any legal foundation and have therefore been rejected by the management of the works.

Q. 6. Has the Works Council abused its rights politically?

A. It is only very rarely that Works Councils have adopted the standpoint imposed on them by the Act, and have confined themselves to their proper legal functions. Virtually without exception, all the works, large and small, hold the opinion that the whole institution of the Works Councils has developed into a Trade Union or political party organisation. Their entire activities were governed by the policy of the Trade Unionists or politicians behind the scenes. The members of the Works Councils regarded themselves primarily as members of their party or their Trade Union, and saw in their office mainly the possibility of training leaders for socialisation to replace the existing leaders. Their activities on behalf of their fellow-workers were also almost exclusively determined by political considerations. To sum up, it may be said that, over most of the field, there has been an appreciable abuse of the rights of the Works Councils, due to their purely political or Trade Union bias.

Q. 7. Has the institution of the Works Council increased the interest taken by the workers in their work?

A. No firm reports that the interest of the employees in their work has been stimulated by the Works Council. On the contrary the opinion is almost unanimously expressed that, owing to the institution of the Works Councils, there has been an appreciable decrease in interest in the fortunes of the works, since the Works Councils are mainly concerned with extracting better conditions of wages and employment for their fellows, and have paid no attention to the fortunes of the works, as should have been their legal duty.

Q. 8. Have the relations of the worker to the employer or to those set above him improved or deteriorated as a result of the legal co-operation of the Works Council?

A. Only one or two works found themselves able to answer this question in the affirmative. Much the greater number hold that the relations have neither improved nor deteriorated. Some works report a deterioration, due to the extravagant claims of the Works Council, which had aroused in the workers hostility against the employer. Also, owing to the special protection which many Works Councils accord to the younger workers, on grounds of agitation, a wedge is often driven between the employer and his employees.

Q. 9. Do you see any further advantages in the existence of a workers' representative body within the works?

A. The great majority of the works reply to this question in the negative. A few, however, are of the opinion that a system of workers' representation, such as existed after the Auxiliary Service Act of 1916, has a real value. Many works hold that a workers' representative body has the advantage of preventing the management from being swamped by requests and proposals from the body of employees. Other works, again, regard the advantage as consisting in the existence of a single body with which all petty matters can be discussed and disputes resolved. It is emphasised, in this connection, that it has frequently occurred that requests and demands have been rejected by the Works Council and have never been brought before the management, with the result that conflicts between the management and the workers were avoided. Some works propose that Workers' Committees, as they existed before the war, should be re-introduced, as they were fully adequate for all purposes. In any case, not a single works considers the now existing Works Councils to be the appropriate form of workers' representation for both sides.

Q. 10. Has the Works Council been given too many rights by the Works Councils Act, and what amendments are desirable?

A. Many works take the attitude that the Works Councils Act should be entirely abolished. They are of opinion that the whole experiment has been a complete failure and should be withdrawn. Other works desire modifications in the Act in the shape of the abolition of Sections 66 (9), 80 para. 2, 84, 71, 96 and 74. All the works are unanimously of opinion that the rights, given to the Works Councils by the Act, go much too far and should therefore be withdrawn, or at least restricted to the exercise merely of economic and social activities.

The above document is of interest, chiefly for the light that it throws on the psychology of the employers and on their attitude towards the Works Councils. In interpreting these answers it must be borne in mind, firstly, that they come from employers who resent any interference with their rights to be unrestricted masters in their own house, and therefore their attitude contains a considerable element of prejudice; secondly, that the answers have been collated by an employers' newspaper with strong propagandist tendencies and the selection made is probably not free from bias; thirdly, that the Ruhr district has seen very troubled times ever since the Revolution, and that the proportion of communists in the ranks of labour and the Works Councils has been higher than in almost any other part of Germany; —hence the employers there have had to suffer much from "wild strikes" and labour unrest, which have often been fomented by the radical Works Councils.

APPENDIX VI

Table of Contents of Works Rules agreed in 1920 for the Rhenish-Westphalian Iron and Steel Industry [1]

I. BEGINNING OF EMPLOYMENT

§ 1. Engagement documents.
§ 2. Medical inspection.
§ 3. Method of engagement.
§ 4. Handing out of the *Arbeitsordnung*.
§ 5. Duties and rights of the worker.

II. GENERAL DISCIPLINE OF THE WORKS

§ 6. Conduct towards foremen.
§ 7. Duties of foremen.
§ 8. Requests and complaints.
§ 9. Clocking in and clocking off.
§ 10. Cleanliness in the works.
§ 11. Changing of clothes and washing, bicycles.
§ 12. Conduct in case of fire.
§ 13. Rules for prevention of accidents, notification of accidents.
§ 14. Illness.
§ 15. Prohibition of noise.
§ 16. Freedom of coalition.
§ 17. Entry into shops other than that of the workers.
§ 18. Leaving of works before close of work.
§ 19. Attendance at continuation school.
§ 20. Introduction of strangers.
§ 21. Prohibition of spirits and tobacco.
§ 22. Right of search on entry.
§ 23. Prohibition of private work and trade.
§ 24. Prohibition of subsidiary occupations.
§ 25. Notices.
§ 26. Notification of thefts.

III. CONDUCT AT WORK

§ 27. Notification of damage to work and mistakes.
§ 28. Handling of tools.
§ 29. Handling of machines, etc.
§ 30. Consumption of materials, water, light, etc.
§ 31. Preservation of drawings and models.

IV. HOURS OF WORK

§ 32. Duration of hours of work.
§ 33. Alterations of hours of work.
§ 34. Interruptions in the conduct of the works.

[1] See p. 157 above.

---

[1] In the case of both § 32 (hours of work) and § 38 (wage rates) the hours and wages are those to which the worker is entitled under the ruling Collective Agreements.

Allocation of Duties between the members of the Executive Committee of the Central Works Council for the German Railways[1]

A. (*Chairman*)

1. General administration of the Central Works Council and representation of the same before the Railway Administration and the Public.
2. Preservation of the rights accorded by the Works Councils Order.
3. Execution and supervision of the rights and duties arising out of the provisions regulating hours of work.
4. Disciplinary and other works regulations.
5. Operation of piece-work and bonus systems in the stations.

B. (*Vice-Chairman*)

1. Deputy for A in regard to administration and representation of the Works Council.
2. General workshop questions.
3. Apprenticeship.
4. Execution of the Collective Wage Agreement.
5. Inspection of materials.
6. Inspection of the utilisation of scrapped material.
7. Scientific works management and reorganisation of the workshops.
8. Piece-work in the workshops (in conjunction with C).
9. Keeping of books concerning expenses to be refunded.

C.

1. Inspection of the condition of machinery, tools and similar equipment.
2. Measures for securing the profitable utilisation of scrapped material.
3. Supervision and control of the co-operation of the Works Councils in the allocation of hours of work in the individual machine shops.
4. Utilisation, training, examination and appointment of personnel.
5. Measures for securing a sound development of piece-work in the workshops.
6. Regulation of the taking on of temporary workers.
7. Regulation of the question of protective clothing.
8. Combating of thefts.
9. Appointments and dismissals.

D.

1. Keeping of all minutes.
2. Control and registration of documents.
3. Supervision of the execution of social legislation in the railway works and other undertakings.
4. Regulation and extension of measures for the promotion of hygiene and the prevention of accidents.
5. Conciliation proceedings, with special reference to decisions.
6. Free travelling.
7. Welfare work (provision of coal and potatoes, housing, leasing of land, sickness and pension funds, etc.).
8. Protection of railway stations.

[1] See above, p. 202.

Resolution of the 12th "Free" Trade Union Congress at Breslau, September 1925[1]

The Congress holds that the active co-operation of the workers and their Unions in the process of production is essential under present conditions. The solution of the economic problems with which the country is faced can only be attained by means of the democratisation of the economic system, coupled with the rationalisation of labour and improvements in the technique and organisation of business.

The Trade Unions have in the past been successful in achieving a certain measure of economic democracy, as a result of their struggle for the collective determination of wages and working-conditions. For through the Collective Agreement the autocracy of the employer in his own establishment is broken. The Trade Unions must therefore continue to strive for the further improvement and perfection of Collective Agreements.

. . . .

The Congress demands from the Reich, the Provinces and the Communes:

(i) Complete and unrestricted recognition of the Trade Unions which, as trustees of labour, should take part on an equal footing with the employers in the organisation and conduct of economic activities, in accordance with the letter and the spirit of Article 165 of the Constitution.

(ii) Speedy transformation of the Provisional Federal Economic Council into a real and organic economic Parliament; speedy erection of Regional Economic Councils in accordance with Article 165 of the Constitution.

(iii) Speedy erection of Economic Chambers for Industry, Commerce and Transport, Handicrafts and Agriculture, to be controlled and administered by employers and employees on equal terms.

(iv) Establishment, in accordance with Article 165 of the Constitution, of self-governing bodies for all industries, with suitable sub-divisions by districts and industrial groups.

(v) Introduction of a systematic statistical record of production, accompanied by scientific investigations into industry and commerce and their mutual relations, but especially into the causes of economic crises. The Trade Unions are to be associated in these tasks.

(vi) Facilities for workers to receive higher education, in order to be instructed in both the theory and practice of economics. Grants to be made to the educational establishments set up by the Trade Unions.

(vii) Maintenance of and increase in the numbers of the economic undertakings in the possession of the Reich, the Provinces, and the Communes; systematic growth of the system of supplying the needs of the population for important necessaries by means of such public undertakings working for the common good.

(viii) Encouragement and support of autonomous productive undertakings operated in the direct interests of the community.

(ix) Systematic support of the Consumers' Co-operative Societies, especially by encouragement of productive undertakings on the part of these Societies.

(x) In conjunction with the Trade Unions, a systematic instruction and education of all male and female employees in establishments, especially of Works Councillors, in regard to the organisation and technique of the

[1] See above, p. 246.

different works departments; the position as to the formation of combines and the special functions of the individual plants within a combine; the connections and agreements between different combines and their purpose and value; the purpose, nature, and consequences of price conventions, cartels, syndicates and similar organisations.

(xi) Extension of the right of co-determination of the Works Councils.

In putting forward these demands the Congress emphasises the fact that the just economic system promised by the Constitution, and the promised co-operation of the wage-earning and salaried employees in the management of industry and commerce, involve a fundamental transformation of the economic system, such as will organise, on a uniform basis, the economic forces that are split up into many isolated units in the capitalist system of exchange economy, and thus will make possible for the first time a control and management of industry in the form desired by the Trade Unions.

The Congress declares that the leadership of the German working classes, in all economic matters, must lie with the Trade Unions. The A.D.G.B., as the common organ of the German Trade Unions, is entrusted with the representation of the broad interests of the workers, which are synonymous with the interests of the greater part of the German people.

The Congress calls upon the workers to take up the fight for the democratisation of industry and commerce, which must be run on collective lines, for practical co-operation in the tasks of the democratic State and the democratic communes, and for the attainment of a dominating influence over legislation and administration in conjunction with the political representatives of the German workers. Political and economic freedom are the necessary conditions for the development of the cultural forces of the workers.

The Legal Liabilities of Members of Works Councils

The legal status of a Works Council in German law is peculiar and is still the subject of controversy. The bulk of legal opinion inclines to the view that a Works Council is a corporation, but one divested of legal personality so far as German private law is concerned.[1] As it is not a legal person, the Council as a whole is not liable for any breach of contract or tort committed by one of its members and, if any action is taken by the Council, involving a tort, those members who voted against such action are exempt from liability. It has repeatedly been held that, if a Works Council injures the interests of one of the employees, e.g. by demanding his dismissal from employment, the employee concerned can bring an action for damages provided that he can produce direct evidence of injury. The action then lies against those members of the Council who are responsible for the injury and, further, against any employees who voted in favour of it, in the event of the Council having acted at the instance, for example, of a majority vote of a Works Assembly.

Again, a Works Council is not liable for torts committed by the employees whom it represents, unless the Council is guilty of the tort or responsible for its commission. The Works Council, as such, is unable to own property or to sue or be sued in the ordinary courts. If a Works Council makes purchases, e.g. of books, office equipment, foodstuffs, etc., which are not authorised by the employer and for which he is not held responsible under the Act, the Council, as such, cannot be sued, but the individual members then become liable and their property can be attached for payment of the debt. Where, as is often the case, the members of a Works Council acquire, out of their private means, books, etc., for the purposes of their office, the ownership of such objects is regarded as divided amongst all the members as co-proprietors, each member having unqualified ownership of his own theoretical share but only a communal share in the objects as a whole.[2] When the personnel of the Council changes, the objects acquired pass normally by tacit consent into the communal or collective ownership of the succeeding members of the Works Council.

Apart from their liability at civil law, the members of Works Councils are also liable, under the terms of the Works Councils Act itself, to fine or imprisonment if they deliberately reveal trade secrets

---

[1] Dersch, *Kommentar zum Betriebsrätegesetz*; Erdel, *Betriebsvertretungen,* pp. 61–68; Flatow, *Kommentar zum Betriebsrätegesetz,* 10th ed. p. 21.
[2] Cf. Flatow, *loc. cit.* p. 107.

communicated to them in their capacity as statutory representatives of the employees

The status of a Works Council in German public law is a different one, for it is undoubted that a Works Council is an entity in public law, but only in the sense that it is a statutory body set up to protect the interests of the workers. Hence it follows that "the rights and duties of the Works Council are not its own rights accruing to it as a Works Council, i.e. as a distinct person in public law, but the rights of the body of workers whom it represents".[1] Thus in the case of a "Works Agreement" (*Betriebsvereinbarung*) the Council itself is not strictly a party to the contract but appears only as the agent of the workers.[2]

[1] Dersch, "The Legal Nature of German Works Councils" in *The International Labour Review*, February 1925, p. 174.

[2] It should be noted that the views of German legal authorities are by no means unanimous on this point.

BIBLIOGRAPHY OF WORKS CONSULTED

GENERAL

AXHAUSEN, G. Utopie und Realismus im Betriebsrätegedanken. Berlin, 1920.

BERNHARD, G. Wirtschaftsparlamente. Wien, 1923.

BERTHELOT, M. Works Councils in Germany. Geneva, 1924.

BRIGL-MATTHIASZ, K. Das Betriebsräteproblem. Berlin, 1926.

FREESE, F. Die konstitutionelle Fabrik. Jena, 1922.

GUTMANN, F. Das Rätesystem. München, 1922.

PICARD, R. Le Contrôle Ouvrier sur la gestion des entreprises. Paris, 1922.

POTTHOFF, H. Die sozialen Probleme des Betriebes. Berlin, 1925.

RÖMER, W. Die Entwickelung des Rätegedankens in Deutschland. Berlin, 1921.

STERN, B. Works Council Movement in Germany. Washington, 1925.

TARTARIN-TARNHEYDEN, E. Die Berufsstände. Berlin, 1922.

TSCHIERSCHKY, S. Wirtschaftsverfassung. Breslau, 1924.

VITALE, A. La Partecipazione degli Operai nell' Ordinamento e nella Gestione delle Imprese pubbliche e private. Milano, 1922.

COMMENTARIES AND LEGAL INTERPRETATIONS

BRAUNS, H. Das Betriebsrätegesetz. München, 1920.

FLATOW, G. Kommentar zum Betriebsrätegesetz. Berlin, 1923.

— Betriebsvereinbarung und Arbeitsordnung. Berlin, 1923.

FLATOW, G. und JOACHIM, R. Die Schlichtungsordnung vom 30. Oktober 1923. Berlin, 1924.

FREISLER, R. Grundsätzliches über die Betriebsorganisation. Jena, 1922.

HOFFMANN, W. Die Betriebsversammlung. Leipzig, 1922.

HÜSING, W. Arbeitgeberschutz im Betriebsrätegesetz. Dortmund, 1921.

KASKEL, W. Arbeitsrecht. Berlin, 1925.

— Das neue Arbeitsrecht. Berlin, 1921.

— Haftung für Handlungen des Betriebsrats. Berlin, n.d.

— Koalitionen und Koalitionskampfmittel. Berlin, 1925.

— Neuerungen im Arbeitsrecht. Berlin, 1924.

KIESCHKE und SYRUP. Betriebsrätegesetz. Berlin, 1921.

KORSCH, K. Arbeitsrecht für Betriebsräte. Berlin, 1922.

NÖRPEL, C. Betriebsrätegesetz und Gewerbe- und Kaufmannsgerichte. Berlin, 1922.

PICK und WEIGERT. Die Praxis des Arbeitsrechts. Berlin, 1925.

— Schlichtung von Arbeitstreitigkeiten. Berlin, 1924.

POTTHOFF, H. Die Einwirkung der Reichsverfassung auf das Arbeitsrecht. Leipzig, 1925.

— Wesen und Ziel des Arbeitsrechts. Berlin, 1922.

— Wörterbuch des Arbeitsrechts. Stuttgart, 1921.

ROSER, H. Die Betriebsräte bei der Eisenbahnverwaltung. Berlin, 1921.

SCHULDT, H. Die Betriebsvereinbarung. Berlin, 1925.

SINZHEIMER, H. Grundzüge des Arbeitsrechts. Jena, 1921.

STIER-SOMLO, F. Kommentar zum Betriebsrätegesetz. Berlin, 1921.

STIER-SOMLO, F. Gesetz über die Betriebsbilanz und die Betriebsgewinn- und Verlustrechnung. Berlin, 1921.

SYRUP und WEIGERT. Gesetz über die Betriebsbilanz und die Betriebs- gewinn- und Verlustrechnung. Berlin, 1921.

ULRICHS, O. Arbeitsordnungen. Berlin, 1921.

UMBREIT, P. Das Betriebsrätegesetz. Berlin, 1920.

WÖLBING, SCHULTZ und SELL. Betriebsrätegesetz. Berlin, 1926.

WORKS COUNCILS AND TRADE UNIONISM

APELT, K. Die wirtschaftlichen Interessenvertretungen in Deutschland. Leipzig, 1925.

BRAUER, TH. Das Betriebsrätegesetz und die Gewerkschaften. Jena, 1920.

BRAUN und MÜLLER. Die Gewerkschaften vor dem Kriege. Berlin, 1921.

ERDMANN, L. Die Gewerkschaften im Ruhrkampf. Berlin, 1924.

GUMPERT, F. Die Bildungsbestrebungen der freien Gewerkschaften. Jena, 1923.

KRANOLD, A. Von den Bedingungen wirklicher Volksbildung. Jena, 1924.

LEDERER, E. Die sozialen Organisationen. Berlin, 1922.

NESTRIEPKE, S. Die Gewerkschaftsbewegung. (3 vols.) Stuttgart, 1921– 1923.

SEIDEL, R. Die Betriebsräteschule. Berlin, 1924.

WINSCHUH, J. Betriebsrat oder Gewerkschaft. Essen, 1922.

WOLDT, R. Betriebsräteschulung. Jena, 1922.

ZWING, K. Soziologie der Gewerkschaftsbewegung. Jena, 1925.

Protokoll der Verhandlungen des ersten Reichskongresses der Betriebsräte Deutschlands. Berlin, 1920.

Protokoll der Verhandlungen des elften Kongresses der Gewerkschaften Deutschlands. Berlin, 1922.

Protokoll der Verhandlungen des zwölften Kongresses der Gewerkschaften Deutschlands. Berlin, 1925.

Protokoll der Verhandlungen des sechzehnten Verbandstages des deutschen Metallarbeiterverbandes. Stuttgart, 1924.

THE WORKS COUNCILS IN PRACTICE
(See also above under General)

Deutscher Textilarbeiter-Verband. Aus dem Tagebuch eines Betriebsrats. Berlin, 1925.

— — Lehrbuch für die im Deutschen Textilarbeiter-Verband organisierten Betriebsräte. Berlin, 1926.

— — Protokoll des zweiten Kongresses der Betriebsräte in der Textil- industrie. Berlin, 1924.

— — Protokoll über die Konferenz der Arbeiter-Aufsichtsräte und der freigestellten Betriebsräte der Textilindustrie. Berlin, 1925.

Deutscher Metallarbeiter-Verband. Protokoll der Konferenz der Betriebs- räte und Vertreter grösserer Konzerne der Metallindustrie. Stuttgart, 1924.

Jahresberichte der Gewerbeaufsichtsbeamten für Preussen, Sachsen, Bayern, Baden, Württemberg, etc., for the years 1920, 1921, 1922, 1923–1924, 1925. Berlin.

NÖRPEL, C. Aus der Betriebsrätepraxis. (2 vols.) Berlin, 1922.

Verband der Bergarbeiter Deutschlands. Protokoll vom ersten Reichs-
betriebsrätekongress für den Bergbau. Bochum, 1921.
WECK, R. Handbuch für Betriebsräte. Berlin, 1921.
WINSCHUH, J. Praktische Werkspolitik. Berlin, 1923.
Zentralverband der Betriebsräte in der Textilindustrie. Die Aufgaben der
Betriebsräte in der Textilindustrie. Düsseldorf, 1921.
— — — Leitfaden für Betriebsratsmitglieder. Berlin, 1922.
— — — Der Betriebsrat in seiner praktischen Arbeit. Berlin, 1925.

PERIODICALS

Die Arbeit.
Der Arbeitgeber.
Arbeitsrecht.
Die Betriebsrätepost.
Betriebsrätezeitschrift der Metallindustrie.
Betriebsrätezeitung des A.D.G.B.
Der Deutsche Holzarbeiterverband.
Gewerkschaftsarchiv.
Gewerkschaftszeitung.
Jahrbuch des A.D.G.B. 1920–.
Jahrbuch arbeitsrechtlicher Entscheidungen, 1920–.
Korrespondenzblatt.
Neue Zeitschrift für Arbeitsrecht.
Soziale Praxis.
Wirtschafts-Informations Dienst.
Die Zukunft der Arbeit, Band 1, Heft 2–3. Jena, 1923.

INDEX

German Federal Railways (*cont.*)
limited powers, 205; new works
rules for in 1922, 203; allocation
of duties on Central Works Council
of, 289
Gooch, *English Democratic Ideas in
the Seventeenth Century*, 5 n.
Graf on officialdom, 71
Gumpert, *Die Bildungsbestrebungen
der freien Gewerkschaften*, 77 n.

Heidelberg, case of dismissal at, 175
Hirsch-Duncker Trade Unions, 34–5;
their outlook compared to Manchester Liberals, 34
Hours of Work Order, Dec. 21, 1923,
59, 110; checked the movement
towards "Works Agreements",
59; and Works Councils, 142–3

Independent Socialists or minority
labour party, 7; influenced by
Russian Revolution, 6–8; their
formation of Workers' Councils,
8–9; their influence on Works
Councils Bill, 9–12
Independent Trade Unions, 35
Industrial Census for 1907, 118
Industrial Courts, 26–7; now called
Labour Courts, 30, 31 (*see* Labour
Courts)
Industrial Unionism, 64; in relation
to Craft Unions, 64–68, 73; effect
of Works Councils in stimulating their formation, 65–8, 73;
favoured by radical-communist
element, 65; led by Metal Workers'
Union, 64, 68; resolutions at
Leipzig Congress of "Free" Trade
Unions in 1922, 66–7
Inflation of currency, colossal in
1923, 40, 57, 107–8, 127, 223–4; and
wage rates, 151; and estimation
of balance sheets by Works Councils, 185–6; its effect on evolution
of Works Councils, 223–4

Joint industrial Alliances, 3–4;
much in common with Whitley
Councils, 4; in relation to Trade
Unions, 4, 36, 61–2

Kaskel, *Arbeitsrecht*, 60 n.

Konzernbetriebsräte, 207–8; their
formation in hands of Trade
Unions, 209; their organisation
most successful in metal and
engineering industries, 209–10;
courses of instruction for, 211 (*see*
Central Works Councils)
Koske, Paul, *Wie beurteilt man eine
Bilanz?*, 184 n.
Krupps, and Central Works Council,
207

Labour, new problems arising with
factory system, 1; influence of
War on, 2–3; measures relating to
after War, 3–4; influence of Russian Revolution on, 5–8; Works
Councils Bill in relation to, 9–13;
cleavage of opinion between Independent Socialists and Social
Democratic labour party, 7–9; problem of leadership, 68–74; growth
of interest in working-class education since the War, 75–82; legislation before and after War compared, 229–30; its hopes and
desires in Germany, 246–7; English and German compared, 247–8;
disunity of German, 248
Labour Courts, 21, 26–7, 29–32;
probable drastic changes in by
Government Bill of 1926, 27 n.,
31–2; Industrial and Mercantile,
27 n., 30, 31; lawyers admitted
to plead in, 32; three stages of,
31–2; their action as to unjust
dismissals, 30, 161–9; success of,
228
Leadership of Trade Unions and
Labour Councils, difficulties of,
70–3, 218; mutual influence of, 74,
218–19
Legal Liabilities of members of
Works Councils, 292–3
Legien, Karl, and "The Great
Charter of Labour", 4
Leipzig Congress, 1922, resolution on
industrial unionism, 66–7
Letterhaus, Bernhard, 134 n.

Maine's *Ancient Law*, 235 n.
"Mandarins" or salaried personnel of
the Unions, 69

300

Printed in the United States
By Bookmasters